Sewing Magic

225 patterns for sewing vintage fashions, accessories, household decor and gifts

Mary Brooks Picken

Bramcost Publications

Copyright © 2012 by Bramcost Publications
All rights reserved
Published in the United States of America

This Bramcost Publications edition is an unabridged republication of the rare original work first published in the 1950s.

www.BramcostPublications.com
blog.BramcostPublications.com
www.Facebook.com/Bramcost.Publications
www.Twitter.com/Bramcost

ISBN 10: 1-936049-69-4
ISBN 13: 978-1-936049-69-1

Library of Congress Control Number: 2012935972

Contents

Introduction 1

Skirts

Square-dance Skirt	7	Box-pleated Jersey Skirt	20
Semicircular Skirts—Long or Short	8	All-around Pleated Skirt	21
Colorful Felt Skirts	10	Jersey Skirt with Unpressed Pleats	22
Circle Skirt with Tie Waistband	11	Striped Skirt	23
Skirt with Matching Stole	12	Back-overlapping Skirt	24
Wool Skirt and Matching Stole	13	Dual-personality Skirt	25
Skirt and Stole from the Drapery Department	14	Novelty Six-gore Skirt	26
		A Swish-swish Taffeta Skirt	27
Double Front Wrap-around Skirt	15	Three-gore Net over Taffeta Skirt	28
Skirt with Bretelles	16	One-seam Skirt	29
Wrap-around Skirt in Wool	17	Corduroy Skirt with Pockets	30
Informal Long Skirt	18	Pleated, Side-pocket Skirt	32
Long or Short Skirt in Wool	19		

Blouses

Boat-neck Blouse	35	Wool Jersey Basics	48
Shawl-collar Blouse	36	A Dark Blouse for a Light Suit	49
Blouse with Portrait Neckline	37	Casual Jersey Blouse	50
Self-trimmed Crepe Blouse	38	Sleeveless Suit Blouse	51
Open-front Jersey Blouse	39	Sateen Blouse	52
Mandarin Blouse	40	Halter Overblouse	53
Tailored Blouse	41	Gingham Blouse	54
Informal Blouse	42	Handy Overblouse	55
Draped Blouse	43	Square-dance Blouse	56
Wool Pullover	44	Dress-up Smock	57
T-shirt Blouse	45	Mother-and-daughter Off-shoulder Blouses	58
Dress-up Blouse of Net or Lace	46		
Lace Overblouse	47		

Dresses

Chemise-type Dress	61	Scarf-trimmed Dress	73
Chemise, Peg-top Dress	62	Sheer Dress	74
Sheath Dress of Nylon Net	63	A Dress to Wear Tomorrow	75
Crepe Sheath Dress	64	Allover Lace Dress	76
Striped Sheath Dress	65	All-purpose Lace or Print Dress	77
A Basic Dress of Jersey	66	Eyelet-embroidery Dress	78
Short-sleeved Basic Dress	67	A Sheer, Cool, Easy-to-wear Dress	79
Tubular Jersey Dress	68	Dress with Velvet Trim	80
Jersey Jumper	69	Nylon Net Dress	81
Slip-on Jumper Dress	70	The "Any-fabric" Dress	82
Shirred Dress in Elastic Fabric	71	House Dress	83
Boat-neck Dress	72	Backless Dress of Metallic Fabric	84

Boleros, Jackets, and Coats

Shoulder Bolero	87	Stiff Satin Evening Jacket	96
Flannel Bolero	88	Dressing Sacque	97
Blazer-striped Bolero	89	Reversible Coverall	98
Spanish-type Bolero	90	Slip-on Coat	99
Striped Jersey Bolero	91	Sheer, Dark Flattery	100
Short Sleever	92	Unlined Coat	102
Plastron Doublet	93	Taffeta Cover-up Coat	103
Quilted Cosy	94	How to Reline a Coat	104
Weskits—Smart and Warm	95		

Stoles, Capes, and Scarves

Fringed Jersey Stole	107	Reversible Circular Cape	118
Two Simple Stoles	108	Unlined Circular Cape	119
Ribbon Stoles	109	Sleeved Cape for Your Shoulders	120
Sheer Stole, Velvet-trimmed	110	Velvet Shoulderette	121
Shoulder Stole of Fake Fur	111	Wrap of a Dozen Moods	122
Fur Fabric or Velvet Cape Stole	112	In the Fashion of Yesteryear	123
Crepe and Lace Capelet	114	Lace Mitts and Scarf	124
Cape Stole	115	Stay-put Scarf	125
Velvet Capelet with Hood	116	One-sleeved Bias Scarf	126
Glamour Cape and Hood	117		

Intimate Apparel

Cover-all Robe	129	Gift Bed Jacket	139
Quilted Lounge Coat	130	Shirred Nightie	140
Summer Negligee	131	Flat-wash Nightie	141
One-piece Negligee	132	Fitted Glamour Nightgown	142
Make-up Cape of Satin-finish Plastic	133	Cool Batiste Nightie	143
Jersey Bed Jacket	134	Petticoat and Camisole	144
Taffeta Make-up Cape	135	Petticoats with Dash	145
Two More Bed-jacket Styles	136	Smocks, Flattering and Practical	146
Bed Jacket from One Yard of Fabric	138		

Dress-up Accessories

Nylon Velvet Shoulder Cape	149	Veiling Charmers	160
Ribbon Accessories	150	Mandarin Hat and Matching Belt	161
More Ribbon Accessories	152	Fake Fur Pillbox, Collarette, and Muff	162
Five-point Scarf. Eyeglass Case	153	Bonnets, Visors, Sunshades	163
The Peplum Story	154	Dress-ups for Your Suit	164
Taffeta Overdress	155	Nylon Velvet Bag	165
Velvet Collarette and Girdle	156	Felt Costume Bag and Belt	166
Ascot Scarf and Muff	157	Drawstring Pouch Bag	167
Velvet-trimmed Tricorne	158	Shirred Evening Bag	168
Matching Hat and Scarf	159		

Aprons

Circular Dress-up Apron	171	Mother-and-daughter Aprons and Scarves	180
Lace Shoulderette and Matching Apron	172		
Crisp, Lace-edged Apron	173	Ruffled Aprons for Mother and Daughter	182
Side-pleated, Braid-trimmed Apron	174		
To the Back with Aprons	175	Father-and-son Work Aprons	183
Plastic Cover-up Apron	176	Heart-shaped Apron	184
House-cleaning Apron	177	Apron for Home Chef or Carpenter	185
Cover-up Aprons from One Yard or Less	178	Four Pretty Aprons	186
		Clothespin Apron	187
		Special Pocket Aprons	188

Clothes for Children

Baby Wrapper and Jacket	191	Bow Drawstring Dress	204
Receiving Blanket	192	Little Girl's Two-toned Dress	205
Carriage Cover and Pillow Case	193	Big-and-little-sister Pinafores	206
Bibs for Babies	194	Cover-up Apron	207
Baby-carriage Cover of Ribbon	195	Play Smock	208
Child's Dress—Easy to Make and Wash	196	A Special Apron for Crayons	209
		Cowboy Bolero and Chaps or Skirt	210
Dress for Small-fry Cinderellas	197	Ruffled Nightie for Your Fairy Princess	212
Youngster's Blouse	198	Nightdress—Big or Little	213
Middy Blouse	199	Little Girl's Robe	214
Child's Jumper and Blouse	200	Little Girl's Accessories	215
Wool Jumper for School	201	Bretelles—Over-shoulder Suspenders	216
Pleated Skirt	202	Ranch-branded Suede Cloth Slipover	217
Circular Skirts for Wee Ladies	203	Ribbon Bows for Little Girls	218

Home Furnishings

Flanged-edge Pillows	221	Cabin or Cottage Dress-up	227
Daybed Cover of Felt and Chintz	222	Dressing Tables	228
New Dress-up Tops for Beds	223	Dress Up Your Windows	229
Lace-trimmed Blanket Covers	224	Dress Up Your Table	230
Summer Bedspread	225	Colorful Felt for Girl's or Boy's Room	232
Bedroom Ensemble	226		

Gifts You Can Make

Santa's Stockings	235	Rainy-day Accessories Holder	250
Card-play Cover	236	Card-table Cover	251
Bean Bags	237	Men's Ascot Scarf	252
Glove and Stocking Protectors	238	Washcloth Scuffs—	
Shoe Covers	240	Mother-and-daughter Dry-off Suits	253
Sailcloth Handy Bag	241	Men's Summer Nightshirt	254
A Rucksack Carryall	242	Bimini Beach Bag and Slip-on	255
Make Your Own Carpet Bag	243	Ponchos Made of Towels	256
Traveling Bath Kit	244	Terry Shaverong	258
Shirt or Blouse Traveling Case	245	Jersey Cardigan	259
Stationery Holders	246	Men's Slip-on of Fake Pony	260
Map Case of Leatherette	247	Night Reader	261
Bathing-suit Bag	248	Hideaway Lap Robe	262
Beach or Camp Roll	249		

Introduction

▶▶▶ THE PURPOSE of this book is to help you to enjoy your sewing, to make practical things, and to acquire sewing skills or to perfect those you have.

GETTING READY TO SEW

Make yourself ready mentally and physically for sewing. First, assemble all your materials just as you would if you were making a cake. Then order the groceries, make the urgent phone call, tidy the house and yourself so that you will not have other things on your mind while you sew.

Have at hand a good tape measure, sharp scissors and shears, pins, first-quality needles in several sizes, chalk, pencil, a pad of paper. Use the pad of paper to write notes to yourself as you go along, such as "piece here," "check this length," "make a French-seam turn," and so forth. When you are assembling a garment, these notes will remind you of the step-by-step plans you made while cutting.

MAKING THE PATTERN

If you have the least doubt about your ability to chalk out the garment on your fabric, then rough it out first with crayon or heavy pencil on wrapping paper or newspaper. Cut out the paper pattern and use it to cut your garment. Cutting from a diagram, you can be sure that the proportions are correct for your size and that the garment will be a good fit. If you are over size 36, buy in your hip and bust size a plain four-gore skirt pattern and a plain blouse pattern with a high neck and set-in sleeves. Adjust these patterns, if necessary, to your measurements. These basic patterns will enable you to adjust the designs in this book to your size, and to enjoy the timesaving and fabric-saving shortcuts this book makes possible.

KEEP ACCURATE MEASUREMENTS

Since the garments in this book are all cut from measurements, it is necessary to have accurate ones to follow. Keep a list of your own measurements always at hand for ready reference.

If your weight varies, a gain or loss of five pounds will make a difference of approximately an inch in bust, waist, and hip measurements; ¼ inch in neck and arms.

Measurements for fitted garments should be taken over the type of foundation garments you expect to wear with them. Remove dress, jacket, or coat, which would distort the measurements. Do not take measurements too tight.

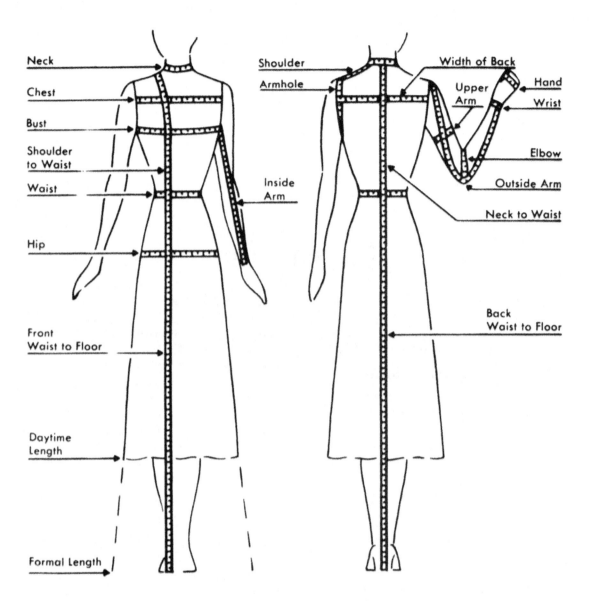

Make all easy enough for comfort. The chart above shows how to place the tape correctly for each measurement.

TIMESAVING HINTS

Always straighten your fabric before you begin to cut. Do this by tearing the ends crosswise or by pulling a thread and cutting on this crosswise thread line. Then stretch the fabric diagonally, selvage to selvage, until it lies smooth lengthwise and crosswise, with all threads even.

Test your machine stitch on a scrap of fabric before you begin a seam or a finish. A little precaution in this regard makes for more uniform work.

Keep your iron near at hand, and press the material before cutting if there are wrinkles. Press each seam before joining it to another. Press edges. Smooth your way with your fabric and it will smooth all your efforts in sewing.

Don't crowd or rush. Remember, sewing is work to enjoy.

SAVE TIME WITH BUNDLE SEWING

Many women have found that they can budget their sewing time with "bundle sewing."

Here's how it's done.

Next time you go shopping, buy the essentials for the item you want to sew. Then, when you have a few minutes, measure and chalk it out and cut. Perhaps you will want to cut several garments or articles at once, while you have a cutting surface available. Now roll all the pieces for each item in an easy roll, ready for the first time you sit down to listen to your favorite radio program or to visit with a friend who drops in.

Then get out your sewing and baste the garment together. Get it ready to fit and stitch. Or, if you did that on a previous relaxing occasion, put in some finishing stitches or make some buttonholes.

Try this plan and you will find that it becomes a relaxing, enjoyable habit. Then, indeed, will all your sewing be fun.

HOW TO GET THE MOST FROM YOUR SEWING MACHINE

A good sewing machine can give a lifetime of service, even if you use it every day. It is always ready for stitching, hemming, binding, gathering, cording, ruffling, and tucking at your direction.

Learn to handle your machine, to put it to work for you. A sewing machine *begs* to be used—to be given the opportunity to make beautiful seams and finishes in attractive garments and home furnishings.

You do not need hours and hours of practice to acquire skill. Twenty minutes of conscientious practice with an unthreaded needle and a piece of ruled tablet paper, and you can learn to stitch straight, to pivot, and to turn a square corner.

Draw some circles on the paper to give you practice in stitching around curves. Try this, your eye following the line of the presser foot. Use this presser foot as a guide in judging distance. See for yourself how easy it is to stitch straight.

Thread the needle and stitch along the stripe of a fabric, then on lengthwise and crosswise threads. Pivot; turn square corners. Cut a true bias, turn an edge, stitch on the edge. Practice until your machine will do anything you want it to do.

Take out your box of attachments and practice with each one, using your machine instruction book. Allow ten minutes to each one so that you really know how it works—how to make full or scant gathers, how to bind a curve, cord a seam, put in a zipper.

Keep your machine closed or covered when it is not in use. Wipe it clean of lint and excess oil. Oil it after each extended use. Keep a supply of needles at hand for quick change when needed. Buy a half dozen extra bobbins so that you always have one for thread of the color you wish to use. Keep your machine near at hand so that you can sew for five minutes or for hours, as your time allows. Do not put it away where it will be difficult to get out again.

Master your machine, and it will pay you dividends year in and year out in lovely things for yourself, your family, and your home.

SMARTNESS FOR ALL THE CLOTHES YOU MAKE

Mental attitudes can have a lot to do with whether or not you look smart in your clothes. Know your best color, best textiles, best silhouette. Experiment—try on clothes. Sometimes a garment proves to be very becoming, though you might never have expected it to be without trying it on.

Decide upon the most becoming dress length for you. When the fashion calls for short skirts, wear yours just a little shorter than *your* most becoming length. When skirts are long, wear yours just a wee bit longer than *your* most becoming length. This way you will never be conspicuously out of fashion; yet you will not depart too far from the length best for you individually.

Decide what kind of shoulder pad is best for you and buy or make several of these. Snap them in for easy removal when garments go to the cleaner.

What is your most becoming neckline? Some look their loveliest in low necklines; others need collars and the tailored look, even in evening clothes. Fashion is not arbitrary. There are no absolute musts. It is your part to *adapt* the really becoming new silhouette to your face, your neck, your shoulders, your bust, waist, hip, and hemline so that you wear the new fashions as they best become you. Never reject a new silhouette simply out of prejudice. Take from it what is good for *you* and use it to look your best.

Avoid hard, clear colors and shiny surfaces if your skin is not clear, or if your hair is subdued in color or is graying. Rather, choose soft fabrics and soft colors so that you yourself will not be eclipsed by your dress.

Be your prettiest self at all times. Do not allow yourself to be sold unbecoming fashions, fabrics, or colors. You and your mirror must decide what is most becoming for you. Look long and consider every angle; then have the courage to modify fashion to suit your needs.

Remember—if your clothes are in good taste and right for you, you will always be attractive and well-dressed.

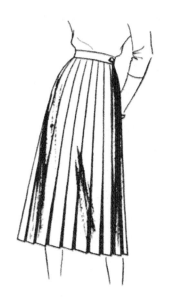

Skirts

Square-dance Skirt

▶▶▶ A DIRNDL, broom, or peasant-type skirt, which is a straight, full skirt gathered into a band, is ever popular—ideal as either a long or a short skirt, good with evening blouse or sweater, and especially a favorite for wear to square dances.

To make, buy four times the length of waist measurement in inches, plus ⅛ yd. for waistband. For a 27-in. waist, buy 108 in. (3 yds.) plus ⅛ yd. for band. You need 1 spool of thread, 1 hook and eye.

Stretch material diagonally to straighten. Measure 4½ in. from one end and cut piece for waistband. Cut this piece crosswise from selvage to selvage and lay it aside for the moment. Pin the two crosswise raw edges of skirt piece together, and make a ½-in. seam, stitching from selvage at one side to within 9 in. of selvage at other side. Make a ¼-in. hem on each side of 9-in. placket opening.

Finish for bottom of skirt: Thirty-six-in. cotton will, according to your height, take a 3- to 5-in. hem, stitched or slip-stitched. For a dinner skirt, use selvage as finish for lower edge. For a really long skirt or to make skirt appear extra full, stitch braid or ribbon over selvage. Some like to use three or more rows of such trimming to decorate the bottom.

To get the length: Having finished bottom edge, put skirt on and tie a tape around your waist. Keep this slightly loose, so that you can pull the fabric up under it. Adjust length as you stand in front of your mirror. Use piece of chalk to mark skirt above cord all around your figure. Remove skirt and lay it out, folded at center-back seam. Pin hem edges together. Cut ½ in. above chalk line, cutting a true line, rather than fol-

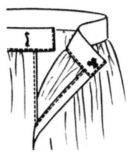

lowing irregular chalk line. Gather skirt fullness, using long stitch, a strong thread, and ruffler or gathering foot. Pull up bobbin thread to condense gathers to correspond to waist measurement. Make band 3 in. longer than waist measurement. Turn fabric back 1 in. on the top of placket so that it will not gap. Remaining 2¼ in. extends under belt on one side, as shown, to ensure holding waistband snug.

Semicircular Skirts

A ruffled skirt made from a full circle or semicircle is feminine and fetching. It is ideal for dancing or for wear with an especially pretty blouse to a cocktail party or to informal dinner parties.

To make a short, semicircular skirt buy 42-in. wide fabric. Two skirt lengths plus one-half the waist measurement is sufficient. For the bottom, buy 12 yds. of 2-in. lace and pleat it with the machine ruffler attachment—or buy 5 yds. of pleated lace. If you prefer ruffles to lace, cut two 2½-in.-wide ruffle strips from the corners of your fabric after you have chalked out the skirt length. Sew these together to make one large circle. Hem the lower edge, gather top edge, and French-seam this ruffle to the bottom edge of the semicircular skirt.

▶▶▶ SEVERAL ILLUSTRATIONS of circular and semicircular skirts are shown in this book. Once you learn to make such skirts, you can vary the length and the fabric and have each skirt quite different.

Taffeta and satin, obtainable in 50-in. widths, work out beautifully for a circular skirt either long or short. The diagram shows this width.

For a short skirt 36- or 42-in.-width fabric can be used. A band of ribbon or a ruffle may be added if you use narrower fabric and want a longer skirt.

Amount of fabric required: Buy in yardage four times waist measurement plus 2 in. (to the nearest fraction). For example, if the waist measures 27 in. and you want a long skirt, you need approximately 3 yds. of 50-in. material; for a short skirt, 2¼ yds. of 50-in. material.

Fold fabric through center crosswise. Pin selvages and the cut ends together.

From the corner point A (see diagram) measure on fold one-fourth the waist measurement plus ½ in. and mark B.

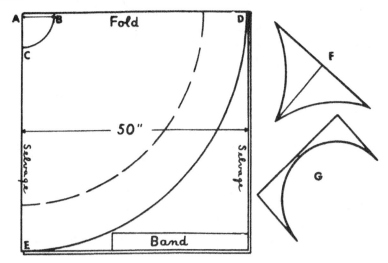

Long or Short

Measure from A on selvage same distance and mark C. For D, measure from B on fold the length of skirt desired plus hem allowance. Measure down on selvage same amount from C and mark E.

Tie a string around a pencil. Holding free end of string at A, draw an arc from B to C and from D to E. Cut on arc B to C for waistline and on arc D to E for bottom of skirt. Stitch selvages together for center-back seam, beginning 9-in. below waistline. Press seam open. Clip curved edge of waistline ¼ in. in, at distances of 1 in. apart. On crosswise edge of remaining fabric cut waistband, as shown. (If a crushed-band effect is desired, cut through double thickness, and seam lengthwise.) Baste band to waistline and fold it over. Fit the skirt, getting the length exactly right; then stitch waistband in position.

Put in hem. A narrow hem is usually the best finish for a circular skirt of this type. Sew hooks and eyes on band to close, and two snap fasteners or a zipper in placket opening.

If fabric is 50 in. wide, the two triangularly shaped pieces that remain after cutting skirt and band can be utilized for a scarf. F and G show two ways these pieces might be put together. A plain rolled edge is used for finish.

A skirt of this type may be made of organdy, either cotton or silk, of taffeta, or of various other fabrics. It may be a separate skirt or be part of a dress with a T-shirt bodice or an attached strapless one. When made of stiff fabric, it may serve as a base for a lace overskirt. Some have lace aprons over them, some have finely pleated silk organza or rayon sheers sewn into a band to wear like an apron.

Colorful Felt Skirts

▶▶▶ COLORFUL SKIRTS of felt are so easy to make. Buy 1⅛ yds. of 72-in. felt, and make the skirt with one seam. It is really no trick at all—no seams to finish. You simply measure, cut, and stitch.

Green, red, royal blue, or purple are favorites in color.

Following diagram, fold felt in half lengthwise with fold toward you. Point A is lower left-hand corner. Points B and C are placed at one-third waist measurement above and to right of A. The length from waist to hem gives you the measurement from B to D and from E to C.

Tie end of string to piece of chalk. Hold other end of string at A and chalk a curve from B to C and from D to E.

If skirt is not as long as desired, chalk bands of width needed, as at F. Mark for waistband as at G. This band can be pieced if lengthening bands cut into right-hand edges. Cut waistline C to B and bottom of skirt E to D. Cut waistband and lengthening bands if needed.

Seam center-back edges, starting 8 in. from waistline to allow for placket. Bottom edge of skirt can be scalloped as illustrated. If lengthening bands are used, lap ends of pieces and stitch to make one strip. Lap skirt edge over top edge of band and stitch. Or, for a more decorative finish, apply a band of contrasting braid to bottom of skirt as at H, then lap braid over felt band and stitch as at I.

Fold waistband in half lengthwise and press. Insert edge of skirt waistline between band edges ¼ in. and pin. Put on skirt and check waistline. Remove. Insert skirt zipper, following directions that come with the fastener. Stitch waistband in position. Stitch across ends and trim close to stitching line. Use snaps or hook and eye to close.

Piece cut out at waistline can be used for two pockets. Pink edges, stitch braid under two side edges, and stitch in position. Rows of bright-colored braid, appliqué designs, or embroidery with yarn and beads can be added to make the skirt gay.

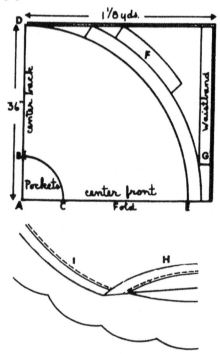

Circle Skirt with Tie Waistband

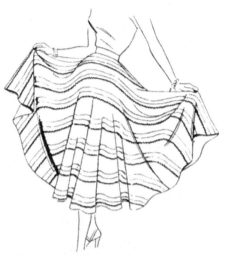

▶▶▶ GAILY STRIPED, printed, or woven-design cottons are ideal for this complete-circle skirt. For fabric needed, measure from waist to desired length, plus one-eighth of the waist measurement. Multiply this by 4 for your skirt.

Straighten fabric and fold in half crosswise. Pin selvages. Mark center of one selvage (A in diagram). B is one-eighth of waist measure from A. From B to corner C mark length of skirt plus 1-in. hem. At A, hold string tied to chalk or pencil and mark two arcs, as shown. Cut on these lines. Piece skirt for length with side pieces, as indicated. For waistbands, mark and cut 2½-in. strips along fold, D, E, F. Seam D and F together, as in G, for front waistband. Cut this to waist measure plus length for tie ends. Use E for back band and cut to waist measurement plus 1½ in.

Stitch around waistline ¼ in. from edge to prevent stretching, and notch edge. Seam selvages together, stitching to within 5 in. of waist. Press seams open up to about 7 in. from waist. From here up press back edge over front to make lapped plackets.

Place wrong side of back band to right side of skirt, centering edges. Stitch, as in H. Fold ends in half and stitch from skirt around ends (I). Turn ends right-side out. Point corners from inside, using an orange stick. Turn under raw edge. Top-stitch around edges (J). Center front band on front edge of skirt and stitch as for back, but leave ends open. Finish edges of ties with narrow hems.

Try on skirt. Bring ends of back band to center-front and mark for hook and eye. Ends of front band go around waist and tie in a bow at back. (For a plain band, cut and make front band exactly like back band.)

Let skirt hang at least twenty-four hours to allow bias to stretch. Try on. Correct any unevenness in hemline and finish with narrow hem.

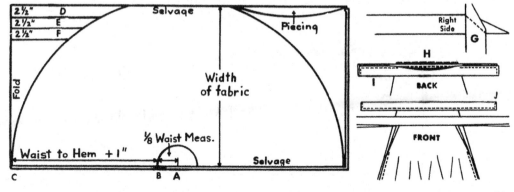

Skirt with Matching Stole

▶▶▶ THIS SKIRT and stole can be made from 3 yds. of 36-in. fabric, for the average figure. A pretty, striped cotton was used for the one illustrated.

Straighten ends. Tear off one skirt length plus 3 in. for hem. Fold this piece in half lengthwise. For waistband, measure in 4 in. on one end and cut through both thicknesses of fabric, tapering to nothing at other end. This shaped gore is used for front. Tear 18-in. strip from remaining length for stole. Cut two back skirt lengths from piece left after stole is torn off. From piece remaining from back skirt lengths large pockets can be made to add to either the skirt or stole.

Stitch selvages of straight gores together, leaving a 7-in. placket at top edge. French-seam torn edges of these gores to shaped edges of front piece. Gather top edge all around. Adjust so that there is slightly more fullness in front of skirt than at sides and back.

Stitch 4-in. ends of waistband together. Cut band to desired waist length, making it approximately 2½ in. wide and equal to waist measurement plus 1 in. for overlap at each end. (See B.) Place center seam at center of front of skirt, right sides together. Stitch around waist. Turn band over and whip the edge down on the wrong side.

Put skirt on. Mark length and make hem. A slip-stitched hem is always best with stripes, as stitching across them shows too much.

Sew hooks and eyes at back of waistband. Clip corners of stole. Make a ½-in. machine hem on both sides of stole and a slip-stitched hem on ends, cutting corners neatly, as in C, and finishing miter by hand, as in D.

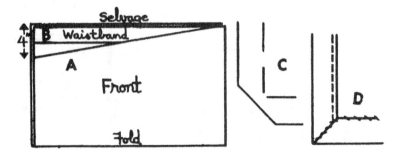

Wool Skirt and Matching Stole

▶▶▶ MANY OF the nice, soft, lightweight wools are 60 in. wide. Choose a pleasing weight of plaid or checked design or plain color. To make both skirt and stole you need only one skirt length plus hem allowance, plus 5 in. for waistband, plus 18 in. for stole. For the average figure, 1½ yds. is ample.

Straighten fabric. Tear off skirt length plus hem allowance, then waistband (see diagram), clipping selvage first, then tearing each piece from selvage to selvage on crosswise grain. The remaining piece is for the stole.

Seam the two selvages of the skirt together, beginning 7 in. (or placket length) down from one crosswise edge. Seam may come at left side or center-back, as you prefer. Press this seam open. Stitch seam binding to bottom edge or turn raw edge ¼ in. and stitch it in preparation for slip-stitching.

Cut from the waistband piece a length for your waist plus 2 in. for overlapping. Tear remainder of this piece in half on crosswise grain and use these pieces to put bands on selvage ends of stole. Finish the crosswise edges of stole with a ⅜-in. hem, or sew a fringe or braid on both sides as a finish.

Lay side or box pleats, as you prefer, in waistline of skirt, spacing all evenly in center-front and center-back to take up waistline fullness. Place right side of waistband to right side of skirt, and stitch it in place. Then bring band to wrong side, turn the raw edge in, baste, then whip it in position, turning and slipping raw ends in at placket edge. Fasten with button and buttonhole or with large hooks and eyes.

Put hem in. Press pleats from waistline down over hips—just to slim the skirt nicely. Your outfit will then be ready for wear with blouses, sweaters, jackets, and to keep you warm and smart. It is ideal for after-ski wear or for weekends in the country.

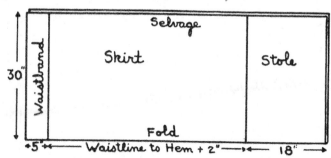

Skirt and Stole from the Drapery Department

▶▶▶ LIKE UNUSUAL fabrics? Want something different? Visit the drapery department of your favorite store and look for a pretty fabric light enough in weight to be ideal for a skirt and stole—something that will go with a sweater or blouse that you have. Look especially for a remnant of 2 to 3 yds. Often you can get them at a worthwhile reduction. For example, the original shown here was a 2-yard remnant. Stripes ran crosswise of the fabric.

To make: Measure off skirt length plus 3 in. for hem and waistline seam. From one end of this cut a 2-in.-wide strip for a belt band. From end of stole piece cut a crosswise strip 5 in. wide; then cut this in half and seam it together to make a pocket. If piecing is done along a stripe or as a tuck, it can look as though intended rather than as a necessary piecing. Put a 1½-in. hem in top of pocket.

Seam skirt; hem placket opening; gather or pleat fullness. Pin this to waistband, and fit the skirt, placing skirt seam at left side. Determine correct length. Pin pocket in position on right side front.

Stitch pocket on. Stitch waistband on. Slip-stitch hem. You have a selvage there to help in making the hemming easy. Use a hook and eye or button and buttonhole for the waistline fastening.

Make a narrow hem all around the stole; or line the stole throughout with a bright color; or hem sides only and fringe the ends. Stole can be very pretty and individual if you give it special attention in finishing.

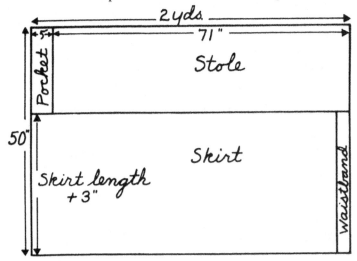

Double-front Wrap-around Skirt

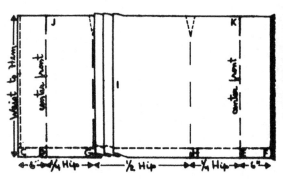
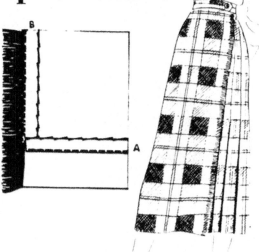

▶▶▶ THIS FRINGED SKIRT is easy to make. Buy a beautiful plaid or another lovely fabric of a pleasing color—a fabric not too tightly woven hangs and fringes best.

For the average figure it requires only one skirt length plus a hem and 2½-in. allowance for waistband. You need ⅞ yd., 1 yd., or 1⅛ yds. of 60-in. material, depending on your height. Straighten fabric. Put hem in bottom, using a seam binding at top of hem, as at A. Cut away selvage on the side that laps over right to left. Carefully ravel out lengthwise threads for about 2 in. so that no crosswise threads are broken. Stitch a strip of straight seam binding along raveled edge, as at B, so that edge cannot ravel farther.

With your fabric thus prepared, make ready to do some arithmetic. Section C to D on the diagram provides 6 in. for underlap; E to F, including fringe, 6 in. for overlap. Spaces D to G and E to H are each one-fourth of the hip measurement. If your hip is 36 in., this accounts for 30 in. from your 60-in. fabric. So you have one-half the hip measurement from G to H plus 12 in. to fold into pleats, which means that you can have six 1-in. pleats or three 2-in. pleats. The pleats can be placed to one side, as at I, centered, or divided between the two sides.

If hip is 40 in., you could have only three pleats; and if hip is larger than 40 in., then you need an extra skirt length, the seam of which can be concealed under a pleat or at center-front underlap. The same principle of overlap should be followed. Make more or fewer pleats as your measurements require.

A dart at each side is indicated in the diagram to take up some waistline fullness. Baste pleats from hem up to hip line. Pin them from hip line up, lapping pleats so that waistline will measure correctly for you. Take this measurement from J to K. When pleats are folded in, baste them. Put skirt on. Lap so that center-front lines meet. Make sure of smoothness over hips. Stitch pleats from hip line to waistline. Then stitch belt band on, right side of band to wrong side of skirt. Bring to right side and stitch. Put a hook and eye at center-front, work a buttonhole at end, and sew a button to correspond on band. Press pleats straight.

Skirt with Bretelles

▶▶▶ WOOLENS ARE really economical to use when they come in 60-in. widths. Buy one skirt length of fabric that has no up and down, plus 3 in. for hem, plus 14 in. for bretelles and waistband. One and one-half yds. is usually ample.

Tear off crosswise a skirt length plus 3 in. Tear remaining strip in half crosswise for bretelles and waistband. Decide how long your bretelles need to be and cut both strips this length. Remaining pieces are seamed together for waistband. If strips are wide enough, turn 1 to 1¼ in. on each edge. You want the finished bretelles about 1 in. wider than your shoulder width. If you need wider bretelles than fabric allows, turn each edge under and face it with grosgrain ribbon or military braid, stitching it so that a generous ⅙ in. shows on each side. Stitch or slipstitch loose edge of facing in place.

To chalk out skirt: Fold in half lengthwise, selvages together. Lay selvages toward you. Following the diagram, measure 7 in. to right of corner A for B. C is one-fourth hip measurement plus 2 in. above B. Locate E one-fourth hip measurement plus 5 in. above D. Chalk and cut line E through C to edge of fabric.

Stitch center-back seams. Bring narrow ends of front and back of skirt together to make the waistline. Baste side seams, beginning left side seam 7 in. below top edge. Lay a box pleat on each side of center-front to make front measure half the waist measurement plus 1 in. Dart back of skirt 2 in. on either side of center-back to make it measure half the waistline. Stitch across pleats to hold.

Put skirt zipper in. Join waistband pieces with seam. Baste waistband on skirt with seamline of band in line with right-hand seam of skirt. Try skirt on. Lay pleats in ends of bretelles and pin in position, crossing them in back, if desired. Check length of skirt. Remove dress. Stitch waistband in position. Since this is a wide band, fold top edge over about 1 in. and whip at ends to hold. Put in bottom hem. Sew bretelles to belt line. To hold them in position on shoulders, tack together from wrong side where they cross in back.

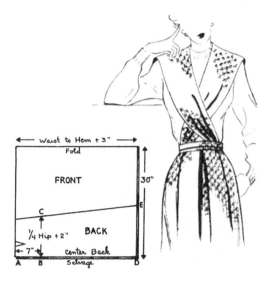

Wrap-around Skirt in Wool

▶▶▶ THE SKIRT shown was made of one skirt length of 60-in. lightweight wool in navy and red with a check about 1 in. square.

Buy one skirt length plus 5 in.; ⅞ to 1 yd. is ample. For waistband, tear off a 2½-in. crosswise strip.

Straighten all ends of fabric and pin selvages together with fold toward you. Measure in from right, along selvage, 7 in. or the distance of your waistline to the largest part of your hips (A in diagram). Measure in from left along fold the same distance (B). Straight out from A, mark one-third of the hip measurement plus 2 in. (C). Straight out from B mark one-fourth of the hip measurement plus 2 in. (D). With yardstick touching points D and C, chalk a line as shown. From point D, shape hip line as broken line shows, ending it 1 in. down from chalk line just drawn. From point C, shape hip line on back in same way. Cut on this broken line, from edge of fabric to D, through C and back hip line, cutting through both thicknesses of fabric.

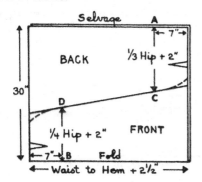

Bring narrowest part of all three gores together at top, joining a bias edge on each edge of front section, making ½-in. seams. Press seams open. Straight edges of back gores are to overlap at back.

Put skirt on, lapping right side over left in back and making certain that seams at each side hang well in line with underarm. Fit to waist by pinning in a dart 3 in. to either side of center-front and 3 in. from seamline on each back gore. Check for depth of hem. Remove skirt.

Stitch darts. Turn a ½-in. hem on each straight edge and finish with seam binding. Turn bottom hem and finish same way.

Measure waistline of skirt and cut belt piece of same length plus 1 in. Fold belt piece lengthwise, right sides in; and stitch ½-in. seam at each end. Clip seams, turn, and press. Pin belt in position on waistline of skirt, right sides together. Stitch. Bring belt over to wrong side, turn raw edge in ¼ in., and hem. Close belt with hooks and eyes at underlap end and overlap end, or with button and buttonhole at both points.

Informal Long Skirt

▶▶▶ THERE ARE MANY times when you do not want to "go formal," but when a long dress gives you a happily dressed-up feeling. Such a skirt can be worn with a shirtwaist, a scarf and bolero, a halter blouse, even a jacket. Suit the top to your mood; the skirt will go along, looking and feeling right in any case.

This is another skirt that can be made from one skirt length of 54- to 60-in. lightweight, pliable wool.

Buy one length, waistline to floor, plus 3 in., one package of matching seam binding, one 7-in. zipper, two hooks and eyes, and one spool of matching thread.

Straighten both ends of fabric, tearing off enough (1½ in.) on one end to make waistband. Bring selvages together, wrong side out, with the fold toward you. Following the diagram, mark point B 7 in. to right of corner A. C is one-fourth hip measurement plus 4 in. above B. E is 7 in. to left of corner D. F is one-fourth hip measurement plus 4 in. directly below E. With yardstick, chalk a line through C and F to both edges of fabric. Cut on this line. Bring E around to C, so that you have a straight edge along a bias edge for side seams. This makes a three-gore skirt with a bias seam at center-back. Stitch, making ½-in. seams, and beginning left side seam 7 in. below top. Press seams open; overcast raw edges.

At waistline, make notches at center-front and 2 in. each side of center-front. Lay a 1-in. pleat each side of center-front at this 2-in. notch. Lay another pleat on each side 1 in. beyond first pleat. Pin these in position.

Pin a 1-in.-wide grosgrain ribbon around waistline, lapping it at left side. Put skirt on and pin pleated top to ribbon. Adjust pleats to waistline and pin all way around. Mark for hem turn.

Remove skirt. Baste skirt to ribbon, and cover this with waistband strip. Turn in raw edges of band and stitch to ribbon, concealing top edges of skirt between fabric and ribbon.

Even the hem, stitch seam binding to top edge, slip-stitch hem. Put a zipper in placket. Sew hooks and eyes at waistline. Press.

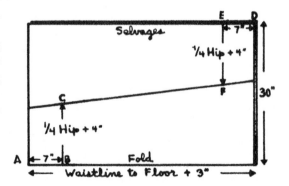

Long or Short Skirt in Wool

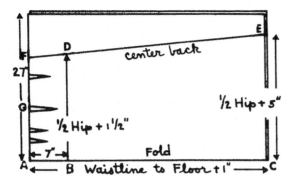

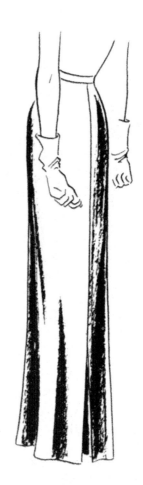

▶▶▶ A NICE, firm wool, such as flannel or tweed, is ideal for this type of skirt. Since these fabrics are usually 54 in. or more in width, you can make it of a single skirt length, waist to hem (long or short, as you want it), plus 3-in. hem allowance. If you plan to wear it with a blouse or jacket of dark or contrasting color, it should be of some attractive color. Otherwise, by all means, buy black.

Imagine how easy it is to make this skirt that has a single seam (at center-back), a few darts or pleats to control waistline fullness, and a hem. Could anything be simpler?

Straighten fabric. Fold in half lengthwise with fold toward you. Mark it for cutting according to diagram, as follows: A is at lower left-hand corner. B is 7 in., or length from waistline to hip, to right of A. C is desired length plus hem to right of A. Measure straight in from B to a distance of one-half hip measurement plus 1½ in. for D; straight in from C to one-half hip measurement plus 5 in. for E.

Chalk line from E through D to F on edge of fabric. Cut along this line. For a short skirt, you may prefer to lay a pleat in center-back instead of making slit shown in illustration. To allow for pleat, cut outside centerback line.

Halfway between A and F, mark for side dart G. The number of darts needed at side front and back depends on difference between waist and hip measurements. Baste side darts and pin fitting darts. Stitch center-back, starting 8 in. from top and ending 10 in. from bottom. Make center-back zipper opening at top of skirt, following directions that come with zipper.

Put on skirt and adjust darts, if necessary. Mark for hem. Finish edge of slit and top of hem with seam binding; slip-stitch in position. Press. Stitch waistline to belting or apply waistband to top of skirt. Use hook and eye as closing. Press.

Box-pleated Jersey Skirt

▶▶▶ THIS EASY-TO-MAKE SKIRT can be worn with separate blouses or jackets to make an ensemble. For the skirt, use a color matching or complementary to the blouse or jacket. Gold and brown, gold and green, rose and brown, blue and black, aqua and navy are but a few of many pleasing combinations.

You need one length (waist to hem plus 4 in. for hem and belt) of 54-in. tubular jersey.

Straighten fabric. Fold in half lengthwise and notch one end for center-back and center-front. Place notches together and lay fabric flat with one fold toward you. For belt, measure and cut a 1½-in. crosswise strip from unnotched end of tube. Measure skirt length plus ½ in.; chalk line straight across for hem.

Take a piece of 1-in.-wide belting, waist size plus 1½ in. Place a pin ¾ in. in from each end of tape; divide section in between into four units with pins. Pin tape to top of skirt, matching pins to center-front and center-back.

Lay 2-in. box pleats on either side of center-front, as at A. Lay a second and a third pleat on either side as shown. Lay an inverted pleat in center-back, making it deep enough so that top of skirt fits tape. Pin pleats. Unpin ends of belting.

When pleats are even, all fullness drawn up, stitch around top of skirt to hold all pleats, stitching along bottom edge of belting.

For placket, cut down 7 in. from top on left-hand side where belting ends. Make a narrow machine hem on both edges of opening. Tack bottom ends of placket securely.

Cut jersey waistband 2½ in. longer than waist measurement. Lay one edge along waistline of skirt, right sides together. Baste and stitch to bottom edge of waistband. Turn in edges of jersey band along top edge and on ends. Pin, then stitch all around waistband from right side. Stitch slowly so that jersey will not crowd in front of presser foot. Press.

Use two hooks and eyes to fasten waistband and one or two small snaps on placket to prevent gaping.

Put on skirt. Check length. Turn raw edge over ¼ in. and stitch. Then slipstitch hem in position.

All-around Pleated Skirt

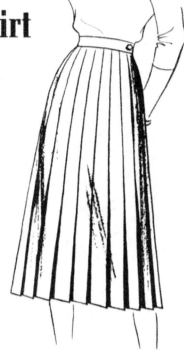

▶▶▶ WHEN FASHION APPROVES pleated skirts, those pleated all way around, as in the illustration, are often favorites. Some skirts have three pleats at each side of center-front and center-back in panel effect.

For an all-around pleated skirt you need three times your hip measurement in fabric width. Sixty-inch woolens make pleated skirts a cinch to make and low in cost, because average figure needs only two lengths. Buy two lengths of 60-in. or three of 40-in. Often, before dividing the lengths, you can take off enough for a belt. If not, buy ⅛ yd. extra for this.

Straighten your fabric. Tear your skirt lengths, allowing for hem. Seam selvages together, leaving one seam open. Put in bottom hem, making this as flat as possible. Finishing with seam binding is best for this, unless fabric is thin. In that case it can be turned and slip-stitched or put in place with blind-stitch attachment.

Pleating skirt: You can use a canvas pleater to lay pleats evenly, as in A. Complete instructions come with the pleater. Or divide your fabric into pleats of the desired depth; pin at waistline. Make all

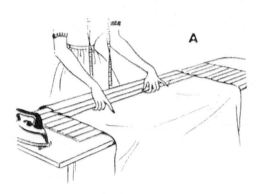

pleats even. Measure, pin, baste, if necessary. Lay out on ironing board and press each pleat its full length. When pleating is complete, baste around hip line to hold pleats. Take a piece of twill tape as long as your waist measurement plus enough to overlap. Divide into quarters, marking with pins. Pin pleats at waistline to this tape, matching center-front, center-back, and sides to pins in tape. From hips to waist overlap pleats slightly, just enough to bring fullness in so as to fit nicely. Baste and press pleats from hip line to waist.

Stitch side seam, beginning at depth of zipper below waistline, usually 7 in. Make a zipper placket or sew two snaps under pleat to hold. Stitch belt band on, right side of belt to right side of skirt. Bring to wrong side; close ends; whip edge in place. Fasten with button and buttonhole or with hooks and eyes. Always fold a pleated skirt and hang in a skirt hanger so that pleats will be straight.

Jersey Skirt with Unpressed Pleats

▶▶▶ GOOD-QUALITY JERSEY, guaranteed against sagging, costs very little. Your skirt length plus 4 in.—about 1 yd.—is ample to make the skirt. This measures about 56 in. around and is large enough for figures with 42-in. hips. For hips larger than 42 in., buy two skirt lengths plus hem allowance and use one-half of tube to add to the skirt. An apron panel can be made from remaining piece.

No cutting diagram is necessary for this skirt.

To cut: Straighten both ends. Measure skirt length, chalk off 2 in. for hem at bottom. Cut additional length off to use for waistline finish.

For placket, cut down on one fold 7 or 8 in. Make a very narrow machine-stitched hem on both edges of this opening. Tack bottom end securely.

Fold skirt in four, beginning at placket and opposite fold. Notch center-front and center-back. Take a piece of tape, waist size plus 1½ in. Place a pin ¾ in. in from each end of tape. Divide center section of tape into four equal parts with pins.

Pin tape to skirt, pins and notches meeting. Now you are ready to lay waistline pleats in position and pin these to tape.

Begin at center-front and lay two 2-in. box pleats each side of center-front. Lay a 1-in. pleat at each side so that placket overlaps it. Now lay two pleats between side and front box pleats, spacing these an even distance apart.

Make inverted pleat at center-back. Lay three pleats an even distance apart on each side of the back.

When pleats are even, all fullness taken up, stitch across top of skirt to hold all pleats. Remove tape as you stitch, so that it will not be caught in stitching.

Cut jersey waistband piece 2½ in. longer than waist measurement. Place crosswise center of this opposite placket opening on waistline. Baste to top of skirt; stitch.

Turn top edges of jersey band over. To hold these, use a strip of the kind of tape you press on. Cut this to the width desired. Lay tape over folded edges of jersey band; press carefully in position.

Stitch waistband from right side, stitching slowly so that jersey will not crowd in front of presser foot. Turn end back on waistband at placket opening; whip down.

Sew two hooks and eyes on band to close it. A small snap fastener may be used 4 in. down from waistband to prevent gapping.

Put skirt on; check length. Turn raw edge over ⅛ in.; stitch this turn, then slip-stitch hem in position.

Striped Skirt

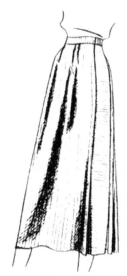

▶▶▶ STRIPED SKIRTS are easy to make when your design is right, and economical, too, when you gain your skirt width in the way illustrated.

This skirt was made of a 46-in. rayon flannel that looks and behaves like wool, but that costs much less. It required only 1¼ yds. Figures with hips larger than 38 in. need 1½ to 1⅝ yds. to provide enough width.

Straighten fabric. Measure down on selvage a skirt length, plus 2½ in. for hem and waistline seam (A in diagram). Clip selvage here and tear or cut on a straight crosswise grain. Then divide remaining piece in half on selvage; clip here (B), and cut or tear in half on crosswise grain. These two pieces make side panels, which run on opposite grain from front and back panels of skirt. Next cut or tear skirt length in half (see broken line in diagram), tearing lengthwise of your fabric to make front and back panels. Now you have four pieces.

Turn lengthwise edges of front and back panels in 1 in. on long sides; baste. Lay these over side panels, as shown at C and D, and baste, beginning 8 in. below waistline. Lay two 2-in. pleats, as shown, on each side of center-front line and center-back, beginning these 1½ in. from center and spacing them 2 in. apart. Measure the waistline and overlap the panels at sides as necessary to have top of skirt correspond in size to waist measurement.

Baste from hip line, or 8-in. point below waist, *up* on all four seams, except on left-side front, which will become the placket. Baste across the pinned pleats. Now you are ready for a fitting. If the soft fullness of pleats seems bulky, pleats may be stitched down as tucks or darts to slim them. Make any adjustment necessary to have skirt fit nicely through hips and at waistline.

Remove skirt and stitch panels, stitching in ⅝ to ¾ in. from panel edge. Stitch from top of skirt to bottom on right side of front panel. On left side of front panel, stitch from placket down. On each side of back panel, stitch from top to within 8 in. of bottom to provide kick pleats at back. Stitch placket free of opening, with line meeting panel line exactly. Pull threads through and tie, so that there will be no apparent interruption in stitching line.

Turn top edge of hem ¼ in. Stitch it by machine; then slip-stitch hem in place.

For belt: Take material left from side panels. Join two pieces. Cut belt to desired width. Slim figure can wear belt 2 to 3 in. wide; 1 in. wide is more becoming to larger waistline. Join belt to skirt.

Sew hooks and eyes on for closing with a snap fastener on placket to prevent gaping.

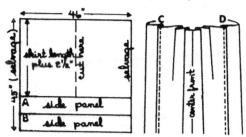

Back-overlapping Skirt

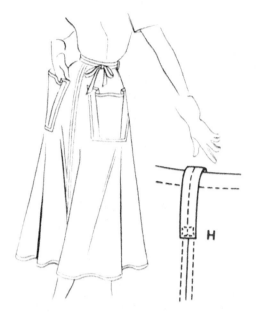

▶▶▶ FOR SPORTS WEAR and especially for quick ironing, this wrap-around skirt is a joy. Made of four gores, it has a deep overlap in back, which makes a slip or petticoat unnecessary. It requires two skirt lengths plus 2 in. for hems, plus ¼ yd. for pockets; 1¾ to 2 yds. is ample.

For pockets, tear off 9-in. crosswise strip. Tear 2-in. lengthwise strip from one selvage for tie belt. Tear fabric length in half, crosswise, and straighten all ends.

Pin crosswise edges of fabric together. Following the diagram, measure in on selvage 9 in., or the distance from waistline to largest part of hips, to locate point A. Measure straight up from A a distance of one-third hip measurement plus 2 in. to locate B. From corner C measure in the same distance as used on diagonally opposite corners to mark D. Straight down from D mark E, at a distance of one-third hip measurement plus 2 in. With yardstick touching points B and E, draw chalk line, as shown, and cut on this line through both thicknesses. Taper off at F and G with a curved line, as shown.

For center-front, join straight torn edges in ½-in. seam. Bring narrowest part of all four gores together at top, joining a bias edge on each of front sections. Make ½-in. seams and use selvages for overlapping at back. Press seams open. Topstitch ¼ in. on each side of seamline.

Finish waistline and bottom edge with ½-in. hems. Turn raw edge of tie strip under selvage, and stitch along selvage full length; cut strip in half.

Use scraps to make two straps 2½ in. long. At each side seam stitch one end under top hem, and bring other end over and stitch, as at H.

Cut two pockets, each 11 in. wide and 9 in. deep. Turn ½-in. hem at top. Lay two pleats, each 1 in. deep in each pocket piece. Turn edges, sides, and bottom in ¼ in. Center a pocket on each front gore 3½ in. below waistline, and stitch in position, stitching on edge, then ¼ in. in on pocket. Stitch ties to end of each selvage at waistline. When putting skirt on, lap back. Bring ties through side loops, and tie at center-front.

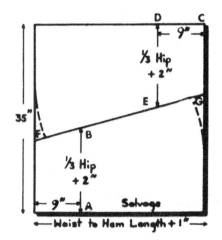

Dual-personality Skirt

▶▶▶ CHANGE IS fashionable, and we like to have something new and different to wear. Here is a way to have two skirts at a cost of one and a half. You need simply three lengths of fabric—one for back, two completely different ones for fronts. Back of skirt illustrated is plain, black rayon crepe; one front is a black-and-white print; ruffled front is of green-and-black changeable taffeta.

Make your skirt long or short. In any event, buy a skirt length of each fabric used. (This is a wonderful way to use remnants.)

For back of skirt: Use a piece as wide as the hip measurement plus 2 in. Fold in half lengthwise. Mark for darts 4 to 5 in. long, as at A in the diagram. If waist measures 26 in. and hips 36 in., divide difference, or 10 in., into six darts to take up fullness at top of skirt. Make ½-in. hem at waistline and a 2-in. hem on bottom edge. Have front edges meet at waistline, also 6 in. below waistline. Sew hooks and eyes at these two points. If it is necessary to cut off some of the width of fabric, then do this on one lengthwise edge only, before marking darts, and make a narrow hem along the one raw edge.

For front made of printed fabric: Use full width and make a large apron. Turn selvages under ½ in. on each side and stitch. Hem bottom. Gather top to equal one-half the waist measurement. Pin and stitch a length of ribbon over gathers. Tie ribbon in bow at center-back.

For ruffled-apron front: Cut a skirt length that equals one-half the hip measurement plus 2 in. in width. Round corners of one end, as at B. For ruffle, cut remaining piece into crosswise strips 3½ in. in width. Seam strips together. Make a ⅛-in. hem on one side of ruffle strip. Gather raw edge. Adjust fullness so that ruffle extends from top of apron on one side to same point on opposite side. Dart or gather waistline so that measurement from side edge to side edge equals one-half the waist measurement. Sew a 2-yd. ribbon across top for tie sash.

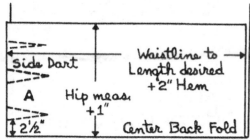

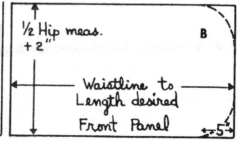

Novelty Six-gore Skirt

▶▶▶ MAKE THIS of two colors of the same print or of two colors that are on good terms with each other, such as rose and blue, yellow and brown, red and black. The one shown is made of a calico print, everfast in color, with three gores in a brown base with yellow and red flowers, and three in a green base with the same yellow and red flowers.

An average figure requires two skirt lengths of 36-in. cotton plus 2 in. for hem. Straighten fabric. For waistband, tear a 2-in. strip from one selvage length of each skirt piece.

Fold each skirt piece so that selvage and lengthwise raw edge come together. With fold toward you, measure up from corner point A a distance of one-eighth waist measurement plus 2 in. to locate B. Measure down same distance from corner C at opposite end for D. With yardstick draw a line from B to D. Cut on this line. Cut the other skirt-length piece in the same way.

Pin skirt together, lengthwise edges of side gores to bias edges of front and back panels. This brings bias edges together at side seams. In stitching these seams, begin 7 in. down from top to provide a placket on left side. Stitch six seams of skirt. Cut bottom corners away to even hemline.

Make zipper placket, following instructions that come with skirt zipper. Gather waistline with long machine-stitch. Adjust gathers to size of waistband.

To make waistband: Using 2-in. selvage strips, cut each strip to measure same as waist measurement plus 2 in. for placket overlap. Lay right sides together and stitch along raw edges and across both ends. Turn right side out and press. Baste gathered skirt to waistband, placing right side of strip to wrong side of skirt. Stitch. Bring second selvage over to right side of skirt, turn it under, and stitch, stitching all around edge of waistband for tailored finish.

Use a hook and eye or button and buttonhole to fasten waistband. Put skirt on. Decide how deep hem should be for becomingness. Pin and check this. Remove skirt. Finish hem first, turning raw edge ¼ in. and stitching. Then slip-stitch hem in position.

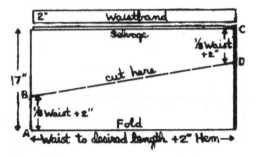

Swish-swish Taffeta Skirt

▶▶▶ EVERY YOUNG WOMAN who likes to dance enjoys a taffeta skirt—especially when it is of two of her favorite colors, and is her favorite length.

Buy two skirt lengths (each measuring from waistline to hem, plus 5 in.) of two different colors of 50-in. taffeta—for instance, one length of cerise red and one a bright navy.

Straighten fabric. For waistband tear a 2-in. strip from one selvage of each skirt length. Fold each skirt piece in half lengthwise, so that selvage and lengthwise raw edge come together. Lay with fold toward you. Measure as indicated in diagram. Chalk line from A to B and cut on this line. This will give you three gores in each color.

Pin skirt together, lengthwise edges of side gores to bias edges of front and back panels. This brings bias edges at sides. Alternate colors so that you have a red center-front and a blue center-back or vice versa. Stitch all seams. Begin left side seam 7 in. down from top to provide placket. Make zipper placket, following instructions that come with skirt zipper. Gather waistline with two rows of shirring. Adjust gathers to size of waistband. For waistband, use 2-in. selvage strips, cutting strips to waist measure, plus 2 in. for overlap.

Lay right sides of waistband together and stitch along raw edges and across both ends. Turn right side out and press. Baste waistband to gathered skirt, placing right side of strip to wrong side of skirt. Stitch. Bring second selvage over to right side of skirt, turn it under and stitch, stitching all around edge of waistband for tailored finish.

Use a hook and eye or button and buttonhole to fasten waistband. Put skirt on. Even bottom edge. Mark for hem. Remove skirt. Turn and slip-stitch hem.

This skirt would also be striking in a black-and-white combination, lovely in green and brown or orange and brown, or nice if made in the school colors of your best beau.

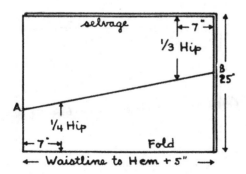

Three-gore Net over Taffeta Skirt

▶▶▶ THE PRINCIPLE of skirt making given here may be varied in many ways. If you want a gathered skirt, simply use two widths of fabric and fold selvages together, and make lines B-C and E-F twice the size indicated for a slim, straight skirt. Your foundation skirt of taffeta, for example, can be made same as net overskirt or according to the diagram.

The underskirt in this instance is a three-gore skirt cut from one skirt length (waist to hem, plus 2½ in.) of 50-in. taffeta. The overskirt is made of two lengths of 72-in. nylon net. Seams are at the side, placket opening on left.

Both skirts can be caught in with one waistband, or they can be made separately so that a skirt of another color may be worn under the overskirt on occasion.

Hem in the overskirt should be made with one turn of the net, then machine-stitched on paper. A narrow machine-stitched or hand-turned hem is sufficient for the underskirt.

Finish the placket openings with hooks and eyes or snaps.

To make the three-gore skirt: Pin selvages together, with fold toward you. Following diagram, measure to right of A 7 in. for B. C is straight down from B at a distance of one-fourth hip measurement plus 2 in. E is 7 in. to left of D. F is one-fourth hip measure plus 2 in. above E. With a yardstick, draw a line through C and F to edges of fabric. Cut on this line. Bring lines A-B around to meet lines C-F and stitch, leaving opening on left side for placket. This brings a straight seam to join a bias at sides, with bias seam at center-back. Even the bottom and top edges of skirt. If waistline is too large, dart fullness in on each side of center-front and center-back. Finish placket and hem, as described above.

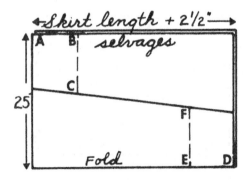

One-seam Skirt

▶▶▶ THE FABRIC MANUFACTURERS have succeeded in making a remarkable rayon fabric that looks like lightweight wool gabardine, and that has all the attractiveness of wool without the cost. This fabric is 60 in. wide and costs much less than wool gabardine. One yard will make a skirt and a cummerbund waistline finish for the average figure.

To cut: Straighten both ends of your fabric. Measure off your skirt length plus 2 in. for hem. Since average finished skirt length today is 27 in., you have approximately 7 in. for cummerbund and pockets. Measure off from one end of the short piece three pocket pieces, each 7 in. wide. The third pocket piece is split into two lengthwise pieces to make the cuffs for the top of the two pockets. The remainder of the piece is used for the cummerbund.

To make the skirt: Stitch the one seam, beginning 7½ in. down from one crosswise edge. Press seam open and put a 7-in. skirt zipper in the placket opening. Stitch matching seam binding to the bottom edge. Turn and pin the hem. Make the pockets neatly as our detail shows.

Fold waistline of the skirt in half, then in fourths, then again in eighths. Cut a notch or place a pin at each fold. Take a piece of seam binding the size of your waist plus 2 in., divide this into eighths as you did the skirt, using pins to mark each eighth. Place tape opposite each mark in the skirt. Then lay soft pleats in the waistline. Bring the ones at center-front and center-back together at the center. Make these 3 to 4 in. deep. Make smaller pleats at sides, but deep enough to take up all of the skirt fullness. Pin tape to the skirt.

Put skirt on; adjust waistline fullness to be becoming to your figure. Pin pockets in position. Check evenness of hem. Remove skirt. Stitch one lengthwise edge of cummerbund to skirt, stitching through the pleats and seam binding. Make a narrow hem on top edge and hems 1 in. wide at side closing. Finish this with hooks and eyes. Slip-stitch pockets and hems in position so that no stitching shows on right side. Press the skirt carefully and it is ready to wear.

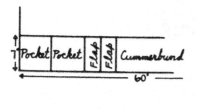

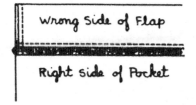

Corduroy Skirt

▶▶▶ CORDUROY SKIRTS are as popular for country as are slacks and are great favorites for school and college wear. The skirt shown requires only two skirt lengths plus hem, one spool of thread, and two buttons.

To make: Straighten fabric. Clip selvage at halfway point and tear fabric crosswise into two even lengths. From one lengthwise edge tear a strip 2½ to 3½ in. for a belt band. This narrower skirt length will be used for the back, the other for the front. For pockets, measure down from top 14 in. and in 5 in. from side, as at A.

with Pockets

From A, cut in to the 5-in. point, then cut straight down to bottom of skirt, B.

The pieces cut out are used as facings for front of pockets, as at C. Stitch these pieces on, right side of strip to right side of skirt front, stitching ¼ in. in from edge, across top and down side.

Clip corners at C. Turn facing to wrong side and press seams open for a good turn. Baste facing pieces on edge after turning. Bring line B over to meet line C on the right-hand side of the skirt. Baste and stitch side seam from bottom of pocket down to bottom of skirt.

Bring front of skirt over back, as in D, lapping front selvage edge under by its full width, so that when you stitch side seam ⅜ in. from edge, no selvage edge will show.

Stitch pocket edges on right side of skirt together, stitching down and keeping them free of skirt. Begin left side seam, E, at bottom of pocket; stitch up 5 in. to F, reverse and stitch down to bottom.

Make two rows of gathers in both back and front of skirt, spacing rows ¼ in. apart. Draw up bobbin threads so that waistline measures correctly.

Divide piece torn off for a belt band into two pieces—one for front, one for back. Back should be long enough to take in back of the pockets. Front band comes one-third of width of pocket flap on each side. Baste right side of band to right side of skirt. Fold raw edge under and fell it down on wrong side. Close ends.

Work a buttonhole in each end of front band. Mark where buttons are to be placed on back waistband. Since skirt opens at waistline on both sides, no placket is necessary.

Determine becoming skirt length, and turn hem. Stitch seam binding to top of hem and slip-stitch hem in position.

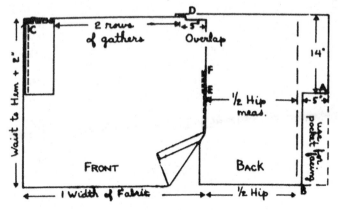

Pleated, Side-pocket Skirt

▶▶▶ AT FASHION SHOWS one often sees models put their hands in side pockets to show skirts to better advantage. Such pockets are a convenience as well as a style factor.

This charming skirt is made from 40-in. moss crepe and requires two skirt lengths plus hem. Straighten the fabric, and, as the diagram shows, divide it crosswise into two lengths. From the back, tear a lengthwise strip 7 in. wide, divide this in half crosswise. These pieces are for the pockets. A second lengthwise strip 3 in. wide is torn off to use for a waistband. Fold each pocket piece as shown, right side in. Stitch one of these along one side and up one-fourth of the distance of the opposite side. On other pocket piece, for left-hand side of skirt, put an 8-in. skirt zipper on the open side to serve as a placket opening. Turn pockets right side out. Clip the pocket seam edge at top of short row of stitching. Beginning at the top of the pocket and top of the skirt, pin the open edges of these pockets to the side seams of the skirt, right sides together. Stitch down to the clipped seam line on both sides of the pocket.

Stitch side seams of skirt from pocket, stitching down to bottom edge. Press seams open. Catch the seam at the bottom of pocket opening with several back stitches exactly in the seam so pocket will not pull out.

Notch center-front and center-back line of skirt at waistline. Fold belt in four and notch for center-front, center-back, and right-side seam. Gather back fullness. Lay front fullness in pleats, as illustration shows. Make sure side seams of skirt come at halfway point in belt band. Put the 3-in. band of fabric on as a belt, stitching it and then slip-stitching edge on inside of band so that no stitching shows on right side. Measure for hem, turn top edge ¼ in., and stitch it; then slip-stitch hem.

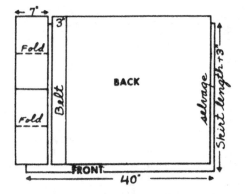

Blouses

Boat-neck Blouse

▶▶▶ THIS BLOUSE can cost very little, as it requires only 1¼ yds. for an average figure; and piqué in good quality is most reasonable. The original was in pink waffle-weave piqué, 35-in. width. It can be worn at any time of day; the same design is striking in taffeta for evening.

Fold fabric as shown in diagram, bringing top selvage toward you and lapping it a distance of one-fourth the bust measure, plus 1½ in. for fullness, plus 4 in. for sleeves. Pin edges together, as at A and B. Halfway between A and B place a pin on selvage at C, and another opposite on lengthwise fold at D. Cut in from fold a distance of half the neck measure, as from D to E. From C measure in each direction half the neck measurement plus 2 in., and place pins at F and G. Measure 4 in. in from selvage for H, I, J, and K. Draw underarm lines as indicated. Cut on those lines. Underarm pieces L and M may be used to make collar, or the long lengthwise strip may be used.

Turn and stitch 2-in. sleeve hems to allow for turn-back cuffs. French-seam underarms, and use a narrow hem at bottom of blouse. Fold collar strip in half lengthwise, right side out, and press. Lay one edge of collar along neckline, right sides together. Pin and stitch. Bring other edge of collar over to wrong side, turn edge under and stitch close to edge. This conceals seam edges inside the collar band. The band collar may be left open at the left side, as illustrated, or closed. A brooch or a corsage may be worn there.

If a fitted blouse is preferred, make a dart on each side of center-front and center-back. Put blouse on and pin in darts. Make a placket on left side. Snaps or a slide fastener can be used for closing.

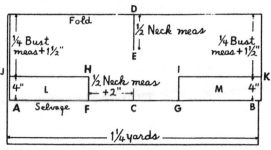

Shawl-collar Blouse

▶▶▶ THE SHAWL-COLLAR blouse is ideal to wear with costume necklaces, with suit or separate skirt. It can have long, three-quarter, or short sleeves, and can be made of many types of fabric. Sheer wool, particularly jersey, is especially good, but so are crepe, taffeta, challis, and metallics. Button the neck high or low and use cuffs or not, as you desire. Buy a fabric that has no up and down—1 yd. of 54-in. or 2 yds. of 36-in. material. Follow the diagram for cutting. You will find the making easy, especially since collar and facing are cut in one with the blouse.

To chalk out: Fold fabric lengthwise, right sides together. Lay out with selvages toward you, if narrow fabric is used, or one fold toward you if jersey is used. The diagram shows the folds as with jersey. B in the diagram is marked 6 in. above corner A; C, 2 in. below B. D is a shoulder-to-waist measurement plus 6 in. to right of A. E is 6 in. above D. Chalk a line B to E to mark center-front line. C, indicated by dotted line, is front edge of blouse. Distance between B and C provides for overlap at center-front. F is one-half the armhole measurement plus 3 in. to right of B and G is one-fourth bust measurement plus 2 in. above F. Draw a straight line F through G to top edge of fabric for H. I is one-half the elbow measurement to left of H. J is one-fourth neck measurement above B. K is 2 in. to right of J. Chalk a line from J through K to I. L is one-fourth bust measurement plus 1 in. above E. Cut out front portion. Lay line B-E of front on opposite fold or selvage for center-back. If selvages, place line B-E a seam's width in from edge. Cut back same as front.

Baste shoulder and underarm, making 3/8-in. seams. Baste back seam also if narrow fabric is used. Try blouse on and shape neck in front as you want it. Curved line indicated on diagram shows how shawl collar is cut. Seam shoulders and underarms; press seams open. Use piece cut out as at M for a facing for back collar. Stitch top edge of collar and back facing together in back. Press seam open. Now press center-front edges back on line C and slip-stitch back facing and these edges all in position. Hem bottom edge of blouse.

There is material enough to make cuffs wide or narrow, as you desire. Stitch these on, and slip-stitch one edge over the joining seam to cover.

Use bound or worked buttonholes and attractive jeweled or self-covered buttons.

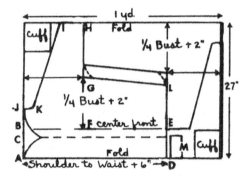

Blouse with Portrait Neckline

▶▶▶ ARTISTS and photographers prefer portrait necklines when they make pictures. Fashion shows them over and over again in the prettiest, daintiest blouses and dresses.

For the blouse illustrated buy 1⅓ yds. of 42-in. taffeta, crepe, dotted swiss, or voile. Straighten both ends. Fold fabric lengthwise through center, selvages together, with fold toward you.

To chalk out: As in the diagram, locate C halfway between A and B. D is one-half neckline measurement plus 2 in. above C. E is on selvage directly above D. F is 2 in. to left of E. G is one-half armhole measurement plus 2 in. to left of C. H is one-half bust measurement plus 3 in. above G. I is straight up from H on selvage. J is one-half neck measurement less 1 in. to left of C. K is straight to left of H on edge of fabric. L is 4 in. below K. Fold on line C-D-E and cut back and front. Cut through four thicknesses from L, rounding the underarm near H, as diagram shows. Cut out to I. Cut neck from J to D to C. If a low neck is desired in the back, measure to right of C 2 or 3 in. and cut back neck from this point to D. Cut shoulder line D to F. The dotted line from F to E shows a way to cut the sleeve hem so that it will be wide enough when turned back. The underarm seams may also be flared, as dotted line shows between K and L, to provide ease over the hips.

Stitch shoulder seams and right underarm seam. Use a bias facing for neck edge. Turn bottom of sleeves up to length you desire and slip-stitch edge down. Stitch left underarm seam and put in an 8-in. zipper, beginning it at waistline.

Draw the fullness down at each side and hold it with shirrings or small pleats. Make this fullness secure, so that you can wear blouse with or without clips.

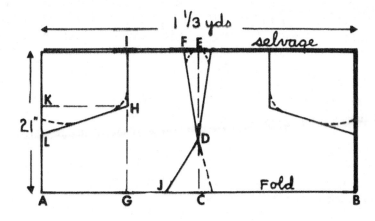

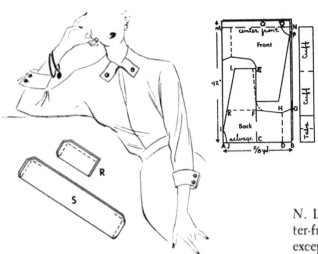

Self-trimmed Crepe Blouse

▶▶▶ TO MAKE the blouse illustrated you need 1½ to 1¾ yds., depending on length from shoulder to waist.

Straighten ends. Cut off 4½-in. crosswise strip for tabs and cuffs. Cut fabric length in half crosswise. With right sides together, pin all edges. Lay one selvage toward you. A in diagram is lower left-hand corner; B is lower right. C is one-half the armhole measurement plus 3 in. to right of A; D is the shoulder-to-waist measurement plus 1 in. from A.

Measure length of shoulder, plus three-fourths of the sleeve length, plus 1 in. Chalk a line this length straight in from C for E, then straight from E to left edge.

F and G are one-fourth bust measurement plus 1½ in. from C and B. H is one-fourth bust measurement from D. Chalk a broken line from D to H. I is one-sixth neck measurement plus ½ in. above A. J is ½ in. to right of A. K is half the armhole measurement plus 1 in. to left of F.

Chalk back-neck curve J-I. Chalk straight from I through K to L on the E line. Then draw L-E, F-H, and H-G. Curve underarm at F. If bottom of sleeve is too wide, taper underarm from F to E (see broken line). Cut out back on lines J-I, I-L, L-E, E around F, through H to G. Mark waistline pleats or darts as indicated by broken line.

On opposite selvage chalk center-front line 1½ in. in, straight across from M to N. Lay selvage edges of back along center-front line. Pin. Cut front same as back except for facing and neckline. Remove back. O is one-sixth neck measurement plus ½ in. to left of N; P, the same distance below N. Draw neck curve P-O. Cut neckline, cutting facing to match curve. Mark depth of front-neck opening Q.

Seam center-front line from Q down. Seam center-back. Press seams open. Turn front facings to right side. Stitch across facings at neckline. Clip corners and curves. Turn facing to wrong side. Press. Stitch shoulder and underarm seams, leaving left underarm seam open for about 7 in. for placket. Face neck and sleeve edges.

Pin waistline fullness in pleats or darts. Check fit. Stitch pleats or darts. Use zipper or snap fasteners for side closing. Hem bottom of blouse. Press.

From 4½-in. strip, cut two 4-in. crosswise pieces for tabs. Cut two cuffs to same measurement as bottom of sleeves, plus 2 or 3 in. Fold tab pieces in half lengthwise, right sides together. Stitch side and one end, as at R. Fold cuffs in half lengthwise, right sides together. Stitch ends, as at S. Clip all corners, press seams open, and turn right side out. Bind raw edges of cuffs.

Check position and length of tabs. Cut off excess. Turn ends in and sew them together. Tack to inside of neckline. Tack cuffs in position. Tabs and cuffs can be changed if buttonholes are made in both and link buttons used at neck and in sleeves.

Open-front Jersey Blouse

▶▶▶ MOST JERSEY BLOUSES are slipovers, finished boat-neck, or have a Peter Pan collar with center-back opening. This one, however, opens down the front. It is ever so easy to make and takes, for an average figure, less than 1 yd. of fabric and 2 yds. 1¼ in. grosgrain ribbon.

To chalk out: Lay jersey out, one fold next to you. For front facings and overlap, measure in 4 in. from fold, as at A in diagram. B is a shoulder-to-waistline length plus 4 in. to right of A. C is one-half armhole measurement plus 3 in. to right of A. Chalk straight across from C to D on opposite fold. E is one-fourth bust measurement plus 1½ in. in from C on this line. Chalk from E straight across to F on left edge. G is 2 in. to right of F. H is one-sixth neck measurement plus ½ in. above A. Chalk from H through G to fold. Chalk straight up from B a distance of one-fourth bust measurement for I. Connect E and I.

To cut out blouse: Cut shoulder line from H through to fold. Cut on fold to D; cut D through E to I, curving underarm on dotted line, then from I through B to fold. Split front fold. Lay this front over back, with fold along line A-B. Cut back same as front except for facing.

To make blouse: Piece bottoms of sleeves of front so that they are same length as back sleeves. Turn under raw edge on front facing and stitch. Turn fronts back 3 in. to wrong side on each side. Baste. Join shoulder and underarm seams, making ⅜-in. seam. Finish bottom edge with ¼-in. hem. Turn a narrow hem in bottom of sleeves or use a scrap of fabric to face them. Fold ribbon in half lengthwise and press. Use ribbon to bind front edges and around neckline, mitering the corners of the ribbon, as at J. After basting and stitching binding in position, slip-stitch front facings in position.

Use swivel, pin-on buttons or bound buttonholes and self-covered or jewel buttons for front closing.

A shirring of elastic thread at waistline will help to control fullness and to keep blouse inside waistband of skirt.

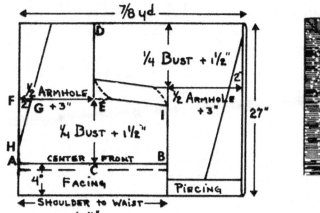

Mandarin Blouse

▶▶▶ EVERY SUIT needs its blouse—its several blouses, rather—and those that are easy to launder are especially desirable.

This one takes less than 1¼ yds. of fabric to make. Buy double the length from shoulder to waist plus 9 to 10 in., depending upon tuck-in desired (usually about 1¼ yds.).

Place lengthwise selvages of straightened fabric toward you. Move one selvage back a distance of one-fourth bust measurement plus 8 in. to mark width needed for bust and allowance plus depth of sleeve as shown in diagram. For example, if bust is 36 in. and you want a 6-in. sleeve, as shown, make fold 17 in. from the top selvage.

On selvage mark center (A). For sleeves, measure both right and left from A one-half the armhole measurement plus 1 in. to locate points B and C. Measure from fold in line with B and C one-fourth bust measurement plus 2 in.; mark D and E. Form sleeves and underarm by cutting from B to D, then straight out to edge, F; and from C to E, and out to edge at G.

Place H on fold straight across from A. Measure from H to I one-fourth neck measurement. Mark J ½ in. to left of H. Measure down from H one-fourth neck measurement for K. Cut from J through K to I to make neckline.

For front opening, cut a facing piece 6 in. wide and 11 to 12 in. long. Place right side to right side of blouse. Stitch from neck down 8 in. and back, as at L. Carefully cut between the rows of stitching. Turn raw edge of facing ¼ in. and stitch free of blouse, as at M. Turn facing to wrong side and baste.

For collar, cut a 2¾-in.-wide lengthwise strip 2 in. longer than neck measurement. Find center of this. Place on wrong side of neck at back; baste and stitch around neckline and across front ends. Turn collar to right side. Turn raw edge under and baste collar. Stitch around collar close to edge, as in N. A button and loop or pin can hold collar at neckline or neck may be left open.

French-seam underarms, leaving left side open from bottom to 4 in. above waistline. Use a ¼-in. hem to finish bottom edge and side placket. Snap fasteners can be used in placket. Finish sleeves with a ½- to 1½-in. hem.

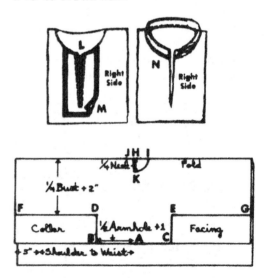

Tailored Blouse

▶▶▶ YOU NEED only 1¼ yds. of 36-in. piqué, broadcloth, linen, or silk to make the front-pleat blouse shown.

For front pleat: Tear fabric in half crosswise. For pleat, cut a 2½-in. lengthwise strip along one selvage of piece for front. Stitch right side of strip to wrong side of fabric on right-hand front. Press seam open, as at A. Fold pleat over to right side, as at B, so that raw edges meet but do not overlap. Press pleat so that seam is in direct center. Stitch ⅜ in. from edge on each side. Make ½-in. hem on left side, as at C. Center front pleat over hem on left-side front and pin. Fold through center. Pin.

To chalk out: Lay folded center-front toward you, as in diagram. Fold over one selvage of back piece to same depth as fronts. Fabric beyond this is for collarband.

D is at center-front of pleat. Measure in from D one-sixth neck measurement plus ½ in. on both back and front for E. F is one-fourth neck measurement to left of D.

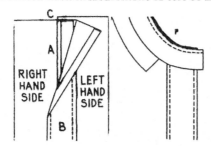

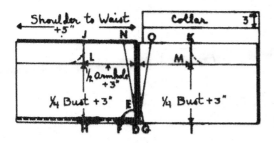

G is ½ in. to right of D. H and I are half the armhole measurement plus 3 in. to left and right of D. Chalk lines straight up to edges for J and K. Measure up on these lines one-fourth bust measurement plus 3 in.; locate L and M. Draw straight lines to left and right of L and M. Curve underarms as shown by dotted lines. N and O are each 2 in. in from line D.

To cut out: Cut front neck from F to E and front shoulder E to N. Curve underarm line at J. Cut back G to E, E to O, and over to K, then underarm from K. Cut about 1¼-in.-width bias from scraps.

To make: Seam shoulders together, beginning at E and using a ⅜-in. seam. Stitch underarm seams, again using a ⅜-in. seam. Clip seam at ¾-in. intervals at underarm curve. Hem bottom of sleeves. Pieces cut from underarms can be used for 2-in. band cuffs, if desired.

Make single stand-up band collar, or, for turnover style, cut it 3 in. wide. Stitch ends of collar, turn right side out, and press. Lay collar to right side of neck. Over this place bias binding, pinning as in P. Stitch collar and bias as shown. Turn collar up and turn bias down on wrong side to cover raw edges. Slip-stitch binding; finish front edges. Use ¼-in. seam to join band to neckline.

Make a ¼-in. hem on bottom edge. Use lengthwise buttonholes in front pleat, and sew buttons on left-hand hem.

Informal Blouse

▶▶▶ SO OFTEN it is desirable to have a gay, easy-feeling blouse to slip on with a long or short skirt at home when you want to look pretty but not "dressed up."

The one shown is especially attractive. It was made of 1¼ yds. of a rayon print crepe 42 in. in width.

Straighten both ends of fabric. Fold lengthwise, with fold toward you.

To chalk out: B on the diagram is at a distance equal to the back length plus 4 in. to right of corner A. C is 1 in. to left of B. E is straight up from B on the selvage. F is 4 in. to left of E. Draw a line from F to B for shoulders. Mark D on this line at one-sixth of neck measurement plus ½ in. from B. Curve a line D to C for back neck. G is one-half the armhole measurement plus 4 in. to left of B. H is one-fourth bust measurement plus 2 in. above G. I is one-half the armhole measurement plus 4 in. to left of F. J is straight to left of H at edge of fabric. Draw lines J-H, H-I, and curve underarm at I, as shown.

Cut from J to H to I, curving underarm as marked. Cut F to D, D to C. Lay this piece over front, center-back fold in line with center-front selvage. Cut front the same as back except for neckline. Cut front sleeve on fold. In the front shoulder seam lay two darts, each ¾ in. wide and tapering to nothing 5 in. below. Begin these darts so that first is one-sixth of the neck measurement from center-front line. Dart fullness is provided in front and back at waistline. Make these as large as necessary for blouse to fit nicely. Center-front darts are caught at waistline, but not stitched. Cut center-front band 4 in. wide, as diagram shows.

To make blouse: French-seam shoulder line and underarms. Apply the center-front band all way around from waistline to waistline. Put a slip-stitched hem, ribbon facing, or lace in bottom of sleeves to finish.

Make a narrow hem on the bottom of the blouse. Cut ties, hem raw edges. Draw fullness in as shown in sketch so that blouse fits around waist, and attach ties at center-front. You may wish to make a nice bow and tack it in place, using a hook-and-eye closing underneath.

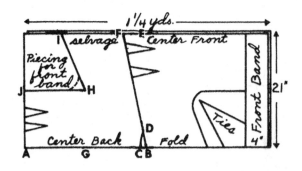

Draped Blouse

▶▶▶ FULLNESS IS ADDED to simple blouses in ingenious ways. This, for example, is just a plain jersey blouse with a boat neck with a strip of jersey coming across back of neck, crossing in front, and extending to waistline in back for a closing. Make drape of matching color, or use two colors, or use a velvet fold on crepe or jersey.

This blouse takes 1¼ yds. of 50-in. tubular, no-sag jersey, using ⅞ yd. for the blouse and ⅜ yd. for the drape.

To chalk out and cut: Straighten both ends. Lay tube out, one fold toward you. From corner A on diagram measure shoulder-to-waist length plus 3 in. for B. C is one-fourth bust measurement plus 1 in. above A. D is one-half the armhole measurement plus 3 in. to right of C. From D draw straight line up to fold for E. F is one-half the wrist measurement plus 2 in. to left of E. For G measure up from A one-half the neck measurement less 1 in. For shoulder, draw line from G to F. Draw a straight line from E to D and from D to H. Curve underarm and slant side seam, as shown by broken lines. Cut from G to F and from B to H, then around to E. This will give you front of blouse. Lay this over back piece, folded edges even, and cut same. Cut folds F to E.

To make blouse: Join shoulder seams and underarms together. Press shoulder seams open. Finish neckline with narrow hem. First turn edge ⅛ in. and stitch; then slip-stitch it in position.

Clip underarm seam at curve. Hem bottom edge of blouse, using narrowest possible hem. Turn edge ⅛ in. at bottom of sleeve; stitch. Turn a ½-in. hem and slip-stitch hem. Press blouse carefully.

To make drape: Cut one lengthwise fold. Turn and stitch a narrow hem on both long edges. Gather both ends of strip, making gathers tight as possible. Put on, cross in front, and bring to center of back. If it is long enough to lap, bind ends with scraps and use hooks and eyes for closing. If more length is needed, add straight 2-in.-wide strips, as at I, stitching over ends of gathers and fastening as shown at J.

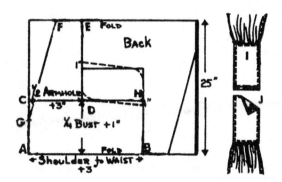

Wool Pullover

▶▶▶ THESE PULLOVERS first became important as an after-skiing fashion, and were worn over sweaters. Then the fashionables started wearing them over blouses. They can be made of rayon in imitation of wool at small cost. One length of 54-in. fabric makes the pullover. Measure length you want yours to be—⅝ to ¾ yd. from shoulder to hem.

Straighten fabric. Fold lengthwise, fold next to you, bringing one selvage edge up on the fabric to a depth of one-half the bust measure plus 3 in., as at A in diagram. C is one-fourth neck measurement to right of B. D is one-sixth neck measurement plus ½ in. above B. E is one-sixth neck measurement plus 1½ in. below A. F is halfway between D and E. G is 1 in. to right of F. H is ½ in. to right of A.

To cut out: Cut front neck from C to D, shoulders D to G to E, back neck E to H. Slash from G to I for armhole, cutting on lengthwise thread a distance of one-half the armhole measurement plus 2 in.

Make hem on center-back edges ¾ in. wide. These can be slip-stitched or machine-stitched. Lap hems as in J. Use snap fasteners or buttons and buttonholes, or turn edges back 1 in. each side and use a full-length zipper. Cut bands for sleeves. Apply armhole band, beginning at shoulder, right side of band to right side of blouse; make ¼-in. seams. Clip every ½ in. around curve at I so that seam will not draw. Seam shoulders, stitching from neck out through shoulder length and band. Turn raw edge of band in and slip-stitch it in place.

Turn hem at bottom; use seam binding at top of hem; slip-stitch in position. Cut a fitted facing for neck. Stitch to right side, making a ¼-in. seam. Clip neck-edge seam all way around. Turn to wrong side; slip-stitch down.

Wear with a narrow leather belt of contrasting or matching color.

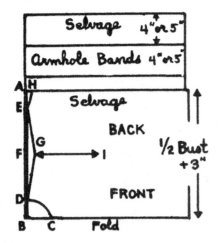

T-shirt Blouse

▶▶▶ PERHAPS one of the most popular blouses is a T-shirt type—chemise, really. Bands of fabric finish neck and armhole. Bands can be of same color or contrasting, as gray on white.

Of 36-in. tricot jersey knit, rayon, or wool, you need 1¼ yds. to make this shirt and ⅛ yd. of trimming color if band is different. Blouse costs little in rayon, more if wool jersey is used.

To chalk out: Straighten fabric. Fold lengthwise, wrong side up with fold toward you. Point C on diagram is halfway between corners A and B. D is ½ in. to right of C; E, one-fourth neck measurement to left. F is one-sixth neck measurement plus ½ in. above C. Draw line D to F and curve neckline F to E. Cut center-back opening about 8 in. deep from D to G. H is one-half the armhole measurement plus 1½ in. to left of C. I is one-fourth bust measurement plus 2 in. above H. J is 3 in. above I. K is one-fourth bust measurement plus 2 in. above A. Draw line K-I, I-J. Shape armhole in curved line at I, as diagram shows. Fold blouse across shoulders. Beginning at line C-F, bring crosswise ends together, and cut back underarm same as front. Pieces cut out at armhole may be used for bands for neck and armhole if shirt and bands are to be of one color.

Cut bands 2¼ in. wide for neck and armholes. Hem back neck slash D to G. Face neck and armholes with bands, taking ¼-in. seam in each lengthwise edge of bands so that they will be finished ⅞ in. wide.

Sleeves may be longer than diagram shows, or surplus fabric may be used for a tie belt, as a tie for the neck, or for a tailored bow on each shoulder.

French-seam underarm seams, beginning at sleeve edge so that band will be even. Make a ¼-in. hem on bottom of blouse. Sew a loop and button for closing to neckline at center-back.

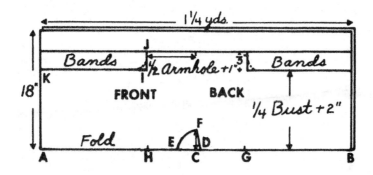

Dress-up Blouse of Net or Lace

▶▶▶ THE COST of a lace blouse depends largely upon the kind of lace used. Sometimes heirloom laces can be used. Generally, however, it is best to buy crisp, fresh lace exactly right for your purpose. You can buy 1½ to 1¾ yds. of 36-in. black cotton net, with a diamond, square, or circle pattern; 2 yds. each of ½-in. and 1½-in. velvet ribbon—all at most reasonable prices.

Fold fabric in half lengthwise, wrong side out. Pin lengthwise edges together. Blouse may open front or back as fashion decrees.

To chalk out: A in diagram is lower left-hand corner. B is the halfway point on fold. One-half the armhole measurement plus 3 in. to left of B is C. Chalk a line straight in to opposite edges from C for D and from B for E. F and G are one-sixth of the neck measurement plus ½ in. from B. H is 1 in. to right of B. I is 3 in. from G.

Measure in from C one-fourth bust measurement plus 3 in. for J; from A one-fourth bust measurement plus 5 in. for K. L is half the armhole measurement plus 1 in. to right of D. Connect K and J, L and I. Mark neck curves F-G-H. Cut out neckline. Cut from K through J to D, curving underarm at J as shown. Cut from L to I. Fold front over back section on shoulder line I-G, center-front fold and back fold even. Cut back same as front.

Center-back fold can be slashed from neckline to bottom edge as illustrated or, if desired, cut only 8 in. down from neckline. Make narrow hem on back edges. Make a narrow turn to right side on neck and bottom of sleeves. Stitch. Make 1-in. hem in bottom edge.

Slip-stitch narrow ribbon over stitching on bottom of sleeves and around neck, leaving long or short tie-ends at neck. Tie wider ribbon around waistline. Tie at back or front. Adjust fullness evenly.

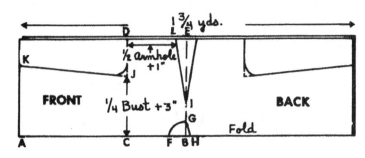

Lace Overblouse

▶▶▶ FOR THAT tired, woebegone dress that is too, too plain or for a new camisole-top dress, try this type of lace overblouse. You need 1½ yds. of 36-in. cotton lace in white, black, or a flattering color. If long sleeves are more becoming to you, piece sleeves with pieces cut from the underarm. Such an overblouse is convenient when your camisole-top dress seems too bare for the occasion or for comfort.

To chalk out: Straighten fabric at cut ends. Fold lengthwise, with fold toward you. Pin selvages together. Following the diagram, mark B at halfway point on fold to right of corner A. C is one-fourth of the neck measurement to left of B. D is one-sixth neck measurement plus ½ in. above B. E is one-half armhole measurement plus 1 in. to left of B. F is on selvage directly above E. G is one-fourth bust measurement plus 2 in. above E on E-F line. H is straight to left edge from G. Cut line H toward G, curving underarm as shown. Cut out to F. Mark I on selvage straight up from B and fold front over this line, center-front fold and center-back fold meeting. Cut back same as front. Cut neck curve C to D, then to B. In fitting, you may want to shape back neck a little, but with lace it is rarely necessary. Slash front on fold to depth desired, usually to waist.

French-seam underarms. Band the neck and center-front with 1-in.-wide lace insertion or ribbon. Make a 1-in. hem in bottom of sleeves and 1¼-in. hem in bottom of blouse.

Sequins may be sewn to the lace to add glitter. Pockets may be added to portion below waistline. A velvet ribbon sash may be used at the waist. These are only a few of the many ways to individualize this type of blouse and make it just right for you.

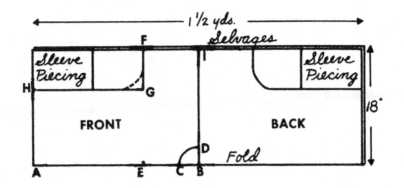

Wool Jersey Basics

▶▶▶ THE BLOUSE SHOWN opens on the shoulder. It is made of one length (shoulder-to-waist measurement plus 4 in.) of 54-in. tubular jersey. The skirt, which requires one length (waist-to-hem measurement plus 3-in. hem allowance) is made as explained on page 20. The blouse and skirt can match or contrast in color. Average amount of fabric needed for blouse is 5/8 yd.

Straighten ends of fabric. Fold tube of jersey in half, lengthwise, so that the two folds come together, as at A. Smooth layers and pin carefully. B is lower left-hand corner, C lower right. D is one-half the armhole measurement plus 2 in. to right of B. E is the shoulder-to-waist measurement plus 1 in. from B. Chalk lines straight across from D to folds and from E to folds. F is one-fourth neck measurement above B.

G is 1 in. to right of upper left-hand corner. H and I are one-fourth bust measurement plus 1 in. above D and C. J is one-fourth bust measurement from E. Connect F-G; H through J to I. Curve underarm at H, continuing line to folds by tapering slightly toward G, as indicated.

Cut out blouse, cutting F-G; I to J around curve at H to folds on edge. Cut both folds at bottom of sleeves.

Separate blouse pieces. Fold front in half lengthwise, shoulder lines matching. Measure from top down on fold one-sixth of the neck measurement plus ½ in. Chalk and cut front neck curve from F on shoulder line to this point.

Cut two 4-in. strips for cuffs, as at K, piecing, if necessary, to get length.

Seam shoulders, beginning 4 in. from neckline on both sides to provide for shoulder openings. Seam underarms and clip curves.

Cut facings for back and front neckline from fabric remaining after cutting cuffs. Cut and apply facings exactly as described for Casual Jersey Blouse on page 50.

Seam ends of cuffs together to form circle. Lay right side of cuff to right side of sleeve, matching seam in cuff to underarm seam. Pin edges together and stitch. Press cuff down. Bring raw edge of cuff to wrong side of sleeve, turn edge under and whip in position. Press cuffs. Turn up to right side.

Finish bottom of blouse with narrow hem.

Use snaps for shoulder openings. Sew buttons in position, sewing through facing or seam allowance to make secure.

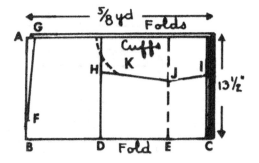

A Dark Blouse for a Light Suit

▶▶▶ A PASTEL SUIT of gabardine may be complemented by a dark blouse of heavy cotton lace. The one shown is made kimono-style, with a few gathers at the shoulders. It may be self-trimmed with cutout motifs of lace, overcast or crocheted on the edges, and sewed to neck and sleeve edge. A pearl bead or a sequin may be added in the center of a lace flower.

Buy 1¼ yds. of 36-in. lace or allover embroidery. Fold lengthwise, wrong side out. Lay out with the fold toward you, and pin edges together at ends and sides.

To chalk out blouse: Point C in the diagram is halfway between corners A and B; D, one-fourth of neck measurement to left of C; E, 1 in. to right. F is one-sixth of neck measurement plus 1 in. above C. G is on edge directly above. Draw a line F to G. Draw neck curve D to F, F to E. H is one-half the armhole measurement plus 1 in. to left of C; I, one-fourth bust measurement plus 2 in. above H. J is directly above I on edge of fabric. K is at edge straight to left of I. Draw lines K-I, I-J, curving armhole at I as diagram shows. Cut on these lines. Fold front over back on line C-G and cut back underarm same as front. Cut neck curve D to F to E; then cut center-back down 7 in. to L. Overcast this cut edge, or face it with very narrow, matching seam binding, or bind with nylon ribbon. Bind neck edge and bottom of sleeves and bottom of blouse.

Seam underarms, using a ⅜-in. seam. Take elastic sewing thread and gather three rows on top of each shoulder, beginning 2 in. from neck and extending out to tip of armhole. This fullness gives blouse a soft look and prevents its being too snug or flat-looking.

Cut motifs of lace from material cut from underarms. Overcast edges of these or crochet a narrow blanket-stitch around edge, using matching thread, of course. Sew these cutout motifs around the neck edge and on sleeves. If lace is such that you cannot cut out motifs to make trimming, then use a pleated ruffle of net or lace such as you can buy at trimming counters.

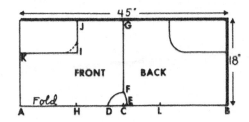

Casual Jersey Blouse

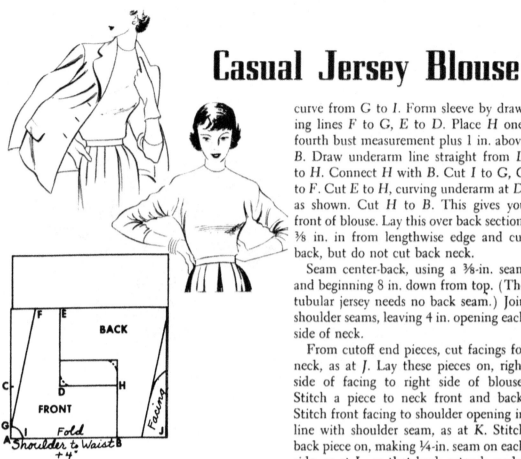

▶▶▶ TRICOT JERSEY in nylon or rayon, or tubular wool jersey is suggested for this blouse. It requires ¾ yd. of 60-in. fabric. The diagram is given for the tricot, but the procedure is almost identical for the wool.

Straighten both ends of fabric. With fold toward you, overlap edge of top piece one-half the bust measurement plus 7 in. from fold, and pin along this edge.

From corner point A measure shoulder-to-waist length plus 4 in. to locate B. C is one-fourth bust measurement plus 1 in. above A. D is one-half armhole measurement plus 3 in. to right of C. E is same distance in from left-edge corner. F is one-half wrist measurement plus 2 in. to left of E. For G, measure up from A one-sixth neck measurement plus ½ in. I is same amount to right of A. Mark front neck curve from G to I. Form sleeve by drawing lines F to G, E to D. Place H one-fourth bust measurement plus 1 in. above B. Draw underarm line straight from D to H. Connect H with B. Cut I to G, G to F. Cut E to H, curving underarm at D, as shown. Cut H to B. This gives you front of blouse. Lay this over back section, ⅜ in. in from lengthwise edge and cut back, but do not cut back neck.

Seam center-back, using a ⅜-in. seam and beginning 8 in. down from top. (The tubular jersey needs no back seam.) Join shoulder seams, leaving 4 in. opening each side of neck.

From cutoff end pieces, cut facings for neck, as at J. Lay these pieces on, right side of facing to right side of blouse. Stitch a piece to neck front and back. Stitch front facing to shoulder opening in line with shoulder seam, as at K. Stitch back piece on, making ¼-in. seam on each side, as at L, so that back extends under edge of front on each side and seams appear continuous. Clip back shoulder seam, as at M, and clip seam edges on curves as shown.

Bring facing to wrong side. Turn outside edge under and stitch free of blouse, as in N. When pressed, facing will hold in place even without tacking stitches.

Clip underarm seam at curve. Hem bottom of blouse, using narrowest possible hem. Turn edge ⅛ in. at bottom of sleeve; stitch. Turn a ½-in. hem and slip-stitch.

Sew loops and buttons or snaps on neck openings. Press blouse carefully.

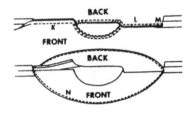

Sleeveless Suit Blouse

▶▶▶ FOR THE BLOUSE shown, measure shoulder to waistline and buy twice this length of fabric, plus 9 or 12 in. for tuck-in. For average figure 1⅓ yds. is ample. You can buy plissé crepe, broadcloth, plain or dotted nylon, linen, plain or embroidered organdie or allover lace.

To chalk out: Straighten fabric. Place wrong side of fabric up, side edges or selvages together, with the fold toward you. Chalk out as diagram shows. B is one-fourth of bust measurement, plus 5 in. above A. Fold fabric so that top selvage is in line with B. D is halfway between A and C. E is one-fourth of neck measurement to left of D, and F ½ in. to right. G is one-sixth of neck measurement plus ½ in. above D, and H is on selvage directly above D and G. I is one-half of armhole measurement to left of H, and J is 3 in. directly below I. K is 2 in. below J. L is 3 in. below B. Chalk a line J to L.

Cut from L to J, J to K, J to I, through top thickness along selvage to H. Fold fabric on line D-H and cut back same as front, except at neck. Unfold, and cut neck F-G, G-E. Cut blouse front down on fold line from E to A. Turn line I-H back to the right side 1½ in. and stitch ends; then turn hem back to position and slip stitch.

French-seam the underarms, and face the under armhole portion with bias binding or a bias scrap of the fabric. Make sure that this finish is secure, and that the ends are caught securely with hand stitches to the hems at each side of the armhole.

Cut two lengthwise facing strips, both 2 in. wide. Stitch a strip each side of front, using a ¼-in. seam. Fold the strip on left-hand side and stitch it on as a band. Use the right-hand side as a facing.

Make a 2½-in.-wide band collar 2 in. longer than neck measurement. Place right sides together; stitch on ends and along one edge. Turn right side out, clip neckline of blouse every ½ in., making clips ¼ in. deep all around neck. Put blouse on. Pin collar on neckline, center-front of collar to center-front of the front facing. Make sure that collar fits smoothly. Remove, re-pin to have true line, baste, then stitch collar in position, concealing neckline seam inside collar. Finish bottom of blouse with a ¼-in. hem. Mark for lengthwise buttonholes in center-fold. Cut and work these. Sew buttons in position on left-front pleat. Press—and your blouse is finished.

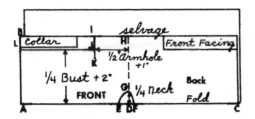

Sateen Blouse

▶▶▶ GRANDMOTHER'S PRIZE PETTICOAT was made of sateen. Cotton satin, some call this lovely old-new fabric. It has sheen, it washes easily, wears well, and looks lovely. It costs more than most cottons, but when you use it economically, as in this blouse, your purchase will prove a good investment.

To chalk out: Take two waist lengths plus 6 in. Fold wrong side out, with fold toward you, selvages pinned together. Point C on the diagram is halfway between A and B, D is on selvages directly above C. E is one-half neck measure to left of C. F is one-fourth neck measure above C. G is 2 in. left of D. Connect G and F for shoulder line and F and E for neckline. H is one-half armhole measure plus 1 in. to left of C. I is one-fourth bust measure plus 3 in. above H, and J on selvage directly above I. K is at edge straight to left of I. Connect J and K, curving underarm at I as shown.

Fold front over so that A and B meet. Cut back same as front. If you do not want neck as low in back, make it distance you desire it below C and connect neckline with F. If you wish blouse to fit snugly, slant line K-I as necessary to take out excess fullness and make a placket at left underarm seam.

Seam shoulder and underarm seams. Cut cuffs 5½ in. wide, so that they can turn back, and twice as long as G to J. Seam cuffs into a tube, turn right side out, press seam open. Place two raw edges of the cuffs to bottom of sleeves; put them on with true-bias facing. Ready-made bias binding pressed flat may be used. Face neckline, clipping binding at shoulders to lie flat and crossing it at center-front for a smooth finish. Stitch binding on; turn it ⅛ in. from edge so that it cannot show. Slip-stitch it into place. Put a narrow hem in bottom of blouse.

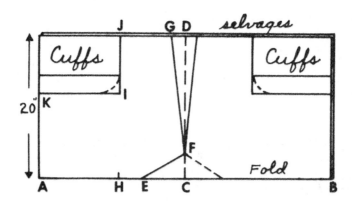

Halter Overblouse

▶▶▶ THIS MAY BE worn over a formal, or under a suit, or with a sweater or blouse. The purpose will determine for you the best type of fabric. Velvet, brocade, satin, or jersey with sequins or brilliants, when in fashion, are right for formal wear; velveteen, corduroy, or jersey for suit wear; and fabric matching the skirt for wear over a blouse or sweater. You can really go up-up-up in yardage price; but since average figure needs only ⅝ yd. of fabric, even expensive fabric is not prohibitive.

Straighten fabric. Fold in half lengthwise, wrong side out, selvages together toward you. Point B on diagram is the front-length measurement (shoulder to waistline) plus 2 in. to right of corner A. C is at upper left-hand corner. D is 6 in. to 8 in. to right of C, depending on depth desired above waistline in back. Measure distance D to E. Place F the same distance below E. To locate G and H, measure from D and F the desired depth of peplum plus seams. (A good depth for average figure is 5½ to 6 in.) Tie chalk on string, and with end of string at E, chalk an arc from D to F, for underarm line and from G to H for top of peplum. Cut on both these lines.

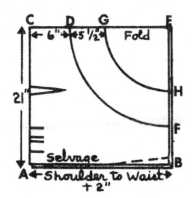

Lay pleats at waistline in front to control fullness under bust. When fitting, pin darts at underarm line. Cut off any excess at center-back, but allow for closing there, using a zipper, button and loops, or hooks and eyes. If, by any chance, waistline is not large enough, a piece can be added from the fabric scraps.

Baste center-front seam, beginning at a point to left of B where you want V to terminate. Turn back selvages for neckline as indicated by dotted line. Finish underarm and back edge with bias facing. From circle of fabric below E, cut a strip 4 in. wide and long enough to extend across the neck at back; make a tube of this, leaving ends open. Slip one shoulder edge into each end of this tube, concealing all raw edges. Fullness along shoulder line B-F may be laid in folds or shirred as you prefer.

The peplum may be lined throughout; or edges may be turned and held back with catch-stitches; or edges may be bound with braid. Fold D-G in peplum comes at center-front. Ends of peplum are toward center-back. Join peplum to waistline when fullness of latter is adjusted to your waist measurement.

Gingham Blouse

▶▶▶ HERE IS an ideal blouse. Make a matching skirt and you will *live* in the outfit.

Blouse requires two shoulder-to-waist lengths of fabric, plus 8 in. for tuck-in at front and back—usually 1¼ yds. For average figure, this leaves enough material from a 36-in.-width fabric to make the bands. A good idea is to buy enough fabric for two blouses: 1¼ yds. of plain, 1¼ of plaid, and make a plaid blouse with plain bands, and a plain with plaid. If you want a single blouse, buy 1 yd. of one fabric and ⅜ yd. for contrasting bands; and cut bands to same size as diagram indicates, but on crosswise of fabric rather than on lengthwise.

To chalk out blouse: Straighten fabric. Place lengthwise fold of fabric toward you, with top selvage (C) at one-fourth the bust measurement plus 3 in. above corner point B.

Be sure fold is on a true lengthwise line. D is at halfway point between corners A and B. E is 1¼ in. to right of D. F is one-fourth of neck measurement to left; G, one-sixth of neck measurement plus ½ in. directly above D. H is on top selvage directly above D. I and J are both 1 in. from H. K is one-half armhole measurement plus 2 in. to left of I. Cut the neck curve from F to G to E. Cut shoulder G to I and G to J. Cut fabric lengthwise full length and through both thicknesses, following top selvage on line C.

To make room for the contrasting bands, cut front through two thicknesses 1 in. from fold, as dotted line on diagram shows, from neckline to left-hand edge of fabric. Stitch shoulders, beginning at neck edge. Make ⅜-in. pressed-open seams.

Cut bands and panels to size as shown. Fold through center lengthwise and stitch across top ends of both front panels and both ends of the collar. Turn these right side out. Stitch back edge of one panel to each side of front opening, beginning ⅜ in. from top on wrong side of opening, and making ¼-in. seam. Now bring free edge of panel over, with raw edge turned under ¼ in., and top-stitch it in place. (Or you can sew band on from right side and slip-stitch free edge of band over joining seam on wrong side.) Stitch collar to neckline so that it comes exactly to joining line of front bands. This should be a ⅜-in. seam, clipped at ½-in. intervals so that collar will set well.

Stitch 3-in. bands to each armhole, applying them from point K to corresponding point on back. Attach these to blouse as you did front panels. Stitch underarm seams, beginning at edge of sleeve bands and continuing to within 3 in. of bottom. Hem these 3-in. edges; also make a ¼-in. hem on bottom edges of blouse. Use button and buttonholes or swivel, pin-on buttons; or work matching eyelets in both front edges and use studs.

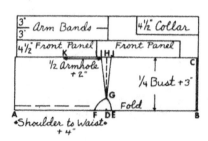

Handy Overblouse

▶▶▶ IF YOU GO to business and like to take off your suit jacket when you get home, the overblouse is your ticket. If you follow the instructions in this book for making the easy-to-do two-, three-, or four-gore skirts, then you can have a new outfit in no time at all.

To make the overblouse, you need two lengths, shoulder to hip, of 36- to 42-in. fabric. Straighten your fabric and lay it out with selvages together toward you.

Point C on the diagram is halfway between corners A and B. D is one-fourth neck measure to right of C. F is on selvage straight above C. G is 1 in. to left of F. Draw a line G to D. E is one-fourth neck measure plus ½ in. from D on line G-D. H is one-sixth neck plus ½ in. from G on line G-D. Connect H and F for back neck curve; E and C for front. Measure down from C one-half the armhole measure plus 1 in. for I, and up from I place J one-fourth bust measurement, plus 5 in. Measure to left on fold from G one-half armhole measurement less 1 in. for K. Measure from A to L one-fourth bust measure plus 3 in.

Cut line D-G. Cut curves H-F and C-E. Lay front selvages over back fold, allowing a 2-in. front hem allowance to extend above the fold. Cut back same as front, cutting from K and curving the underarm at J, then to L at edge of fabric.

Make a ½-in. dart in back, 3 in. deep and tapering to nothing, so front and back shoulder seams will be same length.

Stitch shoulder and underarm seams ⅜ in., clipping curved seams at underarms. Turn center-front line back 2 in. and stitch or slip-stitch it in place. Stitch the cuffs and collar pieces across both ends, turn right-side out and apply to blouse. Conceal neck seam of blouse inside collar. Put cuffs on with bias facing. Hem bottom of blouse, turning length to a point becoming to you. Be sure to have a belt on when you decide this. Finish hem. If desired, lay in pleats or darts at waistline or gather waistline fullness so that it is easy to adjust under the belt. Use snaps to close center-front, or pin-on buttons.

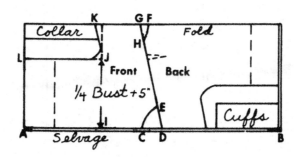

Square-dance Blouse

*Make it pretty, make it gay.
Let it melt his heart your way.*

▶▶▶ CHOOSE A SHEER—voile, swiss, or chiffon—for this pretty blouse. You need 1⅓ yds. of 36-in. or 40-in. fabric. Cotton of nice quality should cost little.

Straighten fabric. For sleeves, cut off one 12-in. strip, on crosswise thread. Fold strip in half lengthwise and cut on fold (see A in diagram).

Cut remaining yard of fabric in half on crosswise thread. For front, fold one of these halves lengthwise so that the distance from one selvage to the fold is one-fourth bust measure plus 5 in. Pin; then cut from B to C. Measure down from B 2 in. (D). Measure along edge from B one-half the armhole measurement less 1 in. (E). Cut on line F.

Fold back piece over to one-fourth bust measure plus 3 in. (G). Cut from G to H. Measure armhole exactly the same as for front and cut on line I. If fabric is 40-in., you need not piece sleeve. If it is only 36 in. wide, then from remaining pieces add a 3-in. strip to each sleeve to provide desired fullness.

Stitch sleeve to front and back of blouse on lines F and I, starting each seam from top edge. (Underarm and sleeve seams are not stitched until after shirring is put in.) If fabric ravels, stitch ⅛ in. from raw edge of neckline and bottom of sleeves; then turn and baste. Put elastic thread on bobbin. Attach ruffler, set for longest possible stitch. Gather around neckline and bottom of sleeves, keeping ¾ in. from edge. (Two or more rows may be added above this hem row. Elastic thread makes it easy to slip blouse on and off.) French-seam underarms, stitching through sleeve and then blouse section. Finish bottom of blouse with 1¼-in. hem.

Lace or daintiest embroidery may be stitched to edges of hems. Narrow velvet bows may be tacked at center-front and on each sleeve.

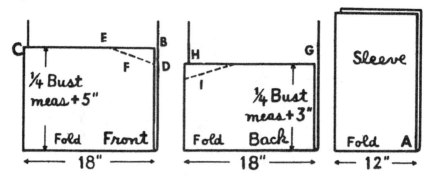

Dress-up Smock

▶▶▶ HERE upholstery ball fringe is used on a smock made of cotton sateen from the drapery department.

You need one length (shoulder to hip plus 14 in., or approximately 1 yd.) of 48- to 54-in. fabric. Straighten fabric. Tear off one 2-in. wide crosswise strip for tie strings. Fold fabric in half lengthwise, with fold toward you.

Measuring from corner A, as in diagram, B is half the armhole measurement plus 2 in. to right. C is the shoulder-to-waist length plus 1 in. from A. D is 7 in. to right of C. Chalk lines halfway across fabric, straight in from B, C, and D. E and F are one-fourth bust measurement plus 1½ in. from B and C. G is one-fourth hip measurement plus 1½ in. from D.

H is 1 in. down from upper left-hand corner. I is one-fourth hip measurement plus 1½ in. from H. Chalk straight across from I to just above E. J is one-third neck measurement to right of A. K is one-sixth neck measurement plus 1 in. up from A. L is length of shoulder from K. M is 1 in. to right of L. N is 3½ in. down from E. O is 2 in. to left of N. P is half the armhole measurement less 2 in. from I.

Chalk neck curve J-K, shoulder K-M, round line to P; then P-O, and O-E. Connect E-F; round hipline from F to G. Extend line straight across from G to edge. Mark 3 in. in from C for paneling of front.

Cut front out, cutting J to K; K through M to P; P around O to E; E-F; F through G to edge. Lay front over back section, center-front parallel with selvage in line with H. Cut sides and shoulder of back same as front except for neckline.

Stitch shoulder and underarm seams. Put on smock and tie tape around waist. Pin in pleats to make front panel. Turn up cuff around bottom to becoming length (about 7 to 9 in. depending on height). Pin. Check curve of cap sleeve. You may wish to shorten it. Remove garment. Crease or chalk 2 in. above bottom fold on inside of smock. Cut on this line. Lay right side of cuff to wrong side of garment and stitch. Turn cuff to right side. Pin.

Fold 2-in. strip in half lengthwise, wrong side out. Stitch raw edges together and across ends. Cut strip in half. Turn both strips right side out.

Make narrow hems around neckline, armholes, and along top of cuff. Turn and stitch ½-in. hems along center-back edges, stitching through cuff section. Lay raw ends of strings under tucks at waistline. Pin. Stitch tucks for about 3 in.

Pin and stitch ball fringe on edges. Stitch cuff flat across top edge at front and back to form pockets. Lap back hems, using snaps to close.

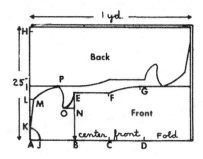

Mother-and-daughter Off-shoulder Blouses

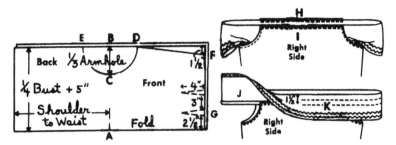

▶▶▶ FESTIVE COTTON BLOUSES for mother and daughter can be made in a few hours. For mother, buy twice the length from shoulder to waist plus ½ yd. for ruffle. For daughter, buy shoulder-to-waist length plus 10 in. for ruffle. Buy two 3-yd. packages of rick rack in contrasting colors, thread for each color, and elastic or tape for drawstrings.

Mother's blouse: Straighten fabric. Tear off two 8-in. crosswise strips for ruffle. On blouse piece measure in from selvage one-half the bust measurement plus 10 in.; tear off lengthwise strip. Fold blouse piece in half lengthwise. Mark center of fold A, as in diagram, and center of selvage B. On either side of A, measure along fold the length from shoulder to waist. For armhole, measure in from selvage one-third armhole measurement (B-C). Measure same amount to right and left of B for D and E. Mark curve as shown. Trim side seam, starting 1½ in. in at F and tapering to nothing at D. Mark darts as at G. Taper underarm and mark darts on back in same way. Cut from F to D around armhole and along underarm of back. Tear crosswise at A for back and front of blouse.

Seam selvages of ruffle strips together to make circle; finish one edge with ¼-in. hem. Apply rick rack over stitching and again 1 in. above. French-seam blouse sides. Finish armholes with narrow hems.

Place wrong side of blouse over right side of ruffle, matching center points, H and I. Stitch edges together across blouse top, as shown. Turn up ruffle and press seam, as at J. Bring ruffle to right side, making a fold 1½ in. above seam.

Press fold. Stitch ruffle to blouse just below seam, as at K. Continue stitching across shoulder section and entirely around ruffle. Make second stitching ¾ in. above first to make casing. Work a buttonhole-type of opening at center-front of casing (on wrong side for elastic, right side for decorative drawstrings).

Stitch darts to shape waistline. Finish bottom edge with 1-in. hem casing and work an opening at center front of it.

Gather at neckline and waistline with drawstrings or elastic.

Child's blouse: Tear two 5-in. crosswise strips for ruffle. Same dimensions can be used for cutting, but allow only 5 in. to chest measurement. Make as above, except that waistline need not be darted.

Dresses

Chemise-type Dress

▶▶▶ USE PLISSÉ CREPE or seersucker for this dress, which needs little or no ironing if patted into shape and dried on a hanger after washing.

For average figure 2¾ yds. is needed.

Straighten fabric at both ends. Tear a 2-in. strip from one selvage edge, full length, for tie and belt. Fold fabric in half lengthwise. For shoulder line mark center on fold, A in diagram, and straight across on selvage (B). From B measure one-half armhole measurement plus 1 in. to locate C. From center fold measure straight across toward C a distance of one-fourth bust measurement plus 2 in. From A measure along fold a shoulder-to-waist length plus 3 in. and mark D. Directly across mark E at same distance as C. Connect C and E with straight line. Cut in from E 4 in., to provide fullness over hips. Cut from C to E to make underarm seam. Cut back exactly like front.

French-seam sleeve portion, underarm, and skirt. Gather lower edge of slash and draw up fullness evenly to fit upper edge, as in G. French-seam slash, tapering seam as shown.

For neck opening cut in from A to a depth of one-fourth neck measurement. Slash along fold from A one-fourth neck measurement plus 3 in. Face this center-front opening with two pieces cut out at underarm. Make a narrow hem across back neckline and 1-in. hem on sleeves.

Fold long strip and stitch through center, as in H. Cut this strip in half—one for tie sash. Turn in all raw ends and whip. Match center of one length to neck at center-back. Overlap ¼ in. and stitch across back neckline, allowing band to stand up. Bring ends forward and tie at a becoming point over front opening.

Put dress on. Tie sash around waist. Raise arms to allow slight blousing. Adjust fullness evenly. Mark becoming hem length. Turn and stitch hem edge. Slip-stitch in position.

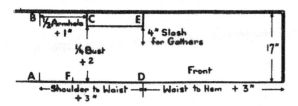

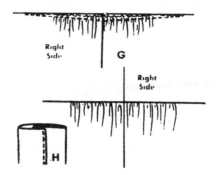

Chemise, Peg-top Dress

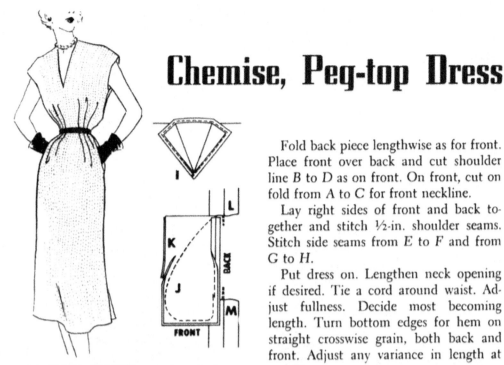

▶▶▶ THIS DRESS requires just one length (shoulder to desired length plus hem) of 54-in. fabric, or two lengths of 40-in. swaggerish gingham, such as was used for the model illustrated. Average requirement 2¾ yds., plus 3 yds. of seam binding and spool of thread.

Straighten fabric. If two lengths are used, cut or tear in half crosswise. Fold piece for front lengthwise, folding it over to a depth of one-fourth bust measurement plus 2 in., with fold toward you. Keep lengthwise grain straight on fold. Cut off any surplus width. This is used for pockets, sash, or added sleeve length.

Locate point A at left end of fold, as in the diagram. Mark B at one-fourth neck measurement above A; and C, one-half neck measurement to right. For shoulder slope, mark D 1½ in. to right of edge, as shown. To right of D measure one-half armhole measurement plus 2 in. for E. Pockets are inserted in side seams.

Mark F for top of pocket 6 in. below waistline. Mark G 6 in. below F. Measure 9 in. from bottom (right-hand edge) for side slits, and mark H. Cut from B to D.

Fold back piece lengthwise as for front. Place front over back and cut shoulder line B to D as on front. On front, cut on fold from A to C for front neckline.

Lay right sides of front and back together and stitch ½-in. shoulder seams. Stitch side seams from E to F and from G to H.

Put dress on. Lengthen neck opening if desired. Tie a cord around waist. Adjust fullness. Decide most becoming length. Turn bottom edges for hem on straight crosswise grain, both back and front. Adjust any variance in length at waistline.

Remove dress. Put hem in. Slip-stitch along edge of side slits, so that finish will be neat. Finish sleeves and neck with seam binding, terminating binding at bottom of neck, as at I (wrong side).

Fold neck edge to wrong side, forming V, as shown. Slip-stitch in position around neck.

Cut four pocket pieces 10 in. long and about 6 in. wide. Seam two pocket pieces together, tapering from top to bottom and along bottom end, as at J. Trim off surplus, as at K.

Stitch one edge of pocket to front seam allowance, making ¼-in. seam. Clip back seam allowance, as at L and M. Stitch back edge of pocket to back seam. Repeat for other pocket. Tack seam top and bottom to prevent tearing out.

Put dress on. Adjust fullness under belt.

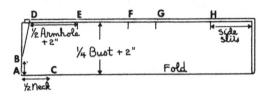

Sheath Dress of Nylon Net

▶▶▶ BUY 50- to 54-in. fabric for this dress. Anyone up to size 38 can make it of one length of fabric. Measure from shoulder to hemline. Add hem and seam allowance. A 50- to 54-in.-wide pleated fabric can also be used, but it is cut on the opposite grain of the fabric.

Fold fabric lengthwise, bringing selvages together at center, as at A in diagram. Measure one-fourth bust measurement plus 6 in. from fold to one selvage. Pin on fold. Lap other selvage over until the measurement from fold to center (A) is also one-fourth bust measurement plus 6 in. Pin on fold. Let longest edge lap under top selvage, as at B. If you use full width, overlap selvages 1 in. for side seam.

Measure from corner C along fold one-fourth neck measurement and along edge one-fourth neck measurement plus 1 in. Draw curve from D to E. Measure from corner F on fold 1 in. and on edge one-fourth neck measurement plus 1 in. Draw curve from F to G. Measure from A 1½ in. (H), then one-half the armhole measurement plus 1 in. (I). Draw line from E to H and H to G. Cut along neck and shoulder line. Mark one-third neck measurement on center-front fold. Mark depth of armhole slash on underside of fabric. Cut away any extra overlap along selvage, leaving 1 in. for side seam.

Mark waistline, as at J. Open out dress. Casing at waistline can be made on right side by applying a ¾-in.- or 1-in.-width ribbon, or a bias strip of self material can be applied to wrong side and a ribbon belt used as illustration shows. Center casing strip over waistline, as at K, and stitch both edges. Stitch side seam from underarm to bottom edge but not across ends of casing.

If slash is desired in side of skirt, leave opening and hem edges or face edges before putting in hem. Stitch around armhole and around neckline slash. Cut between stitched lines, as at L. Stitch shoulder seams together. Make a row of gathers in back and front of neckline. Make a rolled hem on front slash or bind with ribbon. Fold 1-in. ribbon in center and press. Pin and baste around neck and armholes. Stitch, easing into ribbon. Draw elastic through casing and whip ends together. Try dress on. Measure length. Slip-stitch hem.

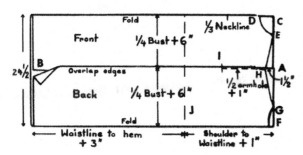

Crepe Sheath Dress

▶▶▶ THIS STRAIGHT, easy-to-wear dress, to use with jackets, boleros, and capes, can be made of silk or rayon crepe. It is a good idea to buy an additional yard to make a matching crepe and lace capelet as on page 114. For the dress, buy enough 42-in. crepe for two skirt lengths plus 4 in. for hem, plus ¼ yd. Cut off crosswise one skirt length plus 2 in. for skirt front. From one selvage, cut off 3-in. belt strip (see A in diagram). From remaining piece, cut a 12-in. lengthwise strip for bodice (B). Then cut off two 4½-in. crosswise strips (C). Remaining piece makes back of skirt.

To chalk out and cut skirt: Fold each skirt length in half lengthwise. Measure 7 in. from ends of skirt pieces D and E. Straight up from D and E, measure one-fourth hip measurement plus 2 in. for F and G. At other ends, measure up from fold one-fourth hip measurement plus 5 in. for H and I. Chalk from H through F to end of fabric and from edge through G to I. Taper side seams from F and G as indicated by broken lines. Mark darts on back and front as wide as necessary to take up waistline fullness. Use pleats in place of darts if preferred. Cut out skirt and baste side seams. Begin basting left-hand seam 7 in. below waistline.

To cut and make bodice: Length of bodice piece is bust measurement plus 2 in. Fold in half crosswise. Baste ½-in. seam on left side for placket. Turn selvage to wrong side 1 in. and slip-stitch for top hem. Lay a long, narrow dart 2 in. down from top of back, as at J. Make this 1½ in. deep at center, tapering at sides. Stitch dart and press toward bottom edge. Place darts or pleats in front and darts in back to correspond to those in skirt. Fullness of bust and size of waist may make these larger or smaller than those in skirt.

To make straps and belt: Fold straps and belt in half lengthwise, right sides together. Stitch, making ⅜-in. seams. Press seam open. Turn right side out.

To fit dress: Pin bodice and skirt together at waistline. Try dress on, adjusting fullness to give a smooth, flat effect. Pin straps over shoulders. Decide on skirt length; remove dress. Stitch darts or pleats. Press. Stitch side seams, then waistline. Make zipper placket, following instruction given with zipper. Slip-stitch straps to hem of bodice. Finish bottom hem with seam binding and slip-stitch in position. Finish off belt with a tailored bow, or point the ends and overlap. Use hook and eye to close.

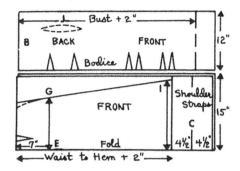

Striped Sheath Dress

▶▶▶ THERE ARE many lovely fabrics with a heavy rib or a woven-in or printed stripe that are ideal for the dress illustrated here. Buy one length equal to the shoulder-to-hem measurement plus 6 in., of 54-in. fabric.

To chalk out: Straighten both ends of fabric. If self belt to tie is desired, cut two 2-in. strips off one end straight across fabric. Fold fabric lengthwise and lay so that selvage is toward you. Fold again, so that you have four thicknesses with selvages on top, as shown in diagram. Measure to right of corner A a distance of one-half the neck measurement for B. C is one-half the neck measurement above A. D is 5 in. above C. E is upper left-hand corner. Measure a distance of one-half the armhole measurement plus 2 in. on folds to right of E for F. Measure ½ in. to right of D for G. Draw curves from B to C and F to G. Connect C and G. For back of neck, locate a point halfway between A and B and connect with C.

To cut: Cut from F to G for underarms and from G to C for shoulders. Lift out the bottom fold, keeping selvages and center-front fold in same position. Cut from C to B for front of neck.

To make: Join shoulder seams, using a ⅜-in. seam; press these open. If you wish neck slightly lower in back, cut it down on broken line from C. Stitch left underarm seam, leaving a 10-in. waistline opening for a zipper. Apply zipper according to package instructions. Use bias binding to bind neck and armholes. Stitch binding on, stitching right side of binding to wrong side of jumper, using a ½-in. seam and easing binding slightly on curves. Turn binding to wrong side so that it does not show on right side, and baste; then slip-stitch it down. Make neat joinings at shoulder seams.

Put dress on. Tie a string around waist; adjust fullness. If desired, stitch three or more rows of elastic sewing thread to hold fullness evenly around waistline. While garment is on, decide on depth of hem. Remove dress. Stitch bias seam binding to top edge of hem, easing it on. Then slip-stitch or machine blind-stitch hem in position.

To make belt, turn raw edges of belt strip in and stitch the turned edges. Sew a tassel or round button to each end. Tie belt around waist.

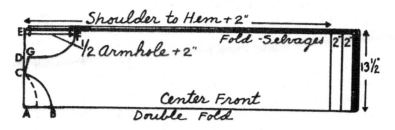

Basic Dress of Jersey

▶▶▶ WHEN YOU WISH for a bright, colorful dress, this simple jersey one can fill the need. It can be made simple and then dressed up as much as you like.

Buy a length of 54-in. tubular jersey—skirt length, plus 3-in. hem, plus ¾ to ⅞ yds., depending on whether you are long- or short-waisted. Cut off skirt length, allowing 3 in. for hem.

Chalk out blouse: Lay blouse length flat on table, with fold toward you. Following the diagram, point B is a shoulder-to-waist length plus 2 in. to right of corner A. C is one-fourth neck measurement to right of A, and D is one-half armhole measurement to right of C. E is one-sixth of the neck measurement plus ½ in. above A. Chalk a line straight up from D to opposite fold (F). G is one-fourth bust measurement plus 1 in. above D. H is one-half the elbow measurement plus 1 in. to left of F. I is one-fourth waist measurement plus 1¼ in. above B. Chalk a line straight up from B, as shown. Chalk a curve from C to E, line to H, line G to I.

Cut neck C to E and shoulder line E to H. Cut fold H to F. Cut from B to I, and to G, curving underarm as dotted line shows, then up to F. Turn front of waist around so that center-front fold is in line with center-back fold. Cut back same as front except at neck. Back neck really needs no shaping.

You have three choices of closing: 1. Use an opening at back neck and left side. 2. Cut a low neck so that dress will slip over head, and use a side opening. 3. Use a long center-back zipper closing. A 20- to 22-in. zipper is needed for this; a 9-in. zipper for side closing. Decide upon type of closing you will use.

Making waist: Seam shoulders and underarms. Press. Use fabric cut from shoulders to make a fitted facing for neck, and 1½-in.-wide facings for sleeves, also a belt, if desired.

Making skirt: Place folds of tube in line with underarm of waist. Lay and pin soft pleats each side of center-front as in the sketch, making these deep enough to take up fullness. Lay same type of pleats in back, but turn these toward center-back.

Put waist on; pin skirt to waist. Adjust waistline so that it is completely smooth all around. Mark hem. Remove dress. Stitch waist and skirt together at waistline.

Put zipper in or finish closing as previously decided. Finish hem, stitching seam binding (not tight) to raw edge. Press, and your dress is ready to wear.

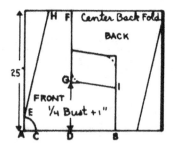

Short-sleeved Basic Dress

▶▶▶ MAKE THIS basic dress of moss crepe, of fine chiffon, cotton, or any other soft fabric suitable to your needs and purse. The average figure needs 2¾ yds. for a dress.

Straighten fabric at both ends. Fold fabric in half lengthwise, with fold toward you. For shoulder line, mark center of fabric length on fold, as at A in diagram. Straight across on selvage mark B. (This divides front and back sections.) From B measure one-half the armhole measurement plus 1 in. (C). Locate CC at same distance to right of A. Measure up from CC toward C one-quarter bust measurement plus 2 in. From A measure on fold the shoulder-to-waist length plus 3 in. (D). Measure straight up from D one-quarter bust measurement plus 2 in. and mark E. Connect C and E with straight line. Curve underarm line at C, as shown.

Cut in from selvage edge to E, and cut in from E toward D to a depth of 4 in. to provide for fullness over hips. Cut from C to E to make underarm seam. For front neck opening cut in from A one-quarter neck measurement. Slash along fold from A one-quarter neck measurement plus 3 in. (F). Cut back of dress exactly the same as front except for neck.

French-seam sleeve portion, underarm, and skirt. Gather lower edge of slash and draw up fullness evenly to fit upper edge,

Moss crepe, jersey, and sheer wool are good for this chemise type of dress. Keep the dress simple in line and decoration.

as in G. Stitch, tapering seam as illustrated, so that right side appears as shown.

Face center-front opening with two pieces cut out at underarm. Face back neckline, and face or hem sleeves, slip-stitching edges down so that no stitching shows on right side.

Put dress on. Tie cord around waist. Raise arms to allow slight blousing. Adjust fullness evenly. Mark becoming hem length. Turn and stitch hem edge. Slip-stitch in position. If desired, mark with chalk or pencil at waistline and stitch a row or two of elastic sewing thread, to ensure even adjustment of waistline fullness. Use a narrow leather or ribbon belt.

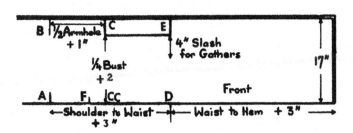

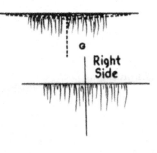

Tubular Jersey Dress

▶▶▶ BUY ONE shoulder-to-hem length plus 5 in., of 54-in. tubular jersey—the kind that does not sag. It comes in beautiful colors. From 1⅜ yds. to 1⅝ yds. is enough to make a dress for a short or a tall figure. Buy 5 yds. of bias binding, ¾ yd. of ¼-in. elastic, and 1 spool of thread.

Straighten both ends of tube by laying a yardstick across, marking with chalk, then cutting on chalk line. Following the diagram, measure in from corners A and B on each fold the armhole depth less 2 in. Cut on folds to these points, C and D.

Stitch bias binding on these slashes, beginning with a ¼-in. seam and tapering to a ⅛-in. seam at the bottom point. Continue binding up other side. Miter binding at point so that it lies flat. When binding has been stitched on both armholes, turn to wrong side, folding the fabric back, as at E and F in the detail. Slipstitch binding down.

Stitch binding to both top edges, making a ¼-in. seam. Turn edges to wrong side ¾ in., as at G, and slip-stitch them down. Run elastic through the casings that top hems provide.

Put dress on; arrange fullness at neck front and back as desired, and pin elastic to hold fullness in place. Later whip elastic ends securely, cutting away any surplus. While dress is on, tie a tape or use a belt around waistline to adjust fullness there. This should look "easy," so lift up arms enough so that dress is straight around figure. Mark for hem. Remove dress. Sew seam binding to hem top; slipstitch it down. Bring ends of casings together and whip. Press dress.

If you want to put elastic at waistline, provide a piece measuring about five-sixths of waist measurement and get 1½ yds. of ¾-in. ribbon. While you have dress on with waistline held in place, mark the line with chalk at bottom of tape or cord. Remove dress and baste a true line all around. Baste ribbon inside dress directly over basting line. Stitch to form casing. Insert elastic and tack ends together at opening. The dress can be worn with or without a belt.

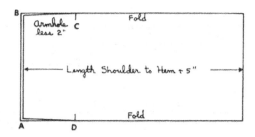

Jersey Jumper

▶▶▶ JERSEY JUMPERS are popular and why not? They are low in cost, easy to wear, becoming, good to wear over last season's blouses or sweaters. Buy the kind of jersey that you know will not sag. You need one length from shoulder to hem plus 6 in. for hem and binding; 1⅝ yds. is usually ample.

To chalk out: Straighten both ends. Cut two strips off one end straight across tube, each strip 2 in. wide. These are used for bindings for neck and armholes. Fold tube length in half lengthwise and lay so that fold is next to you. As in diagram, measure to right of corner A one-half the neck measurement plus 1 in. for B. C is one-fourth neck measurement above A. D is 5 in. above C. Measure one-half the armhole measurement plus 2 in. on folds to right of corner E for F. Measure ½ in. to 1 in. to right of D for G. Draw curves from B to C and F to G. Connect C and G.

To cut: Cut from F to G for underarms and to C for shoulders. Open out, keeping center-front fold in same position.

Cut from C to B for front neck. Leave back neck straight.

To make: Join shoulder seams, using a ⅜-in. seam; press these open. If you wish neck lower in back, cut it down, but only slightly.

Stitch binding on, stitching right side of binding to wrong side of jumper, using a ¼-in. seam. Stretch binding slightly on curves. Turn binding in ¼ in.; baste; then stitch it down. Make neat joinings at shoulder seams.

Put jumper on. Tie a string around waist; adjust fullness. If desired, three or more rows of elastic sewing thread may be used to hold fullness evenly around waistline. While garment is on, decide depth of hem. Remove jumper. Stitch bias seam binding to top edge of hem. Then slip-stitch or machine blind-stitch hem in position.

Use a chain, cord, or narrow belt for waistline.

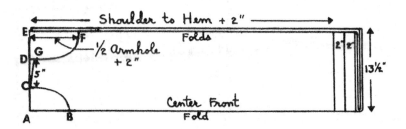

Slip-on Jumper Dress

▶▶▶ EVEN WITH hip measurements up to 42 in., you need only one length, shoulder to hem, plus hem allowance, of 60-in. soft wool fabric for this dress. Provide 9 in. more if sleeve caps and self belt are desired. Usually 1¾ yd. is ample; less is needed for figures shorter than 5 feet, 6 inches. Sleeves, neck facings, and pockets take ½ yd. of 36-in. sateen or velveteen.

Straighten fabric. Fold in half lengthwise. Lay fold toward you. Following diagram, chalk out back by locating point B, 1 in. to right of corner A. C is one-fourth neck measurement plus 1 in. above A. D is one-half the armhole measurement plus 1 in. to right of A. E is one-fourth bust measurement plus 1½ in. above D. F is distance of the back-waist length to right of A. G is 7 in. to right of F. H is one-fourth hip measurement plus 2½ in. above G. Chalk a line through E and H, extending this to both edges of fabric, as shown. Cut out back, cutting B to C and line E-H from edge to edge. Lay the back with its fold parallel to selvages on other side and 1½ in. in from edge. Cut along outside line E-H for front of dress.

Measure left of I on selvage a distance of one-half neck measurement minus 1 in. for J. Measure from I down one-fourth neck measurement plus 1½ in. for K. Mark and cut front neck curve. Cut sleeve pieces to size of armhole plus 1 in.

Seam center-front, beginning 2 in. below J. Pin shoulder seams C and K. Seam sides of front and back together, beginning at E. Stitch down to a point opposite F, or waistline. Leave seams open from waistline to H for pockets. Begin at H and complete each side seam. Fold sleeve pieces in half crosswise. With fold at top of side seam (E), stitch to back and front. Stitch shoulder seams, continuing on through sleeves. Use ⅜-in. seam and press all seams open.

From ½ yd. of contrasting fabric cut facings for neckline and sleeves, cutting on same fabric grain as that of dress. Cut pockets. Lay pockets on wrong side of front, top edge in line with waistline and straight edge along side seam. Baste across top and on curved edge. Baste outside edge of pocket to back seamline. Stitch all facing pieces in position on right side of dress; turn to wrong side and slip-stitch down. Make a narrow tie belt.

Put dress on; tie belt around waist. Adjust fullness and turn hem to desired length. Remove dress; put hem in. Stitch pockets to dress; reinforce stitching for 1 in. at top and bottom of pocket opening. Hem front of pocket opening. Press.

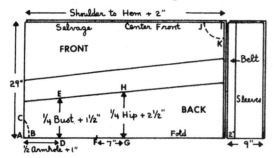

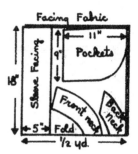

Shirred Dress in Elastic Fabric

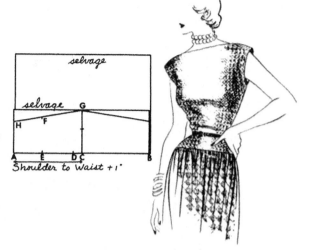

▶▶▶ USE THE new shirred fabric for blouses, for swim suits, and for dresses of the type illustrated. The boat- or bateau-neck dress with shirred fabric top is reasonable in cost, easy to make, and easy to launder, because only the skirt needs to be ironed.

Buy twice the length from shoulder to waist, plus 1 in., of the shirred fabric. Buy plain fabric measuring twice the length from top of hip to hem, plus 6 in., for hem and seam allowance. The model illustrated, in size 16, required 1⅛ yds. of shirred fabric and 1¾ yds. of plain.

Cut the plain fabric in half crosswise and seam the selvage edges to make a two-piece skirt. Press seams open. Gather top edge.

Lay shirred fabric out wrong side up, with fold toward you. Measure from your neck bone out to the point of the armhole on top of your arm. Fold fabric so that you have this width on top. Pin ends so that selvage edges are straight.

To chalk out blouse: Measure from front waistline to shoulder and down to waistline at back, plus 2 in. Mark this measure off on fabric as A to B. Cut yoke section off straight across along selvage marked by G.

C is halfway between A and B. D is 2 in. to left of C; E, half the armhole measurement to left of C. F is one-fourth bust measurement plus 1 in. above E. G is on selvage directly above C. Draw a line from G through F to left edge of fabric to locate H. Cut on line G-H through both thicknesses. Fold fabric on shoulder line C-G and cut back to match front. Unfold on line C-G and slash fabric from C toward G for 6 in., then from C toward D 1½ in. Turn neckline edges down to wrong side, 2 in. on front, 1 in. on back. Clip turned edges at intervals so that they will lie flat. Whip them in place, taking care that stitches do not show on right.

Cut yoke depth from waistline to hip, plus 1½ in. for seams. Measure around hips at top and make length of yoke this measure plus 1½ in. Cut in two equal lengths and dart it at side seams to have it fit easily around the figure. Stitch yoke pieces to front and back waistline of blouse.

Stitch shoulder seams. Stitch the underarm seams, leaving a placket opening on left side if bust is large. Baste gathered skirt to bottom of yoke, side seams meeting. Put garment on and put a belt or cord around figure. Check armholes to make sure that they are comfortable. Make sure that depth of skirt yoke is right for your height and size. It should come slightly below top of your hips. Determine skirt length. Remove dress and adjust. Whip turned edges back at armholes or put them down with flat bias binding. Stitch blouse and skirt together. Turn edge ¼ in. and stitch top of hem, then slip-stitch hem in position. A narrow leather belt seems best for this type of dress.

Boat-neck Dress

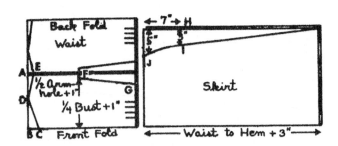

▶▶▶ FOR THIS SIMPLE DRESS buy two skirt lengths, plus 6 in. for hems, plus one blouse length, plus ¾ yd. for sleeves and collar. Three yds. of 42-in. crepe is enough for the average figure.

First, tear crosswise two skirt lengths, each measuring one skirt length plus 3 in. for hems. From one selvage of back length, cut a 3-in. strip for belt.

Tear off waist length plus 2 in. (If figure is larger than 40 bust, omit pleats in back of skirt and obtain a strip from skirt length to add to waist width.

To chalk out waist: Fold selvages of waist length toward center as at A in diagram. Measure in 2 in. from corner B on front fold for C. D is one-half the neck measurement above B; E is 1 in. in from A on selvages. F is one-half the armhole measurement plus 1 in. from E. G is one-fourth the waist measurement plus 2 in. above fold. Chalk a line straight across at F from selvages to front fold. Measure in from front fold on this line one-fourth bust measurement plus 1 in. Chalk underarm lines to edge of fabric as at G. Cut C to D, D to E, E to F, F to G. Place front over back, folds matching, and cut same except to cut back neck down 1 in., rather than 2 in.

Measure width of each sleeve to correspond to size of armhole or line E-F. Cut two sleeves. Remainder of fabric from sleeve piece may be used for a collar, or used to line a velvet or taffeta collar.

Fold both skirt lengths in half lengthwise, laying fold toward you. Measure in 7 in. from ends, as at H. Measure down from H 3 in. for I and along end 5 in. for J. Chalk and cut on a line to shape skirt over hip from J to I and to bottom edges.

Lay a box pleat at each side of center fold, making pleats as wide as your material allows. If hip is 36 in., you can make 3-in. pleats; if it is 38 in., pleats can be only 2 in. For larger hips, pleats must be less deep.

To make skirt: When pleats are in place, stitch them on inside down about 5 in. from waistline. Also stitch across waistline, front and back, to hold pleats securely. Baste side seams, beginning left-side seam 7 in. below waistline.

To make waist: Stitch shoulder seams. Lay soft pleats in waistline in line with pleats in skirt. Baste waistlines of waist and skirt together. Stitch sleeve seams. Baste sleeves in armholes. Baste underarm seams. Try dress on. Consider length, neckline, waistline, and adjust all to fit you. Turn hem of 4 to 6 in. in sleeves, folding this hem back for cuff effect. Remove dress. Stitch all seams. Slip-stitch sleeve hems. Put in skirt hem. Make zipper placket on left-hand side. Cut a newspaper pattern of collar in size desired. Fit it to dress front and back as sketch shows. Cut collar of two thicknesses.

Scarf-trimmed Dress

▶▶▶ FOR THE BLOUSE of this simple dress you need two lengths (shoulder to waist plus 1½ in.); for skirt, two lengths (waist to hem plus 3 in.). Average amount of 42-in. crepe is 3 yds.

To chalk out blouse: Tear off double shoulder-to-waist length plus 1½ in. Fold lengthwise, wrong side out, folding top selvage over to a depth of one-fourth bust measurement plus 7 in., as at A in diagram. Pin. Cut off lengthwise strip for scarf by cutting close to selvage A. B is on fold at lower left corner. C is halfway point on fold. Chalk straight line from C to selvage for D. For neckline, E is ½ in. to right of C; F is one-sixth of the neck measurement plus ½ in. above; G is placed at depth desired in front, or about 7 in. Chalk neckline curves shown. H is length of shoulder less 1 in. from F. I is one-half armhole measurement plus 2 in. to left of C. Chalk a line straight across from I to J at selvage. K is one-fourth bust measurement plus 1½ in. in from I. L is one-fourth bust measurement from B. Connect L-K; K-J. M is 1 in. to right of D. Connect M-H.

Cut out neckline from E to F, around to G. Cut underarm L around to J, curving at K, as shown. Cut from M to H.

Fold front over back section along shoulder line F-H, center-front and center-back folds matching. Cut back shoulder line and underarm same as front.

Stitch shoulder and underarm seams, leaving left side open 4 in. from waistline. Gather bottom of waist to waist measure.

To chalk out skirt: Tear remaining fabric in half crosswise. Pin selvages together. Lay with selvage toward you. N is lower left corner. O is lower right corner. P is 2 in. above N.

Connect P and O. Q is 7 in. to right of P. R is one-fourth hip measurement plus 2 in. above Q. S is one-fourth hip measurement plus 7 in. above O. Chalk straight line from S through R to edge of fabric. Curve hipline to waist, as shown by broken line. Cut skirt front P-O; S-R and along hip curve. Turn front around and lay side edges along line R-S. Cut skirt back same as front.

Seam center-back and center-front. Stitch side seams, starting left seam 6 in. below waist for placket opening. Press.

Pin waist and skirt together at waistlines. Put dress on. Check neckline, sleeves, and waistline. Even bottom of skirt. Mark length. Remove dress. Stitch waistline. Put in dress zipper, following fastener instructions. Face neckline and bottom of sleeves with bias. Turn hem and slip-stitch.

Finish lengthwise edges of scarf with rolled hem. Gather ends; draw shirring up tightly; bind ends. Drape around neckline. Tack ends at waistline and at back of neck.

Make 1 in. belt. Finish with buckle.

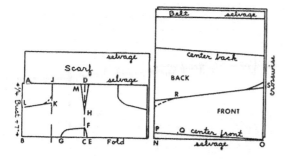

Sheer Dress

▶▶▶ BUY 3 yds. of 42-in. sheer fabric for this easy-to-make dress. A dainty, embroidered handkerchief provides the collar. Choose a small handkerchief and cut a 2½-in. strip, lengthwise grain, from each side for the collar. Use the remainder to make a ½-in. band to finish the raw edges.

Crystal buttons are sewed down the center-front for ornament and to break the width and plainness of the front.

The skirt is made of two skirt lengths of material plus 3 in. for hems, the two widths seamed with a 4-in. placket opening at left side. Gather the fullness at the waistline and baste this to a twilled tape cut to correct waist measure plus 1 in.

To chalk out waist: Straighten fabric. Fold lengthwise, wrong side up, with fold toward you. Depth of fold is one-fourth bust measurement plus 6 in. for sleeves. Point C on diagram is halfway between corners A and B. D is ½ in. to right of C; E, one-fourth neck measurement to left. F is one-sixth of the neck measurement plus ½ in. above C. Extend line C-F straight up to L. Draw line D to F and curve neckline F to E. Cut center-back opening about 8 in. deep from D to G. H is one-half the armhole measurement plus 1 in. to left of C. I is one-fourth bust measurement plus 3 in. above H. J is 3 in. above I. K is one-fourth bust measurement plus 3 in. above A. Draw lines K-I, I-J. Shape armhole in curved line at I, as diagram shows. Fold blouse at shoulder line (line C-F-L), and cut back underarm same as front. Unfold, and cut line D-F and curve F-E.

French-seam underarm seams of blouse, beginning at sleeve edge. Stitch left seam to within 5 in. of waistline. Put blouse on. Check neckline for comfort and becomingness. Lower it if desirable. Tie a cord around waist. Chalk the waistline; pin fullness where you want it. Put skirt on and pin tape on skirt to the blouse. Check skirt length. Remove. Stitch waist and skirt together on wrong side seam at waistline.

Hand-hem back-neck slash D to G. Sew a loop and button for neckline closing at center-back. Hem armholes, making a ¼-in. turn and a 1-in. slip-stitched hem. Pieces cut out at underarm may be used to face sleeves, to extend sleeve length, or to make longer waistline tie.

Finish dress by putting a 9-in. zipper in opening at left underarm. Make waistband ties from the 3-in. lengthwise strips by folding raw edges inside ¼ in. and stitching on ends and both sides of ties. Use a long, double thread and sew buttons to center-front line, continuing thread on wrong side from one button to the next. Baste collar to neckline. Slip-stitch hem in bottom. Press.

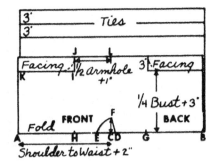

A Dress to Wear Tomorrow

▶▶▶ THIS IS a dress you can make in two hours' sewing time. Buy two skirt lengths, plus one waist length, plus ⅜ yd. of fabric, 2 yds. of velvet ribbon, and 1 spool of thread.

Waist: Tear off crosswise strip of shoulder-to-waist length plus 2 in.; tear this strip into four lengthwise pieces. Hem all lengthwise edges (six) except two selvages. For front, lay selvages together, fabric wrong side out, and stitch from waistline to depth of V, as at A. For back, seam two other strips together in same way. Press seams open. Press all edges to wrong side.

Lay front over back, right sides together. Stitch shoulder seams, as at B, with ¾-in. seam, stitching back at both edges to secure stitching line. Press seams open. Stitch ½ in. from shoulder seam on both sides to form casings, as at C. Insert cord in casings, as at D. When shoulder is drawn up to width you desire, tie a knot and conceal it under shoulder. Tie a bow knot of ribbon over gathers as illustrated.

Matching Bra: Tear a crosswise strip 5 to 7 in. in width, depending upon how long you want this garment. Hem bra piece at top and bottom, using a ½-in. hem. Try on and pin raw edges together. (If bust is larger than fabric width, add a piece to selvage.) Remove bra and hem each end. Sew on hooks and eyes for neat closing. Plan opening at center-front or left side, if you are having a long V at center-back. Dart the lower edges at underarms and under bust to correct fit. Use shoulder straps, if desired.

Skirt: Tear remaining piece of fabric in half crosswise. Stitch selvages together, beginning one seam 7 in. down. Make two rows of gathers at top, adjusting fullness so that there is more at center-back and at each side of the front than at center-front or sides. Adjust waistline fullness to fit a waistband that is 2 in. longer than waist measure. Place wrong side of skirt to right side of band and baste. Turn band to right side, baste, and stitch.

Put on waist and skirt. Hook the matching bra in place. Pin front and back of waist to waistband. Sides may overlap at underarm if desired. Mark hem turn. Remove; stitch waist to skirt band; put in bottom hem by machine or with slip-stitches.

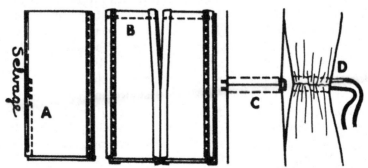

Allover Lace Dress

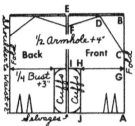

▶▶▶ THE DRESS SHOWN is typical of the semitailored silhouette which can be worn both for service and for semi-dress-up. Skirt may be straight or flared, as fashion decrees.

Buy two shoulder-to-waist lengths and three skirt lengths, plus 6 in. for hems, of 35-in. allover cotton lace. Such lace comes in many colors, and is especially attractive in gray, beige, or navy.

Measure off the two waist lengths, plus 2 in., as the diagram shows. Fold each through center and place selvage edges as shown. If fabric does not hold chalk marks, mark first with pins; then replace pins with tackings of thread to serve as guides in cutting and assembling. B is at a distance of the front length, shoulder to waist, above A. C is the desired depth of front neckline, less 1 in. below B. D is one-fourth neck measurement plus 2 in. to left of B. Measure from D to locate E at the desired depth of sleeve on shoulder. F is 2 in. below E. G is one-half the armhole measurement plus 4 in. below B, and H is one-fourth bust measurement plus 3 in. to left of G. Continue line G-H to desired depth of sleeve; that is, in line with F; and locate I at this point. Curve the underarm from I around H and to point J. Half-cuffs may be cut from underarm section as shown.

Cut F to D, D to C. Lay center-front fold over center-back fold and shape shoulder line F-D and underarm line I-H-J same as front. Cut back neck, making it half as low as front. For skirt, cut remainder of lace into three even lengths. Cut 2-in. strip from one selvage edge of one length for narrow belt. Seam the three skirt lengths together, placing in the center the one from which you have cut the belt strip. Begin the seam on left-hand side 5 in. below top to provide for a placket.

Fold the top of the skirt into eight sections. Place a pin at each fold; then lay four pleats at center-back and center-front, as shown, to take up fullness and so that skirt measures same as waist. Pleats on small-waisted skirt will meet on wrong side; on larger, they may space as detail shows.

Seam shoulder and underarm seams, leaving left-side seam open 5 in. for a zipper. Stitch bias binding to neck and armholes. Turn this to wrong side and slip-stitch down. Cut cuff pieces as diagram shows; stitch them, turn right side out and apply to tops of sleeves.

Baste pleats in top of skirt. Lay soft pleats in waistline of blouse or stitch darts to take up fullness. Put blouse and skirt on. Pin together at waist. Check hem for correct length.

Remove and stitch waist and skirt together. Put 10-in. zipper in left side opening, following package instructions. Put in the hem, make the belt—and your dress is ready to press and wear.

All-purpose Lace or Print Dress

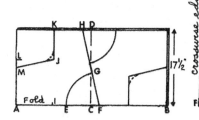
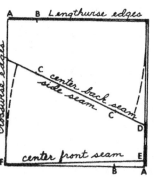

▶▶▶ FOUR YARDS of 35-in. fabric will make this dress for the average figure. An extra skirt length is needed for larger figures.

If fabric is lace, mark this dress out on newspaper to get a pattern to cut by.

For blouse, measure and cut off crosswise a piece of fabric equal to length from center-front waistline over shoulder to center-back waistline, plus 2 in. Fold this piece lengthwise, with fold toward you.

Following diagram, point C is halfway between corners A and B. Mark a dotted line straight up from C to D on edges. E is one-half neck measurement to left of C and F is 2 in. to right. G is one-half neck measurement above C. H is 2 in. to left of D. Draw straight line F to H. For front neck curve, with cord tied to pencil and held at F, swing an arc from E to G.

I is one-half armhole measurement to left of C on fold. J is one-fourth bust measurement plus 2 in. above I. For K, extend sleeve line up from J to edge of fabric. Draw a line to left from J for L. M is 2 in. below L. Connect M and J, curving underarm as shown. Cut from M and around curve J to K. Cut line H to F. Place this front of blouse on back section with centerfold ¼ in. from center-back edges and cut back exactly same as front except at neck. Make this about 4 in. higher than in front. Remove front section and slash sleeve ends of back on fold.

Take two skirt lengths of fabric and pin lengthwise edges together at each side. Point B is 7 in. to left of lower-right corner A. C is one-fourth hip measurement plus 4 in. above B. Locate matching points A, B, and C diagonally opposite, also, as diagram shows. Draw a line through both C's. D is at right-hand end of this line. To fit skirt without fullness at front waist, measure down from D one-fourth waist measurement plus 2 in. for E and draw line E to corner. F. If no back fullness is desired, repeat in back sections. Cut on lines.

Stitch center-front seam, join side seams, and stitch center-back seam up to 7 in. below top. Stitch shoulder and underarm seams. Put blouse and skirt on and pin waistline together. Fit dress, even hem line as dotted lines show, and mark hem length. Stitch top edge of hem; then slipstitch it in place. Put a 22-in. zipper in center-back of blouse and skirt placket.

Cut facings 2 in. wide from cutting scraps and use these to face neck and bottom of sleeves. When stitching blouse and skirt together, sew seam binding in the waistline seam to prevent stretching.

Eyelet Embroidery Dress

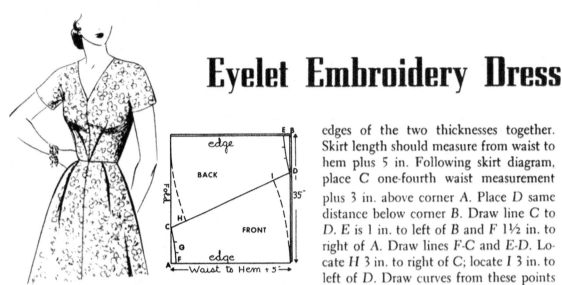

▶▶▶ FOR THIS DRESS, average figure needs 3½ yds. of 35-in. eyelet embroidery fabric.

To chalk out bodice: Measure off twice shoulder-to-waist length, plus 2 in., cut off on crosswise thread, fold, and place fold toward you, lengthwise edges even. Point C is halfway between corners A and B. D is 2 in. to right of C. E is halfway between C and D. F is on top edges directly above C. G is 2 in. to left of F. To draw shoulder line, connect G and D. Place EE one-sixth of neck measurement plus 1 in. above D and draw back neckline on a curve from E to EE. H is 4 in. below G on shoulder line; I is 7 to 9 in. to right of G, depending upon how low you want neck. Connect H and I for a V neck. Or, for an oval neck, place I nearer G, and H 2 in. lower, and draw a curved line to connect H and I. If a high neck is used, make an opening at center-back. J is one-half armhole measurement to left of C; K, one-fourth bust measurement plus 1½ in. above J. L is above K, M to left of K, both on edge of fabric. Make a curved underarm at K. Cut bodice from E to EE, EE to G, L around K to M. Lay back over front and cut underarm to match. Cut front neck as you have planned H to I.

To chalk out skirt: Fold material for skirt crosswise. Smooth fabric and pin edges of the two thicknesses together. Skirt length should measure from waist to hem plus 5 in. Following skirt diagram, place C one-fourth waist measurement plus 3 in. above corner A. Place D same distance below corner B. Draw line C to D. E is 1 in. to left of B and F 1½ in. to right of A. Draw lines F-C and E-D. Locate H 3 in. to right of C; locate I 3 in. to left of D. Draw curves from these points to edge of the fabric, as dotted lines show. Cut on these lines for bottom edge of the skirt. Cut on lines F-C and E-D.

Seam skirt, straight edges together for center-front, straight edge to a bias edge for sides, and two bias edges for center-back seam. Leave a 4-in. placket opening left side front. Lay a pleat in each side, front and back, as at G, to take up 3 in. allowed in each gore; turn pleat in toward center front and back. Seam shoulders and center-front of bodice. Seam right underarm; seam left to within 5 in. of waistline. Lay pleats at center-front of bodice as in the sketch to take up excess fullness; lay pleats in back to match those of skirt. Pin both together at waistline and fit dress. Turn hem. Check neckline and sleeves for becomingness. Remove, and make any fitting adjustments necessary. Face neck and sleeve edges with flat bias binding ¾ in. wide. Stitch same type of binding to top edge of hem and slip-stitch in place. Put zipper in and press dress.

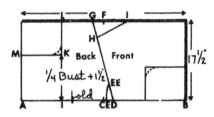

A Sheer, Cool, Easy-to-wear Dress

▶▶▶ FOR THIS cool, fresh dress of cotton voile, the average requirement is between 3 and 3½ yds. An additional ⅛ yd. is needed if sleeve ruffles are used. The finished model has only a belt for trimming.

Measure length from waistline in center-front up over shoulder at side neck and down to waistline at center-back. Tear or cut off this amount plus seams. Cut two skirt lengths plus 3 in. each for hem. Seam these two widths together, stopping one seam 4 in. from end; press.

Fold waist piece lengthwise, wrong side out, selvage edges pinned together. On selvage mark center (A). For sleeves, measure both right and left from A one-half the armhole measurement; mark B and C. Measure from fold in line with B and C one-fourth bust measurement plus 2 in.; mark D and E. Form sleeves and underarm by cutting from B to D, then to F at left edge; and from C to E, then to G at right edge.

Place H on fold straight across from A. Measure from H to I one-half the neck measurement. Mark J ½ in. to left of H. Measure in from H one-fourth neck measurement for K. Cut from J through K to I to make neckline. For back opening, cut 6 in. from J to L on center fold. Cut bias strips 1½ in. wide and join these with ¼-in. seams. With this bias, bind neck and center-back opening. Fold bias in half, baste to right side of neckline, and stitch, as in M. Turn to wrong side and whip, as in N. French-seam underarm seams, leaving left side open 4 in. above waistline.

Run two rows of gathers at each side of front and back of blouse, as at O. Draw up fullness so that waistline equals waist measurement. Gather top of skirt and draw up fullness to waist measurement.

Join waist and skirt. Hem side placket opening and fasten with hook and eye at waistline. Put dress on. Tie a belt or sash around waistline. Decide on a becoming length. Remove dress and put in hem. Press dress. (A 2-in. length for tie sash could be torn from skirt lengths before cutting, if desired.)

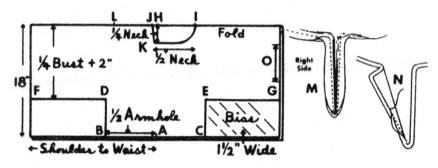

Dress with Velvet Trim

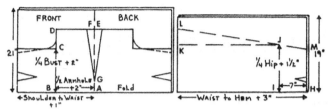

▶▶▶ FOR THIS basic dress buy two shoulder-to-waist lengths and two skirt lengths of 42-in. rayon crepe, plus 6 in. for hems, and 1¼ yds. of velvet ribbon.

Straighten fabric. Tear off length for waist plus 2 in. for seams. From longer piece tear or cut a 2-in. strip from each selvage edge to use for braided belt.

To chalk out waist: Fold waist piece in half lengthwise with fold toward you. A on diagram is at halfway point on fold. B is one-half armhole measurement plus 2 in. to left of A; C, one-fourth bust measurement plus 2 in. above B. D is sleeve depth above C, about 5 in. Draw a line straight up from A for E, on a line with D. F is 2 in. to left of E; G, one-sixth of neck measurement plus 1 in. above A. Chalk a line G to F, F to D, D to C, then straight out from C to edge. Chalk a curved underarm line from D. Cut from D around to left edge, then D to F, F to G, G to A. Cut back piece of waist exactly the same. For waistline darts, as shown at edges, chalk 2 in. wide at bottom and 5 in. deep.

To chalk out three-gore skirt: Divide skirt piece in half crosswise by tearing or cutting on a thread. Fold each half lengthwise of the material. H is at extreme right; I, 7 in. to left; J, one-fourth hip measurement plus 1½ in. above I. Chalk a straight line to left of J for K. L is 4 to 6 in. above this line, depending upon fullness desired. Chalk a line L through J to edge of fabric for M. Mark for dart at waistline, as shown. Cut from M to L.

Keeping front gore folded, lay it over folded back piece, folds touching, then set left end of top fold 2 in. in from left end of bottom fold—this to give greater width to back. Pin front to back and cut along line L-M. Cut on fold of back piece to make two gores which join line L-M of front. Back seam is slightly bias.

To make dress: Apply velvet ribbon to front neck, as in N. Lay right sides together. Stitch down center-front, to depth of ribbon, then back. Slash between stitching. Turn velvet to wrong side. Cut off corners diagonally. Turn raw edge under and stitch free of dress. Baste shoulder, underarm, and the seams of skirt, leaving an opening on left side for zipper. Face back neck edge and make a 5-in. faced slash at center-back. Close with hook and eye. Put waist on; tie a string around waist. Put skirt on; pin it to waist at side seams. Adjust dart fullness so skirt and waist agree in width at waistline. Pin skirt to waist. Mark skirt length.

Stitch seams and darts; put zipper in. Even hem edge. Finish with seam binding; then slip-stitch hem. Face bottom of sleeves on wrong side with velvet ribbon. Turn to right side to make cuff.

Braided belt: Using the 2-in. strips, make three strips, each one-third longer than waistline. Fold each strip lengthwise, wrong side out, and stitch ¼ in. from edge. Turn tubing right side out. Fasten three ends together and braid to make a belt. Turn ends under and whip securely. Use hook and eye to close.

Nylon Net Dress

▶▶▶ IF YOU HAVE a "tired" dress you no longer quite like, cut top off at the waistline, face the top and make a snug-fitting camisole. Take off any extra bulk on skirt or recut the skirt to a slim petticoat silhouette. Sew skirt and blouse together and put a zipper in side. Buy 2 yds. of 72-in. nylon net and make a circular skirt and bolero, as the diagrams show, and you will have a dress to wear when you want to look especially nice.

To cut and make the skirt: Fold material in half crosswise. Pin cut edges together. Mark center of one cut edge A. From A to B mark off a distance of one-eighth waist measurement. From B to C mark length of skirt. No hem is necessary in the net. At A, hold string tied to chalk or pencil and mark the two arcs shown. Cut on these lines.

Cut a placket on left side 7 in. deep, and machine-stitch to prevent stretching. Stitch around waistline ¼ in. from edge to prevent stretching, and notch edge. For waistband use ribbon binding.

To cut bolero, make paper pattern, penciling it out according to diagram as follows: B is shoulder-to-waist length less 3 in. to right of corner A. C is one-half armhole measurement plus 2 in. to left of B. D is one-fourth bust measurement plus 3 in. above C. E is one-fourth neck measurement to left of B, and F 1 in. to right of B. G is one-sixth of the neck measurement plus ½ in. above B. Measure up from G for length of sleeve and locate H. I and J are each 1½ in. from H. Draw a line from D to left to edge of paper. Draw a line straight up from D to connect with line drawn left from I. Draw line to curve front of bolero, as diagram shows; then fold paper on line G-H and cut back same as front, curving the underarm as shown. Cut collar pieces from pieces cut away at the underarm. A seam is necessary in center-back of collar. Lay paper pattern on corner pieces left from skirt and cut out your bolero.

Seam shoulders and underarms. Bind bottom of sleeves, edge of jacket, collar, and one edge of center back with ½-in.-wide nylon ribbon. Lap bound edge of center back over the other half of back and stitch. Baste the collar on, easing neckline of bolero slightly so that it cannot draw. Stitch collar; then turn and slip-stitch raw edge to cover the seam.

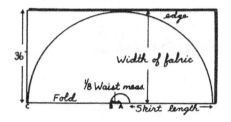

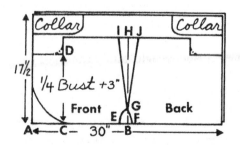

The "Any-fabric" Dress

▶▶▶ MAKE THIS very versatile dress of taffeta, satin, crepe, or jersey. Buy the 50-in. width. It also handles economically in 56-in. tubular jersey, which makes sleeves 3 in. longer and skirt 12 in. wider, since two tube lengths split are used. Buy two skirt lengths plus one waist length— 2½ to 3 yds. is ample.

Straighten fabric. Measure off the shoulder-to-waist length plus 4½ in. Tear or cut off. Remainder of piece is cut in half crosswise, selvages seamed together for skirt. Leave 4-in. placket opening at left side. Top of skirt is gathered with two rows so that it can be drawn up to fit blouse.

To chalk out blouse: Diagram is based on 50-in. fabric. Bring selvage edges together evenly in center, so that there is a fold at each side. Point A is 2 in. down on selvage edges; B is one-half the armhole measure plus 2 in. below A. Draw line straight across from B to folds for C and D. Measure in from both C and D on this line a distance of one-fourth bust measurement plus 1 in. for E and F. Draw a line straight down from both E and F to bottom of fabric. Draw a curved underarm from B to E and F, as dotted lines show.

G and H are at the upper corners. For back neck, measure down from G on fold 3 in. for I, and 5 in. to right of G for J. K and L are each 5 in. from H. Draw lines I to J, J to A, A to L, L to K for neck and shoulder lines. Cut on drawn lines. Cut single thickness of fabric A to B.

Join shoulder seams and right underarm, using a ⅜-in. pressed-open seam. Stitch left underarm seam from B about 6 in. for a left side-seam zipper.

Baste skirt to waist. Try on. Make sure that neckline is becoming, sleeves a good length. Lay two darts each side of center-front and center-back, as on diagram, to take up any excess fullness in waistline.

Decide skirt length. Remove dress. Stitch waist and skirt together. Stitch waistline darts. Put in dress zipper according to instructions provided with the zipper. Put hem in. Turn ½-in. hems in bottom of sleeves and slip-stitch in place.

For neck finish, cut a 1½-in. true-bias facing from pieces cut out at neck. Stitch this on right side, mitering facing at four points: center-front, center-back, and both shoulders. Clip seam. Turn facing to wrong side. Stitch free edge and catch it down at shoulder seams. Use a ribbon or novelty belt, or make one from a 2¼-in. crosswise strip of fabric.

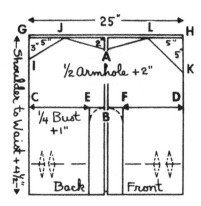

House Dress

▶▶▶ THE EASY-TO-MAKE house dress shown required 3¼ yds. of 36-in. percale. You need one waist length (measure from front waistline over bust and shoulder close to neck to back waistline) plus 4 in. and two skirt lengths plus 6 in. for hems.

Straighten fabric. Tear off crosswise strip of twice the waist length plus 2 in. For skirt, divide remaining piece crosswise into two even lengths.

To chalk out and cut waist: Fold waist piece lengthwise, wrong side out, fold next to you. Measure from corner A, as in diagram, to center, for point B. Chalk a line up to C. Measure right and left from C one-half armhole measurement plus 1 in. for D and E. From fold measure up toward D and E one-fourth bust measurement plus 4 in. for F and G. Draw straight underarm lines out to edges from each of these points. Curve underarms (see broken lines). H is one-fourth neck measurement to left of B; I is same distance above B. J is ½ in. to right of B. Cut J to I around to H for neck; A to H for center-front. Cut underarm curves.

To chalk, cut, and assemble skirt: Lay two lengths with right sides and selvages together. Measure up from corner K one-fourth hip measurement plus 2 in. for L. Place N same distance in from corner M. Draw and cut on line from N to L. Bring selvages at M around to L to join each back gore to a front gore. Seam the bias center-back seam. Even edges at bottom where bias edges extend below straight edges. Fold selvage of right-hand front gore under 1 in. and pin. Lap this over edge of left front gore 1½ in.; pin together, beginning 7 in. below waistline (for placket).

To make waist: Gather back neck to measure one-third of neck measurement plus 1 in. Turn and stitch 1-in. hem on right-hand side of front and ½ in. on left. Stitch a ⅛-in. hem around neck. Lap front edges and pin. Apply rick rack around neck and on side fronts. Join underarm seams. Gather waistline across back and at each side of center-front, beginning 3 in. in from underarms. Gather back waistline of skirt.

Pin back waist and skirt together, matching side seams. Put dress on. Close at front. Lay pleats each side of skirt front to take up fullness. Pin front of waist and skirt together. Decide length. Remove dress. Stitch pleat made by front lap, first top-stitching placket depth, then continuing through to bottom of skirt. Join waist and skirt; put in hem. Make narrow belt or use a contrasting one. Use buttons and buttonhole to close front.

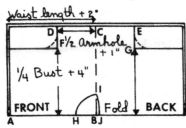

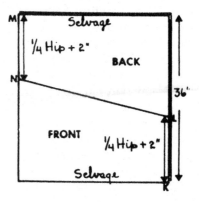

Backless Dress of Metallic Fabric

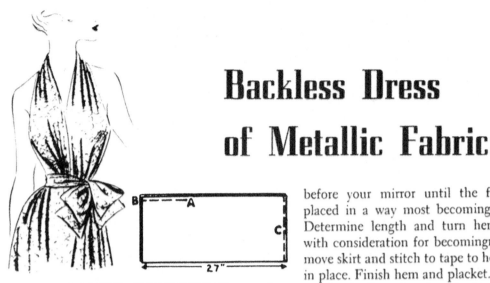

▶▶▶ MANY SHIMMERING, supple metallic fabrics may be found in yard-goods departments, some even encrusted with 24-karat gold. Every inch of these fabrics is valuable, so this design, which takes a minimum of yardage, seems especially suitable to the "minted" fabrics, although it is equally good for satin, taffeta, brocade, embroidery, wool jersey, or fake fur.

Buy two skirt lengths, plus 6 in. for hem, plus ¾ yd. for halter bodice.

Straighten fabric at both ends. To determine bodice length, measure from neck at center-back down over fullest part of bust to waist, adding 3 in. for seams and "take-up" at neck. Mark this length on fabric, pull a thread to guide cutting, and cut bodice piece off. From one selvage of remaining piece, cut a strip for sash, 6 in. wide and full length of piece.

Cut remaining piece in half crosswise, making two skirt widths. Seam cut edges of skirt pieces together; overcast the seam. Stitch selvage edges together, beginning 7 in. below top edge to allow for placket.

Cut twilled tape to size of your waist plus 1 in. Lay skirt out flat with seams at sides (placket at left). Lay soft folds on each side of center-front, as shown in sketch, pinning them to tape. In back, lay folds first at center, then at each side, pinning them to tape. Try skirt on and adjust before your mirror until the folds are placed in a way most becoming to you. Determine length and turn hem, again with consideration for becomingness. Remove skirt and stitch to tape to hold folds in place. Finish hem and placket.

Split bodice piece lengthwise through center. Make a rolled hem on each of the two lengthwise raw edges. Lay the two lengths so that selvages are together and mark on selvage the point above waist where you want V to begin, as at A. Baste from this point to end, B. Baste opposite ends together to form halter, as at C. Put on halter and check it for length. Put a tape around waist and lay folds in front of halter at waistline, pinning them to tape and extending fabric back as far as you want, making sure it is nicely placed for you at front underarm. Remove halter bodice and stitch folds in place, stitching around waistline free of tape. Remove tape.

Stitch center-front seam of bodice and seam at back of neck. Press seams open. Turn under bottom edge of bodice and pin over waistline of skirt, matching center-fronts. Stitch waist and skirt together, beginning at placket in skirt, stitching across front and around to where bodice ends at right side of back. Bind free waistline edge of bodice and of skirt on left side back. Use snaps to hold these edges together.

Slip-stitch a hem in raw edge and ends of sash, or line sash throughout with a contrasting color of taffeta or lightweight satin. Wrap the sash around figure and tie a big generous bow at left side.

Boleros, Jackets, and Coats

Shoulder Bolero

▶▶▶ MAKE THIS BOLERO of fake fur white krimmer, lined with jersey to match dress.

You need ⅝ yd. of 52- to 54-in. fake fur fabric and the same amount of tubular jersey for lining, plus thread, of course.

To chalk out: Fold fabric lengthwise, wrong side out. Pin edges together and lay fold toward you. Mark for cutting, following the diagram. Point B is 4 in. to right of corner A. C is 3½ in. above A. D is 1½ in. to right of C. E is one-sixth of the neck measurement plus ½ in. above B. F is 7 in. above C. G is 7 in. to right of F. Connect D and E with G to get shoulder dart, as dotted lines on diagram show. Tie a string to a pencil and, holding string at E, swing an arc from corner H to edge of fabric above F. Curve front line as dotted line shows; also curve from F to D. Cut on these dotted lines D to F, F around curve to H. Pin shoulder darts, pinning each dart in from G. Put cape on; pin edges together at underarm, and make sure that neckline is comfortable.

Remove. Open darts. Cut lining exactly same size. Pin darts in bolero and lining and baste and stitch these. Cut seams of darts open and press them open. Lay right sides of lining and bolero together. Stitch all around edge, leaving only neck unstitched. Press seam open and turn right side out. Trim raw edge of lining in at neck and whip it down to conceal seam. Put garment on, catch edges together to form bottom of sleeves. Whip these together, and your bolero is done and ready for wear.

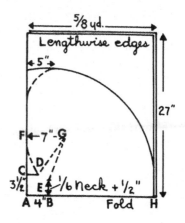

Flannel Bolero

▶▶▶ FLANNEL IS always a favorite for boleros, easy to make and inexpensive. You need only two lengths, shoulder to waistline (usually 1 yd.), of 54- or 60-in. flannel and the same amount of rayon lining of a matching or contrasting color.

To chalk out: Straighten your fabric at both ends. Fold it lengthwise, with fold toward you, and pin ends and selvages together. Place point C halfway between corners A and B; D, ½ in. to left of C; E, on selvage edge directly above C; F, 1 in. to left of E; and G, one-half the armhole measurement to left of F. H is 2 in. below G; I is one-half the armhole measurement to left of D. J is one-fourth bust measurement plus 2 in. above I, and K is same distance above A. L is one-sixth of the neck measurement plus ½ in. above C. Connect J and H. Draw lines C-F and J-K. Draw a line from H to meet line C-F. Connect L and D. Cut from K to J, curving underarm, as shown; cut on to H and to line C-F. Cut L to D. Cut line C-F. Place back over remaining piece of fabric, the back center fold 2 in. from selvage. Cut sleeves of front section to match back. Fold selvages back 2 in. at center-front, and mark front neck curve by measuring to right of F on center-front a distance of one-fourth neck measurement for M, and down on line F-C one-sixth of the neck measurement plus 2 in. for N. Cut front neck M to N.

Cut lining same as bolero except for fronts; make them 2 in. narrower at center-front. Cut cuffs double and long enough to go around bottom of sleeves.

To make bolero: Seam shoulder and underarm seams in flannel and lining, using a ⅜-in. seam. Press seams open. Turn bolero wrong side out and put lining over it. Baste neck edges together; slip-stitch front edges. Put bolero on and pin the double cuffs in position. Even the length of bottom of jacket. If you stand very erect, you may need to shorten the back a little. If shoulders are low, the bolero at end of underarm seam may need to be cut a little to straighten with rest of waistline. Stitch seam binding to bottom edge of jacket after edges have been evened. Turn a hem, slip-stitch this hem in position; then turn a hem in lining, making this ¾ in. shorter than that in the bolero. Slip-stitch this hem in place; catch lining to bolero at the underarm seams. Stitch the cuffs in place on the bolero; turn lining over and slip-stitch it to cover the cuff seams. Turn the neck edge of bolero and lining in toward each other, clipping both edges so that they will lie flat. Then slip-stitch the two together. Work button-holes and sew buttons on center-front, or use swivel pin-on buttons.

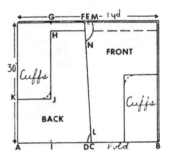

Blazer-striped Bolero

▶▶▶ GAY NINETIES blazer stripes are strikingly different for boleros. The type illustrated is so easy to make that you may want several in different colors of stripes

One yard of 42-in. rayon taffeta or cotton will make a bolero, and the time required to make it is only a short afternoon or evening.

Straighten fabric. Fold wrong side out, selvage edges together, fold toward you.

To chalk out: Point B in diagram is shoulder-to-waist length less 3 in. to right of corner A. C is one-half the armhole measurement plus 2 in. to left of B. D is one-fourth bust measurement plus 3 in. above C. E is one-fourth neck measurement to left of B, and F is 1 in. to right of B. G is one-sixth of the neck measurement plus ½ in. above B. Measure up from G to the distance required for the desired sleeve length and locate H. I and J are each 1½ in. from H.

Draw a line from D to left to edge of fabric. Draw a line straight up from D;

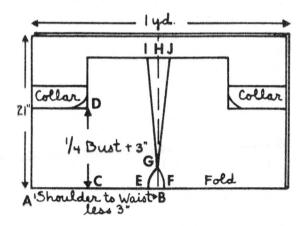

connect this line with the line through I. Turn fabric on line G-H and cut front and back the same, curving the underarm as shown. Cut collar pieces out, as shown, from pieces cut away at the underarm. A seam is necessary in center-back of collar.

Cut line A to E for center-front opening. Cut E to G to F for neck. Use pieces from selvage edges to face center-front opening. Seam shoulders and underarms. Make a 1-in. hem in bottom of sleeves and a 1¼-in. hem in bottom of jacket.

Baste the collar on, easing neckline of bolero slightly so that it cannot draw. Stitch collar; then turn and slip-stitch raw edge to cover the seam.

Spanish-type Bolero

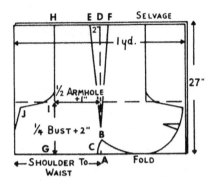

▶▶▶ SPAIN frequently influences our fashions, and we see many adaptations of the Spanish bolero made of fur, of imitation fur, of velvet or tweed, of flannel, of faille, or of lace. You can wear it with a matching skirt or over a dress. It can be made reversible by using the same amount of fabric in two colors or types of fabric.

Buy 1 yd. of 54- to 60-in. fabric or 1½ yds of narrower fabric or if three-quarter sleeves are desired. Buy same amount of lining, unless you are using lace, which is picoted or bound and unlined.

To chalk and cut out: Straighten fabric. Fold in half lengthwise and lay fold toward you. Mark point A in center on fold, as in diagram. B is one-sixth of the neck measurement plus ½ in. above A; C, ½ in. to left of A.

Chalk a straight line up from B to selvage for D. E and F are each 2 in. on either side of D. Chalk lines E to B and F to B for shoulder seams. G is one-half the armhole measurement plus 1½ in. to left of A. I is one-fourth bust measurement plus 2 in. above G. Chalk a dotted line this distance from fold full length of fabric. J is 1 in. to right of edge and 1 in. below dotted line. Chalk line from I straight up to locate H on selvage. Chalk a curved line at underarm. Cut from fold, rounding up to J for back waistline, then through underarm curve and out to H. Cut E to B to C, and B to F.

Lay back over front piece. Chalk front underarm to match. Mark front neckline. Bottom of bolero may be square or curved as is most becoming. Darts may be pinned in in fitting, then stitched and pressed. Cut a lining of same size as outside.

To make: Seam shoulder and underarm seams, using a ⅜-in. seam. Press them open. Bolero may be made collarless or finished with a Peter Pan collar or a straight 1½-in.-wide collarband, rounding ends as shown in the diagram. Turn to right side and press. Lay collar on right side of bolero at neckline, with raw edges together. Stitch ⅜ in. from edge. Place right sides of bolero and lining together. Baste from one shoulder line (through ends of collar) all the way around front and back to other shoulder. Turn right side out through neck opening.

If cuffs are used, make them double and ½ in. wider than finished collar. Sew to bottom of sleeves, seams meeting underarm seam. Whip sleeve lining down over seam.

Ball fringe may be used to trim bottom edge. Slip-stitch it all around or insert edge between outside and lining and stitch.

Striped Jersey Bolero

▶▶▶ BOLERO JACKETS of striped jersey are favored for sports. They are easy to make and effective for wear with shorts and a T-shirt or with a blouse and skirt. One yd. of 54-in. striped jersey plus ⅛ yd. of plain jersey for binding is all that is needed.

To chalk out: Straighten fabric. With a fold toward you, place A at halfway point on fold and measure the length from shoulder to waist to left of A, as diagram shows. B is one-sixth of the neck measurement plus ½ in. above A. C is ½ in. to left of A. Place D straight above A and on opposite fold. E and F are each 2 in. from D. G is one-half the armhole measurement plus 1 in. to left of C. H is on opposite fold straight above G; I, one-fourth bust measurement plus 2 in. above G. Draw chalk lines B-D, B-E. Draw line from I to H; then draw line from I straight to left edge. Locate J 1 in. to right of edge and 1 in. down from dotted line. Extend 8-in. diagonal line down from J to edge of bolero, as shown, and mark underarm curve. Cut shoulder line B-E of back. Place back over front and cut sleeve of front. On center-front, measure to right from A one-fourth neck measurement.

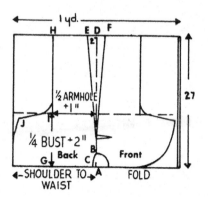

Curve line to B, as shown, and cut on this line to B, then to C. Curve bottom and sides of front as shown. Cut front along folded edge. Cut fold at bottom of sleeves, front and back.

To make: Make a tapering dart in each shoulder front, 4 in. long and 1 in. wide at top. Ease back shoulder line onto front shoulder line so that sleeve lines come out even at bottom. Seam shoulders together, using a ⅜-in. seam.

Cut banding in two strips 2¼ in. wide. Beginning at front neckline and continuing down front, baste strip of banding on, right side of banding to right side of bolero. Ease this around curves, and finish at front neckline and cut banding off. Turn and baste edge of banding back so that finished band will be ⅞ in. wide; turn raw edge in ¼ in. and slip-stitch it down. Bind neck in same way, allowing band to extend over ends of center-front bands so that all raw edges are concealed.

Bind ends of sleeves. Stitch underarms of sleeves. Close at neck with button and loop or with hook and eye.

Short Sleever

▶▶▶ THIS ATTRACTIVE jacket can be made of 1 yd. of 30-in. suedelike woolen. It is ideal for wear over a jersey or woolen dress. Use a scarf, pearls, or chains at the neck, and wear it with or without a belt.

Straighten fabric. Tear off 9 in. on crosswise for pockets and cuffs. For very tall figures, buy 1⅛ yds. and make jacket 30 in. long and pockets and cuffs 10½ in.

To chalk out: Fold through center lengthwise, with the fold next to you. Chalk off 3 in. along selvage for front hems and overlap. From corner A (see diagram), measure to right one-half the armhole measurement plus 5 in. for B. Directly above B draw a straight line up to front line for C. D is one-fourth bust measurement plus 3 in. below C. E is one-fourth bust measurement plus 3 in. above B. F is at top left-hand corner and on center-front line. G is one-sixth of the neck measurement plus ½ in. below F. H is one-sixth of the neck measurement plus ½ in. above A. I is halfway between A and F. Chalk a straight line I to halfway point between D and E. J is 2 in. to right of I.

To cut: Cut from H through J to G, and from J to line D-E. Cut lines D and E, rounding underarm as indicated. For large figure there will be little to cut out between D and E.

To make: Seam shoulders, using a ½-in. seam. Place G and H together and stitch to J. Stitch underarms D and E together. Put jacket on; adjust the 3 in. allowances at center-front for the overlap you desire. Take one small piece cut out at top of shoulders to use as a facing for back neck.

Join cuffs to armholes, right sides of cuffs to right side of jacket, using a ¼-in. seam. Turn to wrong side; press seam open. Seam underarms of cuffs. Catch-stitch raw edge to seam to avoid bulk. Stitch on top fold of cuffs ½ in. from edge.

Turn edges of pockets ¾ in. on all four sides. Catch-stitch these turned edges back, taking stitches so that they do not show on right side. Place pockets on each side, in a position that is becoming to you. Stitch ½ in. from sides and bottom, pivoting at corners. Pull threads through to wrong side. Thread your needle and take a few securing stitches on wrong side at each side of top of pocket, so that stitching cannot pull out. Turn bottom edge of jacket and catch-stitch hem in position.

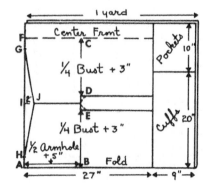

Plastron Doublet

▶▶▶ FOR WEAR over a sweater, to protect a blouse, for extra warmth, or for dress-up, a plastron doublet qualifies. It requires only ¾ yd. of fabric. Made of velveteen or felt, it is inexpensive—of gingham or imitation linen, still more so. It can be attractively made of any of a dozen fabrics and would provide ideal use for a remnant.

To make it of 36-in. fabric, split the ¾-yd. lengthwise through center. Fold two pieces lengthwise and lay end to end, with folds toward you. For front neckline, measure one-half the neck measurement plus 1 in. from corner A to point B. C is one-fourth neck measurement above A. For back neckline, make same measurement as A to C on front to mark D, and 1 in. down on fold of back mark E. Mark and cut a curve from B to C; then from D to E. Slant shoulders about 1 in. on front and back, as dotted lines show.

Stitch shoulder seam from neck edge out. Face neck edge and sides with flat bias binding. Slip-stitch a 1-in. hem in bottom.

Put garment on and tie tape around waistline. Mark for loops and buttons as shown in the sketch. Sew an elastic loop on each side of back at waistline, as at F, and buttons on front, as at G. Loops come over buttons and hold garment in position. If desired, a belt may be worn, or darts may be used at each side, front and back, to make more fitted at waistline.

Pockets can be added each side of center-front at bottom. Strip cut from side when 54-in. fabric is used may be cut in two lengthwise, seamed on crosswise ends or faggoted together, edges fringed. Or piece may be hemmed or ribbon-bound and made into a very nice scarf to wear with your plastron doublet. The doublet is ideal for wear at football games, for skating, or for any outdoor occasion when arm freedom and, at the same time, chest protection are desired.

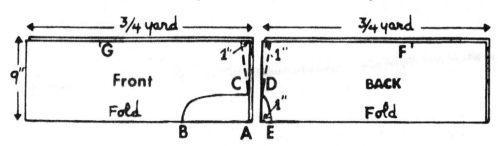

Quilted Cozy

▶▶▶ LET THE winter winds blow! You'll never mind them if you are snugly warm with a short quilted cozy under your coat. A gay ribbon scarf like the one illustrated makes the cozy permissible to wear even after the coat is off.

The jacket takes only 1 yd. of 36-in. quilted fabric—wool, rayon, silk, or cotton—in black or in the gayest color you can find, as suits your mood and purpose. Imagine how nice to have that ribbon (1 yd., 6 in. wide) sewed in place across the back of the neck to tie in a jiffy and look "put" when you want it to. For extra warmth, as well as for easier finishing, line the jacket throughout with jersey or with a sheer crepe.

Straighten fabric. Fold in half lengthwise, with fold toward you. Mark A the lower left-hand corner, as in diagram. B is at halfway point on fold. Straight across from B on opposite edge is C.

D is 2 in. to left of C; E is 2 in. to right of B. Chalk a line from D to E. F is one-half the armhole measurement plus 3 in. to left of E. Chalk a line straight in from F to opposite edge. G is one-fourth bust measurement plus 1½ in. in from F. H is one-fourth bust measurement plus ½ in. from A. Connect G and H. Round underarm as shown. I is 1½ in. from D. Chalk a line from I straight across to edge at J for center-front. K and L are one-fourth neck measurement from I. M is one-fourth neck measurement from E. Chalk neck curves, making back neck ½ in. to left of E on fold.

Cut from D to E; from H through underarm curve (G) to edge of fabric. Lay back over front section, shoulder lines matching, and center-back fold matching chalked center-front line. Cut out front underarm. Separate front and back necklines. Cut front sleeves on fold line and cut piecing for front of sleeves as at N. Lower edge of back and front can be darted if a more fitted effect is preferred.

Cut lining exactly the same except that you allow no lap at center-front.

Stitch piecing to front sleeves. Press seams open. Stitch shoulder and underarm seams in both quilted and lining fabrics.

Lay lining over quilting, right sides together, seams matching. Stitch around bottom of sleeves and down front edges. Turn front hems back 1 in.; then stitch around neckline. Press seams open. Turn right side out. Press. Turn bottom edges in toward each other. Slip-stitch together.

Lap front 1 in. and use snaps to close so that there will be no bulk. Tack center of 1 yd. of ribbon at back neckline, if desired.

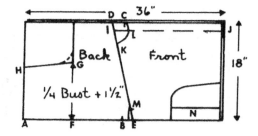

Weskits—Smart and Warm

▶▶▶ FOR WEAR over a blouse that is tailored to a T, or over a sweater, or for extra warmth under a suit or coat, this fake-fur waistcoat is ideal.

Make it out of ⅝ yd. of fake fur, and you will have enough left for a scarf or a pair of mittens. Line throughout with sheer rayon crepe, and thus you will have no finishing to do on edges. Fake fur, lining, buttons and all can be bought at a surprisingly low cost.

Straighten ends of fabric. Fold in half lengthwise, wrong side out. Pin edges together with fold toward you. As in diagram, mark A at lower left-hand corner. B is one-half the armhole measurement plus 2 in. to right of A. C is at the distance of shoulder to waist from A, on fold. D is lower right-hand corner. Chalk a line straight from B and C to opposite edges, and mark E and F. G is one-fourth neck measurement above A; H is length of shoulder above G. I is one-fourth bust measurement plus 1 in. above B; J the same distance from D. K is one-fourth waist measurement plus 2 in. above C. L is 1 in. to right of A.

Mark armhole curve from H to I. Draw line L to G, and connect G and line H, as shown. Connect I-K and K-J. Mark for 1-in. waistline darts as indicated on line C. Decide depth desired below waistline and mark this depth as at M. Chalk center-front line straight, as at N, 1½ in. in from lengthwise edges.

Cut out back except for line M. Lay back over front, center-back fold along center-front line N. Mark and cut front shoulder, armhole, and underarm same as back. Remove back. Mark front neckline, darts, and shape bottom edge as desired. Cut neckline (line O).

Pin or baste shoulder seams, underarm seams, and darts. Put on; lap fronts 1 in.; check shaping of bottom edge and fit of waistline. Remove. Cut bottom edge, back and front, allowing ⅜-in. seam. Remove pins or basting. Lay on lining fabric and cut it the same.

Stitch shoulder and underarm seams and darts in both fabrics. Lay right sides together and seam neckline, fronts, and bottom edges, leaving a small opening at lower center-back for turning. Press seams; clip corners; turn right side out. Press. Whip edges of opening together. Turn armhole edges in toward each other and slip-stitch together.

If you wish to avoid making buttonholes, use snaps and pin-on swivel buttons.

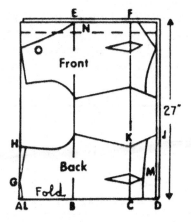

Stiff, Satin Evening Jacket

▶▶▶ SATIN JACKETS in white, pastels, or bright colors with dark linings are practical, comfortable, and easy to make.

You need, for average figure, 1½ yds. of 50-in. stiff satin fabric, plus same amount of taffeta for lining.

To chalk out: Straighten ends of satin; fold lengthwise, wrong side out, with fold toward you. Pin ends and selvages together. As on diagram, mark point C halfway between corners A and B. D is 1½ in. to right of C; E is on selvage edge directly above D; F is 3 in. to left of E. Draw line D to F. G is ½ in. to left of D; H is one-sixth of the neck measurement plus 1 in. above D on line D-F. Draw curve H to G. I is one-half the armhole measurement plus 1 in. to left of C; J, one-fourth bust measurement plus 2 in. above I. K is on selvage directly above J. L is one-fourth bust measurement plus 5 in. above A. Connect L and K, curving around underarm at J. M is 1 in. to right of L on line L-J. Cut A to M, M around curve to K. Cut F to H, H to G. Place back section on front, with center-back fold on selvage edges of front. Cut front same as back except at neck. Measure on selvages from F one-fourth neck measurement for E, and place N on shoulder line one-sixth of the neck plus 1 in. below F. Draw and cut front neck curve E to N.

To make: Piece sleeves to make them as long as you desire or make double turnback cuffs. Cut lining same as coat, piecing lining sleeves, also. Join piecings in ⅜-in. seams. Press seams open. Baste shoulder and underarm seams of jacket and try jacket on. Make sure that sleeves are correct in length. You may want to fit shoulder seam a little, taking out some from the shoulder down, or you may want a little less fullness under the arm. After the fitting, rebaste to correct the lines. Make changes in lining to match outside. Then stitch jacket and lining as basted and press all seams open. Clip seam every ½ in. on underarm curves. Turn coat wrong side out and slip lining over it.

Turn coat edges at front and bottom 1 in., and turn ½ in. at neck. Baste all around edges; then slip-stitch lining in position.

If desired, braid, ribbon, or sequins may be put on front and around neck. Tinsel thread is ideal for decorating such a coat and can easily be used on your own sewing machine.

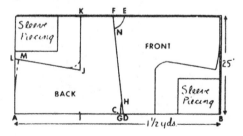

Dressing Sacque

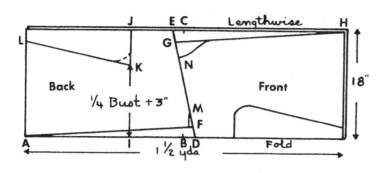

▶▶▶ OUR GRANDMOTHERS wore beautiful dressing sacques for dinner, tea, or informal occasions at home. Since their day the dressing sacque has gone places—out for dinner, for bridge, canasta, or the movies. It has been made of all sorts of fabric. Imagine how lovely this is with black cotton lace over coral-pink rayon satin. Pockets can be big or little, and the length short or long, whichever is most becoming to your hip line.

You will find 1⅜ yds. to 1½ yds. of 36-in. lace ample, unless you want a longer garment or long sleeves. Buy the same amount of satin for lining. For binding with ribbon, you will need 5 yds. of 1-in. velvet ribbon in the same color as the lace.

Straighten lace. Fold in half lengthwise, wrong side out, with fold toward you. A in diagram is lower left-hand corner. B is at halfway point on fold. Straight across from B is C, on opposite edge. D is 2 in. to right of B; E is 2 in. to left of C. Chalk a line from D to E. Measure on this line 2 in. from D for F; 2 in. from E for G. Chalk from A to F and from G to H.

I is half the armhole measurement plus 2 in. to left of B. Chalk straight across to J on edge. K is one-fourth bust measurement plus 3 in. in from I. L is one-fourth bust measurement plus 6 in. in from A. Connect L, K and J. Curve underarm as indicated. M is one-sixth neck measurement plus 1 in. above F. Curve back neck as shown. Pin edges of back pieces together.

Cut lines D-E; F-A; L around curve at K to J. Lay back pieces over front section, shoulders even and A-F in line with G-H. Cut front same as back except neckline. N is one-sixth neck measurement plus 1 in. from G. Curve front neck from N down on line G-H to depth desired. Cut fold at bottom of sleeve. Cut back neck curve as marked.

Straighten, fold, and cut lining fabric to match lace. Lay wrong side of lace pieces over right side of matching lining pieces. Pin together. Lace and lining are to be seamed together as though one fabric. Stitch center-back seam, shoulders, and underarm seams. To hold fabric edges together, stitch ¼ in. in on sleeves, neckline, and fronts, and around bottom. Bind all edges with 1-in.-wide velvet ribbon or 1¼- to 1½-in.-wide strips of lace cut from underarms. Straight strips can be used for binding, unless lace is very heavy; in that case, it should be cut on bias.

Cut pockets. Bind top edge only, or all around. Stitch in position desired.

Use snaps to close.

Reversible Coverall

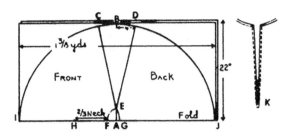

▶▶▶ BUY 1⅜ yds. of 45-in. rayon gabardine—the kind that looks and feels like wool—1¼ yds. of 54-in. clear plastic fabric, and thread to match the gabardine. Also buy or cover four buttons of about the size of a nickel.

Straighten fabric. Fold in half lengthwise, right sides together. Mark exact center of fold (A in diagram). On selvages directly above A place B. C and D are each 4 in. from B. Measure one-sixth of the neck measurement plus ½ in. in from A for E; to left of A for F. G is ½ in. to right of A. Mark neck curves. Draw lines from E to C and E to D. I and J are at the ends of the piece. Draw a curved line from I to C and D to J. Cut out neckline; then cut E to C, E to D, I to C, D to J. Now lay the wrap out, right side down, on plastic cloth and cut a lining exactly the same as top.

Stitch shoulder seams in both fabrics; press seams open; lay fabrics together, seams to outside. Use paper clips to hold them in position. Stitch ¼ in. from all outside edges except the neck. Carefully pull right side out through neck opening. Smooth flat. Press outside edge on gabardine side, using a press cloth and moderately warm iron.

Cut center-front opening down from F to H a depth of two-thirds of the neck measurement. Turn raw edges in. Begin at point H for this and taper the turn-in up to ¼ in. at neck. Baste both sides carefully. Clip neckline every ½ in., making clips ¼ in. deep. Use extra pieces for a double collarband. Cut a 2¼-in. strip on true crosswise grain. Stitch one edge to right side of neckline with a ⅜-in. seam. Whip other edge down on wrong side. Stitch center-front opening ⅛ in. from edge. Stitch from neckline down to K; pivot and stitch back up to the neckline. Pull threads through and tie.

Top-stitch ⅜ in. in from edge all around the wrap. Work four buttonholes or have them made at your sewing center, or make three loops and sew hooks on.

Prepare two strips of fabric, each ½ in. wide finished and long enough to extend from center of buttonhole on one side to center of the one on opposite side. Sew buttons to each end of each strip. Tack these in place on right-hand side.

Measure down from shoulder seam on each side about 7 in. and tack edges of cape together to form sleeves. Do this with a bar-tack.

98

Slip-on Coat

▶▶▶ IT IS ever so convenient to have a lightweight coat to slip on over a wool dress or suit when the weather is just too chilly for comfort without a wrap and a top coat is too warm.

For the coat shown, plaid rayon in imitation of wool for the lining and rayon gabardine for the outside, make a happy combination and cost surprisingly little. You need only 1¾ yds. of each fabric in a 54-in. width.

To chalk out: Straighten the crosswise edges of both fabrics. Work with lining fabric first. Fold it wrong side out, with selvages together and fold toward you. Point C in diagram is halfway between corners A and B. D is 2 in. to right of C. Draw a straight line up from C for E. F is 2 in. to left of E. Draw a line for shoulders, F to D.

G is ½ in. to left of D and H is one-fourth neck measurement plus ½ in. above D. Connect G and H for back neck curve. Mark I one-sixth of the neck measurement plus ½ in. from F. Beginning at I, round the front neck curve to E, as shown. Cut from G to H; H to F; from I to E.

J is one-half the armhole measurement plus 2 in. to left of G; K, one-fourth bust measurement plus 3 in. above J. Draw straight line up from J through to selvage. L is one-half the armhole measurement less 1 in. to left of F. M is one-fourth the bust measurement plus 8 in. above A. Connect M with K, K with L. Draw a curved line at underarm, as shown. Lay the back over the front and cut front underarm to match. Bottom edges below armhole may be curved slightly, as shown, to give an even edge here.

Cuffs may be as wide and as large as you desire them. Those on the model are 7 in. deep and wide enough to go around sleeve (or the armhole measurement less 2 in.).

Cut the top of coat in the same way as plaid lining. Seam shoulder and underarm seams of each. Press seams open. Clip seams on underarm curves. Put right sides of two fabrics together, stitch around front. Turn right side out. Seam short ends of cuff together; join to sleeves, catching coat and lining in seam. Slip-stitch raw edge of cuff in position; conceal all raw edges. Even bottom line of coat. Turn a hem in coat fabric about 1½ in. deep and slip-stitch this in place. Make a hem in lining 2 in. deep. Slip-stitch this to outer fabric. Tack lining to top at underarm seams. Press coat—and it is ready to wear.

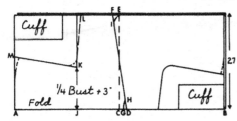

Sheer, Dark Flattery

▶▶▶ THIS SHEER organdy or nylon duster is made from 4 yds. of 42-in. fabric.

Straighten fabric; fold in half crosswise. Pin selvages together and lay fold to left, as shown in diagram.

For the back, measure to left from corner A one-half the armhole measurement plus 4 in. (B). To left from A on selvage measure back length plus 2 in. (C). Measure straight up from C one-half the bust measurement plus 4 in. (D). Directly above B measure one-fourth bust measurement plus 2 in. (E). With yardstick, draw line from D through E to edge of material. Mark F 2 in. to left of edge. Measure up from A one-fourth neck measurement for G. Draw shoulder line F to G. Curve bottom line. Cut along this line C-D. Then cut up to F and over to G.

For fronts, draw a straight line from D to selvages. Three in. below edge mark H, or center-front line. Measure one-fourth neck measurement below H for I; curve to J one-sixth neck to right of H. K is one-half the armhole measurement plus 4 in. to right of H. Measure down from K one-fourth bust measurement plus 3 in. for L. Straight down from center-front line on edges measure one-half bust plus 6 in. for M. Draw a line from M through L and mark N on C-H line. Two in. to right of N mark O. Make shoulder line from I to O. Make O to P same length as side back. Curve bottom line. Cut out fronts, cutting straight across from I. Then turn front hem back and cut front neck curve.

For sleeves, measure up from corner Q on fold armhole measurement plus 10 in.

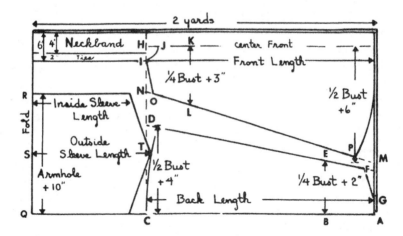

(R). Place S halfway between Q and R. Measure your full outside-sleeve measurement in from S for T, and inside-sleeve measurement in from Q and R. Connect these three points for top of sleeve. Cut out sleeves.

Cut neckband and ties along selvage, 4 in. and 2 in. wide, as shown.

This coat can be made for a really large figure, as indicated. For smaller sizes fabric as narrow as 36 in. may be used.

For tier-tucked sleeve, stitch a 2½-in. hem. Two and one-half in. above stitching line make 2½-in. tuck; stitch. Press tuck toward hem.

Remove center-back selvages and make a French seam. French-seam shoulde seams together. Join top of sleeves to coat, matching point to shoulder seam. French-seam sides and sleeves in continuous

Here is another sheer coat. Make it of georgette or nylon net, following diagram and instructions for Unlined Coat on page 102. Only changes are to cut straight to right from D on diagram (page 102) and to make shorter sleeves. Make a 6-in. tuxedo roll on front and neck edges, with matching cuff trim.

seam. Turn under 3-in. front facings and stitch. Turn neck edges of this fold in and stitch across.

Match center of neckband to center-back seam. Stitch neckband to back neck, using a ¼-in. seam. Fold in half and stitch across back. Other edges are left free and hemmed.

Put on coat and even the bottom. Make a slip-stitched hem. A ribbon sash or patent-leather belt may hold duster at waistline.

Unlined Coat

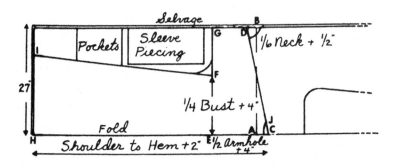

▶▶▶ USE RAYON FAILLE to make this coat to wear the first warm days of spring over a suit or dress, and for cool days the spring and summer through.

This simple, unlined coat—hem-length—is made of 3 yds. of 54-in. fabric, plus 10 yds. of grosgrain ribbon. For a three-quarter coat or a shortie, buy two lengths of 54-in. fabric. You can use the same diagram and instructions to make it of organdie or net with equally good results.

To chalk out coat: Straighten fabric. Fold lengthwise; lay fold toward you. A on diagram is halfway point on fold. Chalk a straight line from A to selvage for B. C is 2 in. to right of A, and D 2 in. to left of B. Chalk a line from C to D. E is half the armhole measurement plus 4 in. to left of C; F, one-fourth bust measurement plus 4 in. above E. Continue line E-F on up to selvage for G. Measure distance E to F. I is this distance plus 5 in. above corner H. J is one-sixth neck measurement plus ½ in. above C on line C-D. Mark a curve from J to ½ in. to left of C. Chalk a line G through F to I, curving underarm.

To cut out coat: Cut from I toward F and curve to G; D to J and back neck curve. Place back over remaining piece of fabric with center-back fold on selvage line of front, slanting shoulder lines meeting. Cut out front same as back except for neck. Remove back. To mark front neck, measure down from shoulder along selvage one-fourth neck measurement plus ½ in. and place pin. Measure from selvage down along shoulder line one-sixth of the neck measurement plus ½ in. and place pin. Mark and cut in curved line from pin to pin.

Cut front sleeves on fold line. Cut sleeve piecings as indicated. Cut 2½-in.-wide lengthwise strip for stand-up collar.

Assembling: Use ⅜-in. seams for shoulder and underarms. Baste these, beginning shoulder seams at neck. Neck edge can be held in slightly with a row of stitching ¼ in. from edge. Put garment on and mark for hem. Remove garment. Stitch shoulder and underarm seams; press open. Fold stand-up collar strip lengthwise, right-side in. Stitch ends; turn right side out. Stitch piecings to end of each sleeve; press seams open.

Stitch ribbon on right side along front center edge; also on bottom of sleeves. Press ribbon to wrong side so that no ribbon shows and slip-stitch free edges.

Apply standing collar to neckline. Turn edge and machine-stitch top of hem; slip-stitch hem. Press garment carefully. Use ribbon to tie collar at center-front, or a hook-and-eye closing may be used.

Taffeta Cover-up Coat

▶▶▶ DON'T SAY you have no coat for your summer dresses. Make one of 2 yds. of taffeta in two hours' time.

Straighten crosswise ends of fabric. Open out full width. Fold in half crosswise with selvages together. Pin. On fold mark center point A. Measure from A one-fourth neck measurement each way, as at B-B. Measure from A to C one-third bust measurement. Measure straight down from C to D one-third bust measurement. From fold, measure down on selvage from corner E to F one-third bust measurement plus 3 in. From lower left edge, measure in from selvage 3 in. (G to H). Draw straight lines F to D, D to H. Measure 3 in. from H to I on line D-H. From center of bottom edge, J, draw a slightly curved line to I. On top length of fabric only, cut from J straight up to A, and cut on fold from A to B on both sides of center. Through both layers of fabric cut from J to I up to D and over to F. Fold the cut-out side on center-back line, and cut both sides exactly alike.

The pieces K are added to bottom of sleeves. Gather wide end of each (L) to fit opposite end (M). Make French-seam turn.

If tie belt is desired, use pieces N to make it. Use pieces O as 1-in. bias facing for back neckline. Turn ¼-in. hem on underside of front turnbacks. Stitch or slip-stitch this from neckline to hem. Turn front turnbacks to wrong side and stitch along bottom edge, as at P. Turn back to right side. Begin at neck edge, B, and top-stitch, as shown, making two pockets on each side of front. Keep stitching line about 1 in. from both edges of turnback. French-seam underarms. Add cuffs to sleeves. Place fullness on inside of arm, as illustration shows. Hem bottom of coat. Press.

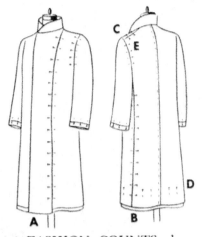

How to Reline a Coat

▶▶▶ FASHION COUNTS show that almost all cloth coats are lined and that they are worn for an average of three years. All fur coats are lined and each averages seven years' wear. In time, therefore, new linings are in order for most coats. If measurement around bottom of coat is no more than two widths of lining fabric, you will need only two lengths (shoulder to hem), plus one length for sleeves. Rayon satin or taffeta or crepe are good materials. Choose fabric that will slip over a dress easily and not cling. Match coat color as closely as possible, unless fashion decrees contrasting colors.

Rip old lining out. Where edges are turned under, press them out smooth. Use old lining for pattern to cut new.

Before putting in new lining, if sleeves of coat are worn at bottom, turn the hem edge inside out and stitch a narrow seam on wrong side, for a new edge and a sleeve just a little shorter than before. This works on fur as well as fabric.

Be sure to check hem so that coat is even all around. Sometimes turning the edge only ½ in. and getting a new and even line will give a coat a newer look.

Straighten fabric. Lay original lining on new fabric so that grain remains the same in old lining and new. Use old lining as pattern and cut the new.

Fold a pleat in center-back. Baste and press this in. Pin side fronts in position, as shown at A, turning edge of lining over front facing. Bring front lining back to side seam B and up on shoulders C. Baste front to shoulders and side seams of coat. Turn side seam edges on back of lining and lap these over side seams of front lining, and pin, as at B, placing pins crosswise to hold securely. Turn and pin neck edge of lining under all around.

Stitch underarm seam of sleeves. With heavy-duty thread, baste pressed-open seam to coat seam. Secure ends of basting, as this basting stays in. Because there is much pull on the lining as a coat is put on and off, the basting definitely helps lining to hold in place.

At armhole, baste body lining to armhole seam all the way around. Bring sleeve lining up over this. Turn raw edges in and pin, as shown at E. Turn edge of lining under at bottom of sleeves and pin.

When lining is completely pinned, with all raw edges except bottom concealed, and while coat is on form or figure, place pins 6 in. above bottom and all around coat, catching both coat and lining together, and spacing these pins about 6 in. apart.

Remove coat. Lay it out on table. Slip-stitch front edges, shoulders, neck, and bottom of sleeves. Slip-stitch side seams and armholes as inconspicuously as possible.

Turn bottom edge of lining for hem to fall halfway up depth of coat hem. Press and slip-stitch it in position.

Give coat a good steam pressing after lining is in place so as to place the lining inside the coat. Coat must always dominate the lining. Sometimes a good pressing of a relined coat by the local tailor is worth the cost.

Stoles, Scarves, and Capes

Fringed Jersey Stole

▶▶▶ OF ALL THE versatile stoles designed in the fashion capitals of the world, the wool jersey ones are loveliest. The soft jersey drapes so gracefully that it lends itself to varied effects when wrapped around the neck, about the shoulders, crossed in front or on the left shoulder. Make one for yourself, and your mirror will help you to find the most becoming way for you to wear this periodic fashion favorite.

The stole shown was made from 2½ yds. of fine wool tubular jersey, and two hanks of yarn. The cost will depend upon quality of jersey and fringe you use.

To make: Straighten fabric. Seam one end. Seam opposite end, leaving an opening 6 in. wide. Clip corners. Turn jersey right side out through the 6-in. opening. Point corners out true, and press ends. Turn edges in and slip-stitch the 6-in. opening so that both ends appear the same.

To make the fringe: Use a darning needle large enough to carry four yarn threads. Cut the skeins into 24-in. lengths. Thread four lengths into needle. Beginning at one corner, make the fringe as shown in the details. A shows how needle is inserted ¼ in. above edge. Pull thread through and draw ends even at bottom. Now ⅜ in. from this first, draw a second needleful through until ends are even, and make a knot, as at B. Space insertions of needle ⅜ in. apart and do this across one end of scarf. Knot each needleful as shown in B. When yarn is in place, take four yarns from one group and four from the adjoining group and loop these together, as at C. Continue looping, as shown, across end. Keep loops about 1¼ in. below edge of stole and on an even line. When entire row is finished, fringe opposite end. When all is done, smooth fringe out and press lightly over knotted part to smooth it into position.

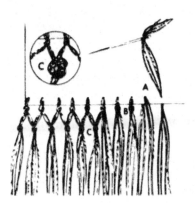

Two Simple Stoles

POCKET STOLE FOR SUITS OR DRESSES

Pocket stoles are convenient and attractive. This one in ivory nylon is appealing, and you can make it with only 1¼ yds. of 45-in. fabric.

Split nylon lengthwise through center. Pin two crosswise edges together, beginning at selvages. Stitch this in a ⅜-in. seam. Fold stole lengthwise, selvage edge to the cut edge, and stitch these edges together, ¼ in. from edge. Stitch across one crosswise end. Press all seams open.

Turn the stole right side out, turn raw edges in and slip-stitch the open end. Press the stole carefully, making sure the seamed edges are perfectly even.

For the pockets, turn the bottom ends of the stole up 7 or 8 in. at each end, as shown. Slip-stitch these to each side so that they will hold securely, as our detail shows.

If desired, work a buttonhole in the center at top of each pocket and button the pocket to the stole to hold it in position, or simply sew a button or use a swivel pin-on, to hold pocket in place.

STOLE WITH FRINGED ENDS

▶▶▶ TAKE A PIECE of Far Eastern-type silk. It usually is narrow. Buy as much length as you want for your stole. Pull crosswise threads at each end to make fringe as deep as you like. Take some of the raveled threads and whip a line along the top of fringe so that it will not ravel farther.

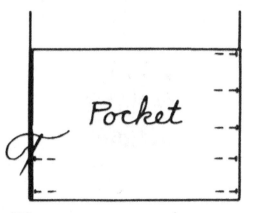

Ribbon Stoles

▶▶▶ THESE RIBBON STOLES go over a basic dress as the proverbial duck takes to water, and are as pretty as can be. They take no time at all to make and the materials needed are as follows: For A you need 2 yds. of 7-in. rayon taffeta ribbon and 4 yds. of 1½-in. satin ribbon. For B, 4 yds. each of two colors of 3-in. ribbon is required, in velvet, satin, or taffeta. Buy a spool of thread to match each color. Use thread in needle to match top ribbon and thread in bobbin to match the under ribbon.

Buy a pretty color combination—green taffeta with gold velvet, king's blue with darkest navy, black with scarlet or with kelly green, or two shades of purple.

To make A: Divide narrow ribbon into two even lengths. Lap each edge of the wide ribbon over one edge of each narrow strip about ¼ in. Stitch. Crease a ½-in. hem in both ends. Hem with fine stitches. Fold ends over about 5 in. to make pockets. Whip edges together or stitch close to edge on each side.

To make B: Divide each 4-yd. length of ribbon into two even lengths, which will give you four strips each 2 yds. long. Fold each strip in half, bringing edges together

to form points, as at C. Starting 8 in. from point, stitch inner edges of one strip together, as at D. Stitch second strip in the same way. Overlap two outside edges and stitch, as at E. Pull other ribbon strips halfway through loops. Fold these strips into points, as at F. Lap edges and stitch as on opposite side. Make rolled hem on ends, or simply even edges.

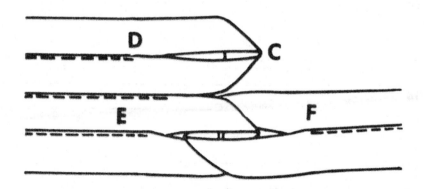

Sheer Stole, Velvet-trimmed

▶▶▶ RAYON SHEERS are inexpensive and colorful and are especially attractive when trimmed with bands of ¾- to 1-in.-wide rayon velvet ribbon. You need 1⅓ or 1⅜ yds. of sheer 40-in.-wide fabric, and 10 to 12 yds. of ribbon. Satin, metallic or any novelty ribbon can be used instead of velvet, if preferred.

You can make this stole in about two hours.

Straighten crosswise ends and tear or cut fabric in half lengthwise. French-seam two crosswise edges together, seaming so that selvages are along one lengthwise edge. Make a ⅛-in. hem on other edge and on both ends.

Diagram A: Divide each side into six even parts, and ends into two, as shown. Chalk lines diagonally from side to side, as shown. Lay ribbon over lines and cut into lengths needed. Stitch all diagonally placed ribbons in position, stitching one edge only. Stitch ribbon all around outside edges, mitering corners, and covering cut ends of ribbon. If desired, ribbon can be run diagonally both ways (crisscrossed) before edges are finished.

Diagram B: Divide ends into quarters and chalk lines from end to end. Stitch ribbon along the lines. Finish edges of scarf as described above.

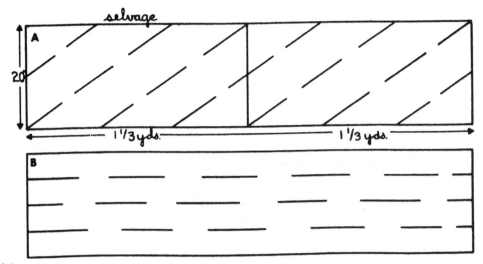

Shoulder Stole of Fake Fur

▶▶▶ WHEN THE SUIT is not quite warm enough, or the coat too tailored for a dress-up dress, have at hand a stole like this.

Buy 1 yd. of one of the flat fake-fur fabrics and 1 yd. of 50-in.-width lining fabric or 2 yds. of narrower width. Use wool jersey, crepe, taffeta, or satin for lining, depending on the effect desired. Make all of one color—black, brown, gray—or line with a contrast—royal blue with black, for instance.

Cut fur fabric in half lengthwise. Seam two crosswise edges together, as at A. Press seams open. If 50-in. lining is used, tear in half lengthwise and seam together, as for fur fabric. If lining fabric is narrow, use 2 yds., and cut to same width as stole.

Lay right sides of fabric together, center seams of stole and lining meeting, as at A. Stitch ⅜ in. from edge all around, leaving an opening, as at B. Clip off corners, as at C. Press all seams open. Turn stole right side out, flatten it, square out corners, and press. If a pile fabric is used, such as velvet or velveteen, press it on a velvet board or steam it so that no pressing marks can show. Close the opening with slip-stitches.

If desired, patch pockets, convenient for handkerchiefs or gloves, can be made and stitched to the lining at one end before top of lining is stitched to stole.

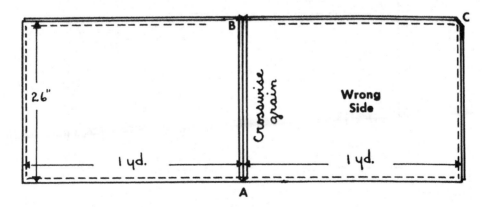

Fur Fabric or

▶▶▶ BUY FAKE FUR, velvet, velveteen, or wool crepe for this attractive cape stole. Buy either a 50-in. taffeta or a 54-in. tubular jersey for lining.

Straighten your fabric. Fold it in half lengthwise, wrong side out. Lay the fold away from you, as in diagram. Measure a distance of the length from shoulder to waist to left of corner A for point B, and 2 in. to left of B for C. D is one-sixth of the neck measurement plus ½ in. above C. Measure 20 in. from left-hand edge for E. Chalk a line 1½ in. in from lower edges to E and a second line in 13 in. for F. G is 9 in. above A. Connect G and B. Draw curve from B to D and connect with E for front neckline. Broken line shows continuation of facing. If a high neck is desired as for the velvet stole illustrated, simply round the corners at front neck and do not turn facing edges back.

Tie string to chalk. Hold end of string at D and chalk on edge at G. Draw arc from G around to connect with line F.

Cut garment, cutting B to G, around

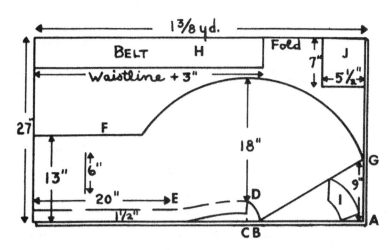

Velvet Cape Stole

curve, along line F to edge of fabric. Cut from B to D, out to C and down front neckline.

Cut belt of desired width from lengthwise strip, as at H, and a back neck facing, as at I. Cut welt pieces for pockets from fabric at J. Remainder of fabric may be used to make a matching turban, if desired.

Mark position of pockets; then follow steps below.

(K) Lay pocket piece over pocket position, right sides together. Stitch, making a box 6 in. long by ½ in. wide. Slash through center of the box and into the corners, as shown.

(L) Draw fabric through to wrong side. Form even welts and baste diagonally. Press carefully. From right side, stitch close to welts, again making an oblong box.

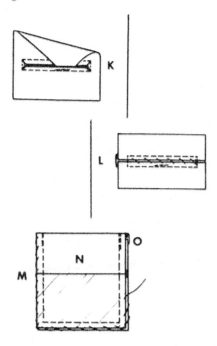

(M) Press welt piece N down over opening. Stitch lining piece to each edge. Even the length of pouch pieces. Stitch edges, reinforcing top of pocket on both sides, as at O in the detail. Press.

Cut stole lining to same size as outside, except 1 in. narrower at center-front. Stitch center-back seams in both fabrics. Lay fabrics together, wrong sides out, and seam all way around except neck and center-front lines. Press seams open. Turn right side out; stitch back neck facing in position. Turn raw edge of facing and front edges under ¼ in. and slip-stitch facing to lining. Press carefully.

Make belt, turn right side out, and make a buckle covered with fabric or use a metal or leather-covered buckle. A large hook and eye at waistline of stole is a convenience.

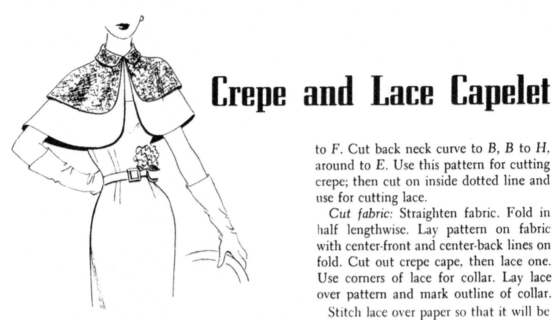

Crepe and Lace Capelet

▶▶▶ IMAGINE making this lovely capelet from just 1 yd. of 42-in. crepe and ¾ yd. of 36-in. lace.

Cut paper pattern: Using a piece of paper 21- by 36-in. long, draw pattern as follows: Divide one 36-in. edge in half, as at A in diagram. B is one-sixth of the neck measurement plus ½ in. above A. Tie a string to a piece of chalk. Hold end of string at B; draw an arc from corner C through D to corner E. Shorten string 5 in. and draw another arc, as indicated by broken line for bottom of lace cape. Round corners on front as shown. F is one-fourth neck measurement to left of A, and a curved line F to B makes front neck. Draw back neckline from B to a point ½ in. to right of A. A Peter Pan type of collar is indicated by dotted line 2 in. outside neckline. G and H are 3½ in. to right and left of D. Draw line from B to G and from B to H. Cut on front curved line around to G, G to B around to F. Cut back neck curve to B, B to H, around to E. Use this pattern for cutting crepe; then cut on inside dotted line and use for cutting lace.

Cut fabric: Straighten fabric. Fold in half lengthwise. Lay pattern on fabric with center-front and center-back lines on fold. Cut out crepe cape, then lace one. Use corners of lace for collar. Lay lace over pattern and mark outline of collar.

Stitch lace over paper so that it will be nice and smooth.

Make cape: Join shoulder seams and press seams open. Bind all edges (unless you prefer to picot them) by cutting bias 1 in. wide from corners of crepe and using this for edges of crepe and lace. Apply double fold French binding. Fold bias in half lengthwise. Stitch fold on right side, raw edges together, taking very narrow seam, as at I. Turn folded edge to wrong side and whip in position, as at J. Baste two capes together at neckline. Join these permanently with a bias binding or facing. Or attach Peter Pan collar which has been cut from crepe and lace. Bind its edges and put collar on with a narrow bias facing. Crepe may be sewn to neck edge and lace whipped over the seam. Use a hook and eye at neckline to close.

This design is good for velvet, felt, even tweed. Can be lined or made of single thickness, with edges hemmed, faced, or bound with military braid.

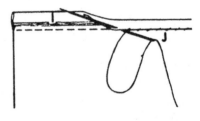

Cape Stole

▶▶▶ MAKE A dashing cape stole from only ⅞ yd. of 52- or 54-in. fabric. Cost depends on type of fabric used. Make it of taffeta, wool, or other favored fabric.

Fold fabric lengthwise. Straighten ends. Pin selvages together. For front sections, measure up from corner A along edge 24 in. to locate B (see diagram). Measure along selvage 22 in. (C). Tie a string to piece of chalk or lead pencil. Hold string 2 in. to left of A. Starting at B, mark semicircle to C. Measure up from selvage 11 in. (D). Mark a line to left to meet circle edge. Round off sharp corner (E).

For back section, measure to right from corner F 25 in. and mark a 10-in. arc. Mark a straight line from arc to arc, as at G.

To mark neckline, measure in from A and F one-fourth neck measurement, as indicated by broken lines. Mark with basting.

With tailor tacks, mark six ¾-in. darts (three on each side), as indicated.

Begin darts at neckline and taper each to nothing. Cut fronts from D through E, up to B; cut back along G and bottom curve. Seam edges A-B and G together, stitching only to neckline, thus giving back neckline petal effect. (If plain neckline is preferred, cut away ¼ in. above basting.) Press seams open and overcast raw edges. Try on cape and adjust darts if needed. Stitch darts, fastening threads securely at ends. Press. Lower corners of stole may also be rounded if desired. Finish all edges with a rolled hem. (Rolled hem will face out on petal collar.) If selvage is attractive, use it as a finish and hem only raw edges.

Fabric left over may be used for pockets at lower ends of stole, or for a shaped facing if no collar is desired.

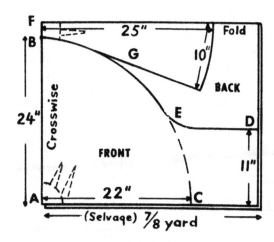

Velvet Capelet with Hood

▶▶▶ THESE FLATTERING capelets are ideal to wear for a little extra warmth. The hood is easy to pull up over the head when you are dashing to or from a car, so convenient in the theater to drop down out of way of those behind you. Make this of jersey; line with plastic. Make it of taffeta and unlined. The model illustrated required ¾ yd. of velveteen, ¾ yd. of rayon crepe, and one spool of thread.

Take a piece of paper 27 by 36 in. and make a pattern. Fold in half lengthwise and lay fold toward you. Place point A at lower left-hand corner as in diagram. Mark B 4 in. above A, and C 2½ in. to right of A. Draw a line B to C.

Locate D at upper left-hand corner. Measure 10 in. to right of D for E, 6 in. to right of E for F, and 6 in. to right of F for G. Draw a line B to E. Measure in on this line 3 in. for H. Draw a curve from H to F, then from G down to right-hand edge of paper. Cut from C to B, B through H around to F, then from G on curved line down to bottom edge (I). J is halfway between C and I. Draw a curved line H to J to locate casing through which ties will be run to control fullness. Use this pattern to cut both outside and lining of hooded capelet.

Straighten fabric. With fold of fabric toward you, place fold of pattern along it and cut around pattern edge, except fold. Repeat with lining.

Open out both fabrics. Place right sides together and pin edges together all around. Lay over a piece of tissue paper and stitch each side from B through H, F, G, and around to I. Press this seam open all way around, and clip seams, doing this ever so carefully. Turn right side out through opening B to C. Seam hood of capelet on this line; then slip-stitch lining together over this last seam.

Make a casing 1 in. wide, making first stitching ½ in. above line J to H. Make second stitching 1 in. below first stitching.

Since your lining fabric is wider than velveteen, you have enough material along one edge to tear two 2-in.-wide strips, each ¾ yd. long. Join these on crosswise, and then fold edges together. Stitch, using a ¼-in. seam on all raw edges. Turn tie string right side out and insert this in casing. Do this by opening the seams at H just enough to slip ties through.

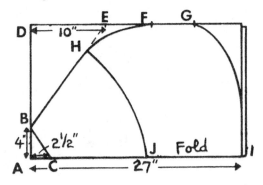

Glamour Cape and Hood

▶▶▶ THE CAPE and hood of filmy lace and net can be worn everywhere—at cocktail parties, in the restaurants, even at the theatre. They are flattering, less expensive than hats, and easier to manage when dining or dancing.

This lace cape with hood was made from ¾ yd. of 35-in. gossamer-type lace and 2 yds. of ½-in. wide velvet ribbon.

Take a piece of paper 27 by 36 in. and make a pattern. Fold in half lengthwise and lay fold toward you. Place point A at left-hand lower corner, as in diagram. Mark B 3 in. above A. Locate E halfway between upper corners C and D. F is halfway between E and D; G is same distance below D that F is to left of D. Draw a curved line B to E, F to G. Cut on these lines.

Put the hood on; bring it over hair as you want it. Tie ribbon around the neck over the lace, pin lace to the ribbon. Line will come about as dotted line shows.

Finish edge of cape and hood by stitching edge ⅛ in. from edge all around; do this over paper to prevent tightening of stitching line. Turn stitched edge, making a rolled hem, and whip this down, or take to your local sewing shop and have all edges picoted. Gather fullness under ribbon. Do not make this tight, as it should appear loose and easy. Tack ends of ribbon at edge of hood so that they will hold.

The photograph shows the same design made of velvet.

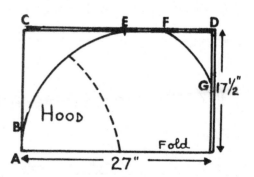

Reversible Circular Cape

▶▶▶ THE CAPE shown was made of one side dark blue, the other steel gray Shantung—completely reversible and delightfully wearable when just a suggestion of a wrap is needed. Make it of organdie, chiffon, lace, or taffeta—even piqué or denim. Choose a fabric right for your needs and colors to complement your wardrobe.

Two yds. of 40-in. material were used—1 yd. of each color. Cape is slightly longer over shoulders than at front and back. The extra 4 in. in fabric width make this possible. If a 36-in. fabric is used, buy ¾ yd. of each fabric and make a smaller cape.

Fold one of the fabrics lengthwise and pin edges together. Lay fold toward you and mark center of fold A, as in diagram. Measure in 3 in. from A for B. Tie end of string to a pencil or chalk, hold other end at B, and draw an arc from edge C to D. Cut on this line.

Measure in from A one-fourth neck measurement to E and to right on fold (F). Measure 1 in. to left of A for G. Draw neck curves. Cut out neckline and slash fold to H for center-front.

Fold, mark, and cut second fabric in same way. Open circles out flat and lay right sides together, center-fronts matching. Stitch edges together, starting at I, stitching all around bottom edge and up to J.

Clip off corners and along seam edge, as shown. Press seam open. Turn right side out through neckline. Baste close to turned edge and press. Baste neckline edges together ¼ in. in. Clip edges in ⅛ in.

The narrow collar can be made of either color. Cut two strips 2½ in. wide from fabric piece, as shown in corner of diagram. Make length the size of neckline, or longer to allow for tie ends. Seam ends together. Fold in half lengthwise, right sides together. Stitch across ends. Turn right side out and press. Pin and baste one edge of band to neckline. Stitch, turn other edge of band under, and whip in position.

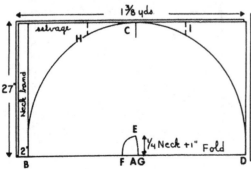
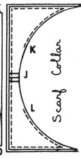

Unlined Circular Cape

▶▶▶ TAKE 1⅜ yds. of 54-in. wool fabric. Straighten both ends. If a straight, tie neckband is desired, tear off 2-in. crosswise strip, as in diagram. Then pin selvage edges together. Mark center of fold (A). Tie a string to chalk or pencil, hold free end of string at A and pencil at B, and draw arc from B to C on opposite edge and from C to corner D. Cut on this line through both thicknesses of fabric.

Measure in from A one-fourth neck measurement plus 1 in. (E). Measure to left of A one-sixth of the neck measurement plus ½ in. for F, to right of A ½ in. for G. Draw curves from F to E and to G. Cut G to E and around to F for neckline.

Slash fold F to B for center-fronts. Lay a 2-in. inverted pleat in center-back—G to D. Finish front edges with ¾-in. slip-stitched hems. Make narrow hem on entire circular edge of cape. Finish neckline with straight neckband and ties, or with scarf collar. Sew snap fastener or hook and eye at cape neckline to close.

Scarf collar: Use four corner pieces to make a scarflike collar. Place right sides of two pieces together and make seams 2 in. long, as at H. Repeat with other two pieces, as at I. Trim off short ends beyond ⅜-in. seam allowance. Press seams open. Place right sides of these corner pieces together, seams over each other, as at J, and pin. Measure one-third of the neckline from each side of J on curve and mark K and L. Stitch from L to point, around square corners to opposite point, and up to K, using a ⅜-in. seam.

Press seams open. Turn collar right side out and press. Place center-back seam of collar over center-back pleat at neckline. Baste and stitch under edge of collar to neckline. Make ¼-in. hems on front neckline. Turn under top edge of collar and whip over seam edges. Tie pointed ends of collar scarf-fashion.

Straight neckband collar. Use the 2-in. crosswise strip previously cut. Fold on crosswise; stitch ends and sides up to within 7 in. of center. Turn right side out, place right side of strip to right side of neck of cape, and stitch. Slip-stitch raw edges in position.

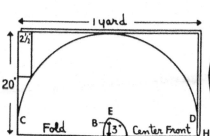
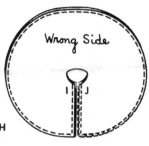

Sleeved Cape for Your Shoulders

▶▶▶ HOW OFTEN have you sat playing bridge or canasta, or in a movie, and wished you had something to put over your shoulders, something that would not slip off, that would look attractive with whatever dress you were wearing, be easy to handle, and have just enough warmth for comfort?

A sleeved cape of fake fur is ideal for the purposes mentioned. If of a conservative color, it can be worn through spring and summer with suits and dresses.

Sleeved cape illustrated was made from 7/8 yd. of 54-in. fake fur.

For the cuffs tear a crosswise strip 4½ in. deep and the full width of 54-in. fabric. Divide this evenly into four pieces, each slightly more than 13 in. Place right sides of two of these pieces together; seam two crosswise edges and across one end. Turn right side out.

Seam ends of cape piece up from selvages a distance of about 10 in., as A to B in diagram. Turn right side out. Gather across bottom of each sleeve at selvage as at A; then put cuffs on, making them the size you like them. They are large enough for ends to extend out about 2 in. as illustration shows.

Finish neck and bottom edges with 3/8-in. grosgrain ribbon, as at D. Stitch this ribbon to the raw edge, lapping a scant ¼ in.; then slip-stitch free edge of ribbon to fabric.

Two brilliant buttons added to each cuff can dress this cape up and help make it gay for evening. Cape color may be bright red, royal blue, silver gray, black, or what you choose.

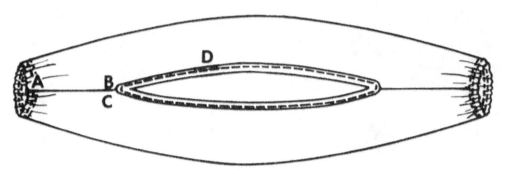

Velvet Shoulderette

▶▶▶ THESE SHOULDERETTES are as easy as A B C to make, are cozy to wear, flattering, and ever so practical.

You will want one to wear with your dresses, also one to wear as a "hug-me-tight" instead of a wrap. There are many fabrics suitable to this design. The original was made in deep king's blue nylon velvet—very lush, very useful.

Buy ⅝ yd. of 40- or 50-in. velvet or 54-in. wool. The difference in width simply makes sleeves come down farther on your arms. Very tall girls may need as much as ¾ yd. of fabric.

Straighten fabric. French-seam crosswise edges together, stitching from each selvage in about 8½ in., as at A and B in diagram. Fold raw edges under and make slip-stitch hems on both sides of 24-in. opening (C). Turn selvages over at each end and slip-stitch them down to make a casing. Insert elastic in each casing and draw up fullness to fit arm. If you prefer, turn selvages at each end and baste. Then stitch two rows of elastic thread over turned-back selvages.

Turn right side out, and your shoulderette is ready to have your arms inserted and for you to enjoy.

If you make this of a lightweight flannel or jersey, and sleeves are longer, you may wish to fold in three darts on each sleeve so that they come to underside, as at D. Ribbon or jeweled banding may be used to ornament the sleeves at bottom edges. A lovely pin at left-side front may be used to hold shoulderette in position on figure.

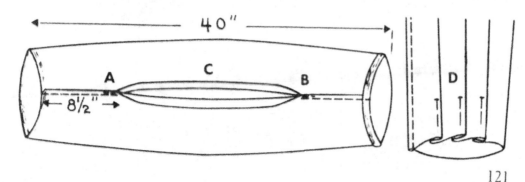

121

Wrap of a Dozen Moods

▶▶▶ WHEN YOU have a dress you need a casual wrap for, try this one that is so easy to make, so smart to wear. Drape it to suit you, your dress, your occasion. Make it of rayon, taffeta, or faille.

Take a square of fabric and fold it diagonally so that you have a true bias fold. Cut on this fold. Lay two selvage edges together and join in a plain seam.

Make a ⅜-in. hem on long crosswise edge, point to point. Sew ball fringe or ribbon on two bias edges. To do this, turn raw edge over ¼ in. to wrong side. Baste, then sew or stitch fringe or ribbon in position by stitching along each edge of finishing medium, as at A, so that raw edge of wrap will be securely held and concealed.

Now for the draping. If you wear your hair severely and wish to look demure, then by all means wrap the wrap with the seam coming directly down center-back. If you like dash, like to be different, do this: Tack an 8- to 12-in. length of ribbon or strip of fabric two-thirds of the way up on seam, as at B. Secure the other end of ribbon to top end of seam at edge of wrap, as at C. This will help to control drape—make the wrap easily manageable when being worn.

This design is good also for soft cashmere, jersey, even organdie. Suit your fabric to your need for a wrap for a favorite costume, and drape it on you in front of your mirror until you wear it gracefully and it is becoming to you at all angles.

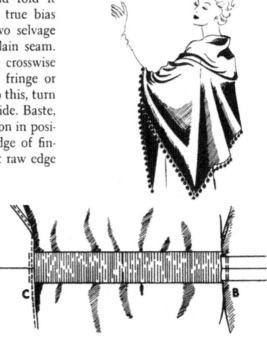

In the Fashion of Yesteryear

▶▶▶ DURING CIVIL WAR years calico cost more than now. Women dressed up in calico then and wore the fabric proudly. You can do the same today if you choose a pretty print and make your ensemble according to the instructions given here.

Buy 5 yds. of 1½- to 2-in. bright-colored fringe in the drapery department, and 4 yds. of 36-in. calico (percale, it is called today). Straighten both crosswise ends of fabric. Tear off 1 square yd. for your stole shawl. Tear a crosswise strip 3 in. wide from one end for waistband. Divide remainder into three even lengths and seam these in a circle, leaving a placket opening 7 in. deep at the top of one seam. Gather top of skirt, pushing more gathers to center-front than at sides and back. Stitch band on and use a button and button-hole or hooks and eyes as a finish for waistline closing. Put skirt on; decide on its length. Remove it, turn hem, then machine-stitch or blind-stitch it in place.

For the stole shawl, fold diagonally, as dotted line on diagram shows. Cut on this line. Place one of the triangles over the other right sides together, with corner B over corner A. Stitch ¼ in. from edge all around the three sides, leaving opening in diagonal side to turn. Turn to the right side and close opening with whip-stitch.

Stitch the cotton fringe over the hem on the two side edges, easing it on so that it cannot be tight on any point. Shape the corners nicely to make fringe lie flat. Fringe covers the hem and makes a neat finish.

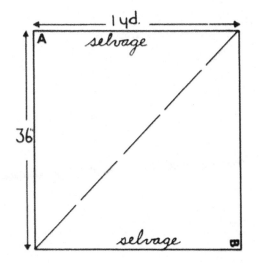

Lace Mitts and Scarf

▶▶▶ WHEN YOU WANT an effect with little sewing effort, try this! Buy 1½ yds. of 34-in. lace in medium-small pattern, soft enough to drape over shoulders. Make these in any color or, bride or graduate, choose white.

As in the diagram, measure up from corner A 24 in. on one cut edge. Place pin. Measure down from corner B 24 in. and place pin. Fold over to make true triangle at each corner and cut around lace design on each folded line.

Take one corner piece and shape a mitt. Distance from C to D is hand measurement around knuckles; E to F, forearm at largest part. Space from C to G and from G to H is 1 in., from H to I, 1½ in. Cut one thumb part, fold half over and cut other side. After cutting one mitt, lay it over other triangular piece and cut second mitt. Stitch the mitts, using scant ¼-in. seam and stitching twice to hold securely. Always stitch lace over paper to prevent puckering. The needle readily cuts the paper away.

Cut two 3-in. strips of narrow elastic for use on underside of wrists. On wrong side of each mitt, sew one end to seam and other 4 in. away from seam, then catch-stitch elastic in position, as in J.

Raw edges of lace may be machine-stitched, but it is quite correct to cut around the lace pattern and wear with raw edges showing on all edges of scarf and at top and bottom of mitts.

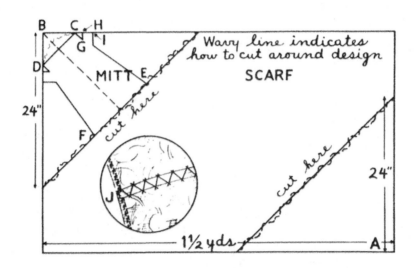

Stay-put Scarf

▶▶▶SCARVES and stoles are lovely, but they do need handling to keep them always smartly in position. This scarf is simple. Tucks and belt hold it in position. Business girls can wear it and look "well-put-together" throughout the day.

If you use a 54-in. tubular jersey, such as was used in the model, you need ¾ yd. to 1 yd. of fabric. The length depends on the proportions best suited to you.

Cut jersey along each lengthwise fold. Bring right sides of two crosswise edges together and make a ⅜-in. seam. Press seam open. Fold in half lengthwise, wrong side out, and pin raw edges together. Measure in 4 in. from raw edges on center pressed-open seam and mark point A, as in diagram. Chalk a line on either side of A, tapering to ends as at B and C. Baste on the chalked line, then stitch on basted line. Stitch across one end. Cut along stitching line, B-A-C, allowing ⅜-in. seam. Clip corners to eliminate bulk. Press seams open. Turn right side out. Crease on seamline. Turn edges of open end in toward each other and slip-stitch. Press, and scarf is ready to mark for tucks.

Tucks placed at back of neck and waistline will control fullness. Three tucks ½ in. deep, about 4 in. long, and 1½ in. apart, as at D, give a smooth effect at back of neck. Put scarf on. With belt around waistline, chalk waistline. Decide on amount of fullness to take up in tucks and divide amount into three or four tucks, as at E. Tuck should extend halfway above and below waistline.

If you wish to make scarf of silk or rayon, buy the same amount of 50-in. satin or taffeta. Make it as you do the jersey one.

This is a practical way of adding color to a somber dress. The same cutting pattern can be used to make the scarf without tucks. Made of wool, it is a warm scarf to loop at neck and wear for protection under your coat.

Some women like to buy gold or silver initials and wear them on such a scarf. Others decorate it with costume jewelry or tuck a boutonnière into the waistline.

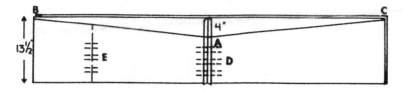

One-Sleeved Bias Scarf

To cut out: Straighten fabric. Lay it flat, with one raw edge toward you. Point A is at upper left-hand corner. B is 10 in. to left of lower right-hand corner. Chalk a line diagonally from A to B. Using this line as a guide, measure and outline scarf pieces as indicated on diagram. Cut out on heavy outlines.

To make: Bring edges C and D together so that front and back are lapped, as in E. Seam edges at F to make shoulder line and edges at G to form underarm. Turn seams to inside and press. Finish all edges with narrow rolled hems.

▶▶▶ THIS IS a new twist on an old idea. Have you despaired of keeping a scarf on your shoulders and attractively draped? The sleeve effect in this scarf is your answer.

You need 1 yd. to 1⅛ yd. of 50-in. taffeta. Follow the same diagram for cutting a yard of fabric, but make the diagonal ends shorter.

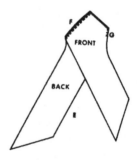

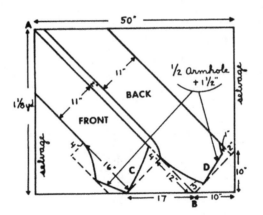

Intimate Apparel

Cover-all Robe

▶▶▶ THIS SOFT, flattering cover-all, boat-necked robe is easy to make, cozily comfortable.

Buy a tube of jersey in a length equal to your measurement from shoulder to floor, plus ⅜ yd. Straighten fabric and cut off two crosswise 2-in. strips for binding neck and sleeves. Cut off 12 in. for sleeves.

To chalk out robe: Fold tubing as shown in diagram, fold next to you. B is one-half the neck measurement less 1 in. above corner A. Place sleeve piece along creased folds as shown, lapping for a ⅜-in. seam. Measure in from edge 2 in. for C. Draw a line B to C for a shoulder seam.

To make: Slash folds C-D and E-F of sleeve piece. Stitch underarm seam of each sleeve, D to E. Join sleeves to garment along line E-F. Stitch seams B to C. Bind boat neck, as in G, using a 2-in. strip, stitching strip to wrong side, bringing edge over to right side, and stitching. Bind bottom of sleeves.

Put robe on. Tie a cord around waist. Adjust fullness. Turn hem.

A silken cord with tassels, such as you can buy in the drapery department, in a contrasting or matching color, makes an ideal waistline finish. Narrow strips of fabric can be sewed on each side, as at H, to hold cord in position. Usually straightening your fabric will give enough material for these, or there will be enough left from bindings to make them.

Use bias binding at top edge of hem, so that it will not appear tight. Stitch binding on, then slip-stitch it in place.

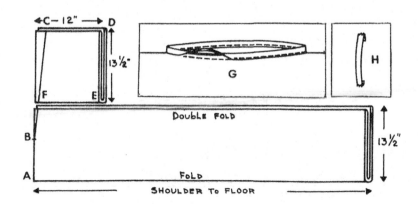

Quilted Lounge Coat

▶▶▶ FOR A lounge coat of quilted chintz, challis, or satin, in any length and lined as brilliantly as desired, you need two lengths of fabric (shoulder to desired length), plus ⅓ yd. for sleeves, plus ¼ yd. extra if you wish to have big, hold-everything pockets—with the same amount of lining. The coat illustrated required 2⅝ yds. of quilted chintz and the same amount of percale lining.

To cut: Straighten fabric. Cut off 12-in. crosswise strip for sleeves and ¼ yd. if pocket piece has been provided. Pin lengthwise edges together.

Place point A at exact center on fold and B 1 in. to right. C is directly above A on edge, and D 1 in. to left of C. Draw line B to D for shoulder line.

Draw center-front line parallel to selvages, 1 in. in from edge. This allows for ¼-in. front seam with ¾-in. lap.

Measure a distance equal to the armhole measurement less 3 in. to right of B for E; same distance to left of D for F. Draw straight down from F, up from E.

On these lines measure up one-fourth bust measurement plus 4 in. for G; and down from center-front line one-fourth bust measurement plus 4 in. for H. Draw lines H to J and G to I. Cut on these lines, curving underarms as indicated.

Measure in from B one-sixth of the neck measurement plus ½ in. for K. Measure down from D one-sixth of the neck measurement plus 1½ in. for L. M is one-fourth neck measurement to right of D.

Mark back and front neck curves. Cut out neckline and along shoulder line K to L. Cut fold B to E.

Cut lining in same way as top. Divide sleeve piece lengthwise into four pieces. Seam one 9-in. edge to each sleeve. Make pockets 9 in. deep and about 11 in. wide.

Then join back shoulders to fronts. Since backs measure 1 in. more than front, ease these in, pinning to hold in fullness. Stitch shoulders and underarm seams. Prepare lining in same way and stitch to coat. Lay right sides of coat and lining together; pin carefully on all edges except at bottom of center-back. Leave open about 15 in., so that coat can be turned right side out with all edges except this opening finished. Then slip-stitch the opening.

Line pockets in same way. Turn right side out. Close opening and catch or stitch them in position on coat.

To hold lining in position, stitch ¾ in. from edge on right side all around coat.

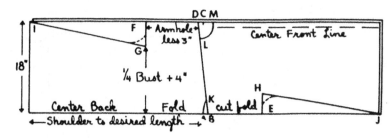

Summer Negligee

▶▶▶ SEERSUCKER IS ideal for this kimono style of negligee, since it washes easily and requires no ironing when hung straight for drying. The negligee shown requires 4 yds. for the average figure.

Measure from shoulder to floor in stocking feet. You need twice this length, plus 1 yd. for sleeves and sash.

Straighten material. Cut off 24 in. for sleeves and cut in half, lengthwise (A in diagram). Cut off two 6-in. crosswise strips (B) for sash and front band piecing. From one of these strips cut a strip 1 in. wide (C). Turn raw edges in on 1-in. piece and stitch. Cut it in two for belt carriers. From remaining piece, cut a 6-in., full-length strip from one selvage edge (D), for front band. Measure in from other selvage two-thirds of bust measurement (for 36-in. bust, use 24 in.), as at E. Cut off extra width.

Fold kimono piece in half crosswise and place pins to mark shoulder line. Center sleeve pieces, as at F, one on each side. Have selvage at bottom of sleeves. French-seam sleeves in position. For center-front opening, make lengthwise slash (G). At shoulder line cut 2 in. each side of center-front for neck, H. Measure down from neck 8 in. Place pin. Cut off points to make neckline, I and J.

Pin belt carriers in 7 to 9 in. below sleeve. French-seam sleeves and underarms from bottom of sleeve to bottom of kimono, catching ends of belt carriers in underarm seams, and stitching back over carriers to insure their not pulling out. Make 6-in. hem in sleeves to provide turnback cuffs. Make 1½-in. bottom hem. Cut 8-in. length from one of the strips (B) and seam it and strip D together for front band and collar. Pin and stitch band to center-front edges, starting at hem, going around neckline, and back to hem on opposite side. Turn in and stitch across bottom ends to finish them.

Seam remaining B strips together for sash. Fold full length and stitch. Press seam open and turn right side out. Turn ends in and stitch. Slip belt in belt carriers, and your kimono is ready for wearing.

Any washable fabric is ideal for this type of garment. The formula works equally well for children, but make bands and sash half as wide as for adult.

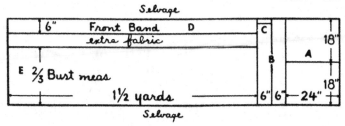
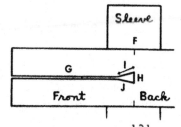

One-piece Negligee

▶▶▶ THIS NEGLIGEE is easy to get into, easy to launder, easy to pack, inexpensive to own. It is all in one piece and requires on the average only 3 yds. of fabric.

Buy two lengths, shoulder to floor, of washable 36- to 42-in. fabric. The model was made of nylon seersucker.

Straighten your fabric. Fold through center lengthwise. Place point A at halfway point on fold, as in diagram. Measure up from A one-half the neck measurement plus 2 in. for B. C is the length from shoulder to waistline to right of A. D is on selvage directly above C. E is one-half the front waist length less 2 in. to left of D (7 in. in diagram). F is one-fourth waist measurement above C on line C-D.

For neck, cut from fold on a crosswise thread from A to B. For waistline, cut D to F, F to E, through both thicknesses of fabric. Make two 1-in. tucks on either side of front panel, as at G, stitching across tucks to hold. Cut ¾-in. strip to face top edge of two side fronts. Turn ⅛ in., then ⅜ in. for a hem on neckline and two side backs (line D-F on cutting diagram). Turn ⅛-in., then ¼-in. hem on line E-F for sleeves. If desired, sleeves may be French-seamed halfway from H to I, and edges from H in hemmed separately.

Run ⅛-in. elastic in back hems, as at J, making elastic one-fourth waist measurement on each side of negligee. (If you prefer, stitch two rows of elastic thread in the turned edges to control this fullness.) Catch elastic so that it will hold securely. Sew a large eye at J and a corresponding hook at same point on opposite side.

Put negligee on. Hook the elastic part at center-front waistline. Then bring side front edges around to back. Panel front and back of negligee by laying folds at end of slash, as at K and L, so that excess fullness is taken up. Remove garment. Stitch these folds for 1 in. at waistline, so that they will hold.

Make tie strings of strips ⅝ in. wide and each as long as fabric from D to F. Turn in all raw edges and stitch. Sew these ties on either side of front at points M and N.

Put negligee on again. Hook the back edges together at center-front. Bring front edges to center-back and tie the strings. Now you are ready to determine length. Some like a negligee to the floor, others to the ankle. Make yours to suit you, and turn and finish the hem accordingly.

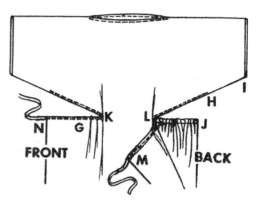

Make-up Cape of Satin-finish Plastic

▶▶▶ OPAQUE PLASTICS come in a lovely range of colors and handle almost like fabric, with the happy exception that they require less effort in sewing, since they have no grain and do not fray.

This make-up cape in silver blue is pretty with its ruffles. The colors and prices of plastics by the yard will intrigue you into making capes for yourself or for gifts.

Straighten fabric by stretching, if necessary, so that it will lie square and true for marking and cutting. Use a yardstick to get a straight line. Trim cut ends, if this is needed, so that edges are straight.

To mark and cut: Fold plastic on table as indicated in diagram, with fold toward you. A is lower right-hand corner of fold; B, 16 in. above A; C, 16 in. to left of A; D, 16 in. from C. Mark points E and F one-fourth neck measurement from C.

Tie a string to chalk or pencil and, with free end of string held at C, draw half circles E-F, D-A. Cut on these lines. Cut on fold from D to E for front opening of cape.

Open remainder of plastic out and with yardstick and chalk or pencil, measure off the six 1¼-in. strips indicated—one for neck binding and ties, and five for ruffles.

To bind neck: Mark center-back neckline of cape. Fold binding strip in half crosswise and mark center. Measuring from center of strip as marked, place top edge of strip around neckline of cape and baste ¼ in. from edge. Set machine for large stitch and loose tension and test on a scrap of plastic; then stitch band in place. Bring free edge of band up over neckline and just below stitching line and stitch it in place, thus completing the neck binding, with tie ends left free.

Ruffles: Join and gather the ruffle strip, as in G; then baste it in place on cape with large stitches, beginning at neck on one side of front and continuing around cape and up other side. Stitch ruffles in place, remove bastings—and you have a pretty cape that will make a welcome gift or that will serve you yourself nicely when you are putting on or removing make-up.

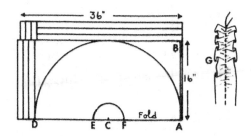

Jersey Bed Jacket

▶▶▶ HERE IS a wonderfully soft, warm, comfortable bed jacket to be made in a flattering pastel of wool jersey. This fabric comes in a range of beautiful colors which will surely inspire you to make one or more of these jackets for gifts.

All you will need is 1 yd. to 1⅛ yds. of 54-in. tubular jersey and a spool of matching thread.

To chalk out: A is at center or halfway point on fold (see diagram). B is 1 in. to right, C is directly opposite A on edge, and D 1 in. to left of C. Chalk a line B to D. E is one-sixth of the neck measurement plus ½ in. above B and F one-fourth neck measurement to left of B. G is one-sixth of the neck measurement plus ½ in. below D. H is one-half the armhole measurement plus 2 in. to left of A. Draw a straight line up from H to fold on opposite side. I is one-fourth bust measurement plus 3 in. above H on this line. Mark curve at underarm as at J.

Cut on shoulder line from B to D. Cut sleeve and underarm, cutting on dotted line; cut front neck, curve F to E.

Lay front over back, shoulder lines and folds matching. Cut back underarm same as front. Cut back neck G to C Material cut out at underarms provides the 4-in.-wide strips for center-front, around the neck, and bottom of sleeves.

Cut on fold for center-fronts. If desired, curve front neck as shown. Cut on folds at bottom of sleeves. A finished band 1½ in. wide for front and neck is comfortable and generally becoming. A band too wide may crowd at neck—too narrow may look skimpy.

Piece front band to make it necessary length, doing this so that seam comes at center-back or at shoulder seam. Press shoulder seams open. Apply right side of band to right side of jacket. Stitch, using a ¼-in. seam. Apply right side of sleeve band to right side of sleeve and stitch, using a ¼-in. seam. Stitch underarms, stitching straight through sleeve ends. Press seams open. Turn raw edge of band back over seam at bottom of sleeve and hem, putting in a ½-in. bottom hem. Turn front band to wrong side and hem edge down.

If there are additional pieces left from underarm, make a pocket or two, first cutting to size desired and applying a 1-in. band at top of pocket. Turn raw edges under and slip-stitch pocket from wrong side so that no stitching shows on right.

A little yarn or silk embroidered motif, or initials embroidered on, can add to beauty of this type of jacket, or tiny brilliants sewed at intervals on the front can help to make it gay.

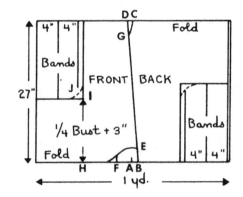

Taffeta Make-up Cape

▶▶▶ MAKE-UP CAPES with tied strings and with edges just meeting don't always give the desired protection from powder, stray hairs, etc. This cape can be lapped 1 to 2 in. at front, back, or on shoulder, whichever is most comfortable.

You need ⅜ yd. of 50-in. taffeta.

Straighten fabric. Lay out flat with one 50-in. edge toward you. Point B in diagram is 27 in. from A, or lower left-hand corner. Halfway between A and B is C. D is one-sixth of the neck measurement plus 1 in. from C. With string and chalk draw curve from D to edge on both sides. Then draw half circle from A to B. Cut on bottom curve and cut out neckline. Lay straight edge A-B of half circle on opposite straight edge E-F, and cut out second half circle.

Seam two straight edges together as from E to G, making a narrow French seam. Make 1-in. hems on two other straight edges. Bind neckline and bottom edge, using a rayon bias binding in a matching or contrasting color. Put cape on and check lap at neckline. Sew two snap fasteners to binding at neckline, as

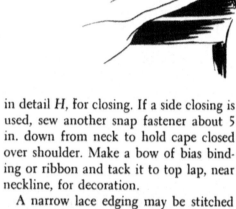

in detail H, for closing. If a side closing is used, sew another snap fastener about 5 in. down from neck to hold cape closed over shoulder. Make a bow of bias binding or ribbon and tack it to top lap, near neckline, for decoration.

A narrow lace edging may be stitched to edges except around neckline, or bottom edge only may be trimmed. Full lace on along bottom edge so that it will be flat on curve. To do this, draw up slightly a thread in top edge of lace, as at I, and stitch to edge of binding, as at J.

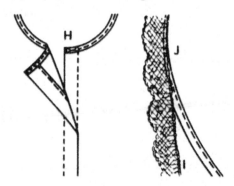

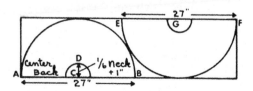

Two More

▶▶▶ *Washable Bed Jacket:* Make this of 1 yd. of pastel batiste, of wool or cotton challis, of crepe de chine, even of velvet. Trim with lace, embroidery edging, or ribbon binding.

Fold fabric through center lengthwise; pin selvages together. Mark center of selvage with pin (A in diagram). Mark center of fold (B). On either side of A measure one-half armhole measurement plus 2 in. for underarm (C and D). Directly in line with these points measure in from fold one-fourth bust measurement plus 1 in. (E and F).

Measure in from fold at edges of fabric one-fourth bust measurement plus 2 in. (G and H). Draw a line from C to E, then to G, curving underarm as indicated. Do the same on opposite side. Cut along these lines. Slash in from fold at B, to a depth of one-fourth neck measurement. From B cut straight along fold for center front opening. Top and bottom corners can be rounded.

French-seam underarms, clipping curved edge (I in detail) after first stitching is made, so that seam will not pucker after second stitching.

Make very narrow machine hems around neckline, along front edges, and around bottom. Stitch narrow lace edging on hems. Draw up thread in edge of lace at corners so that it can be eased around corners, as at J. Finish bottom of both sleeves in same way.

Quilted Coolie Jacket: If you like extra warmth in a bed-jacket, this should just suit you. It is double-breasted, has a standing collar and long sleeves. The model shown required 2 yds. of quilted satin and it was lined with rayon satin.

You need two lengths (shoulder to waist) plus 5 in., plus ⅜ yd. of 36-in. quilted fabric, and the same amount of lining fabric.

Straighten fabric. Fold in half crosswise, wrong side out, bringing selvages together. Lay with two selvages toward you and with fold on right-hand side.

Following the diagram, A is lower left-hand corner. B is the length from shoulder to waist plus 5 in. from A. C is one-half the armhole measurement plus 3 in. from B. If distance from B to C is too short, move B to left by amount needed for correct measurement (which will simply shorten skirt of jacket by this amount).

D is one-half armhole measurement plus 3 in. to right of A. Chalk straight

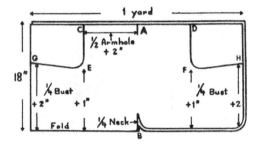

Bed-jacket Styles

across from D to opposite edges (E), and straight in from B about halfway across fabric. F is one-fourth bust measurement plus 2 in. from D. G is one-fourth bust measurement plus 3½ in. from B. Connect F and G. Curve underarm (see broken line).

H is ½ in. to right of A. I is one-sixth neck measurement plus ½ in. in from A. Measure from neck down arm to sleeve length desired and mark J this distance from I. K is 4 in. to right of J. Chalk neck curve H-I, then lines I-K, K-L. Cut out backs, cutting H-I, I-K, K-L, L through underarm curve at F to G; G-B.

Measure in 3½ in. from E for M. Chalk straight across to N for center-front. Lay back over front section, H-B edge matching center-front line M-N. Cut front underarm and shoulder lines to match back. Remove back. O is one-sixth neck measurement plus ½ in. to left of N. P is same distance below. N. Mark and cut front neck curve, continuing line on slant out to selvage. Front lap can be left straight or tapered in from E, as indicated.

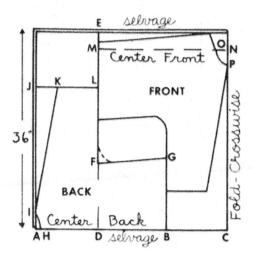

Cut lining in same way as quilted fabric. Seam shoulders and underarms in both fabrics. Measure around neckline from center-front line to center-front line. Using this measurement, cut straight collar 2 in. wide and length needed plus seams. Cut cuffs to width desired and length to fit sleeves. There is enough fabric to make pockets if you wish. These can be lined and stitched in position before jacket is lined.

Fold collar in half lengthwise, wrong side out, and stitch across ends. Clip corners, turn right out, press. Lay collar on right side of neckline, raw edges together and center of collar matching center-back neckline. Baste and stitch in place. Stitch ends of cuff pieces together. Line each cuff.

Lay lining over jacket, right sides together, and pin. Stitch fronts and around neckline, through collar. Clip corners. Turn right side out. Turn bottom edges in toward each other; slip-stitch. Stitch cuffs to bottom of sleeves. Press jacket.

Use snaps to hold laps in position. Loops or small frogs can be used to trim collar and front closing, as illustrated.

Bed Jacket from One Yard of Fabric

▶▶▶ CHOOSE CHALLIS, crepe, flannel, or satin in a plain or printed fabric, in a becoming color, and in fabric right for the warmth you want.

The model illustrated required 1 yd. of printed, washable rayon satin, one spool of thread, and two skeins of embroidery floss, each in a different color.

Straighten fabric at both ends. Fold wrong side out selvages together; lay out with fold next to you.

To chalk out: A is at lower left-hand corner on fold, as in diagram. B is 19 in. to right of A on fold. D is 19 in. to left of top right corner C on selvage. Chalk a line D to B. Measure down from D on this line one-sixth of the neck measurement plus ½ in. for F and one-fourth neck measurement to right of D for E. Chalk a curved line F to E. G is ½ in. to left of B; H, one-sixth of the neck measurement plus ½ in. in from B. Chalk back neck curve.

Measure up on line B-D one-fourth bust measurement plus 3 in. for I. J is straight out to left of I at a distance of one-half the armhole measurement plus 3 in. Chalk a straight line to left of I to edge, then straight up to selvages from J. Curve underarm as shown.

To cut: Cut G-H, then H-F, and F around to E. Cut out underarm on back, cutting on curved line. On front, cut B to H.

Keeping front and back pieces folded, center the back fold over selvages of front with shoulder lines even. Cut front underarm to correspond to back. Remove back piece and cut on fold of front (bottom of sleeve). Darts ¼ in. deep may be placed 1½ in. from center-back fold on each side, if it is desired to have jacket fit close to neck.

To make: French-seam underarm and shoulder seams, taking first ⅛-in. seam to right side, then a ¼-in. seam on wrong side. Turn raw edges at neck, bottom of sleeves, and bottom of jacket—first ⅛ in., then ¼ in. Turn selvage edges along front ¼ in. Now with double thread of embroidery floss, baste edge all around with running stitches about ⅛ in. long, basting from wrong side so that edges will be caught, as at K. From right side, with second color of embroidery floss, make a twisted running-stitch by catching thread in each running stitch, as at L. This makes a sturdy, attractive, washable finish, especially good for lingerie and for children's clothes.

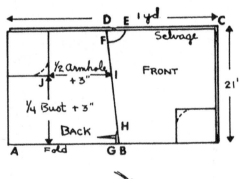

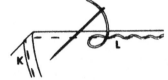

Gift Bed Jacket

▶▶▶ WHEN PUT TOGETHER, this looks as if it were made of a circle, but it really isn't, as diagram shows. To make, you need only 1 yd. of 36-in. fabric, if 2¼ yds. of 4-in. lace banding is used to trim, or 1⅛ yds. of fabric if lace is omitted. Use wool, rayon, or cotton challis—any lightweight pretty fabric suitable for a dainty, lace-trimmed accessory such as this. The model sketched was made of very lightweight blue wool crepe with cream Alencon-type lace to trim.

Mark out a pattern on paper, because once you have made one of these jackets, you will want the pattern to guide you in making many more for gifts or to sell. Shape and cut pattern according to measurements given on diagram. Round corners.

If lace is used: Fold paper back on dotted lines A and B. Line A should come at selvage edge when pattern is placed on fabric for cutting, as you will want to use that edge as a finish. Make a tiny, rolled, hand-finished hem across shoulder line on back (B), also on shoulder line on each front piece (C). Stitch or hand-sew lace over back shoulder line (B). Apply lace down each center-front (A) in same way.

To join front and back pieces: Lay one front corner (D) to back corner (E). Seam front piece to free edge of lace on back piece, beginning seam at outside edges and sewing in toward neck opening; do same with second front piece. Hem entire outside edge. Put garment on and pin edges together at F. Remove and tack at this point.

If lace is omitted: Bring corners D and E together and French-seam shoulder lines. Use narrow ribbon binding or narrow lace on all edges, or turn edge and finish with blanket or featherstitching. Finish to suit your taste and purpose, and wear this garment often. It can dress up your nightie, keep your shoulders warm, and prove ever so becoming.

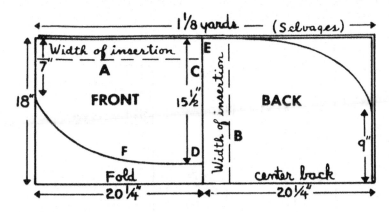

Shirred Nightie

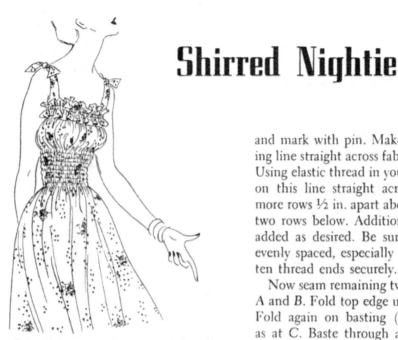

▶▶▶ SHEER, SHIRRED, and cool, this was made for summer sleeping comfort. Elastic thread makes shirring easy and gives perfect fit. Cost depends on fabric selected. Buy enough for two lengths, shoulder to floor, plus ¼ yd. for shoulder ties—a total of approximately 3 to 3¼ yds.

For ties, tear two 4-in. strips crosswise. Tear remaining fabric in half crosswise. Seam two selvages together. Begin stitching 7 in. from top raw edge, as at A. Turn to right side, clip seam, and stitch remaining 7 in., as at B. Press seams open.

To mark for top edge of ruffle, place a basting or crease with iron 5½ in. from top edge on a crosswise thread. Fold edge down on this line to right side. Decide at what point you want waistline to come and mark with pin. Make a second basting line straight across fabric at this point. Using elastic thread in your bobbin, stitch on this line straight across. Stitch four more rows ½ in. apart above first row and two rows below. Additional rows can be added as desired. Be sure that rows are evenly spaced, especially at selvages. Fasten thread ends securely.

Now seam remaining two selvages, as at A and B. Fold top edge under 2 in. Press. Fold again on basting (or crease) line, as at C. Baste through all thicknesses 2 in. from top edge. Stitch with elastic thread on this basting and ½ in. above, as at D.

(Or make a casing by stitching on basting line and again ½ in. above. Work opening like a buttonhole in center of one width. Run 2 yds. of ribbon through. Adjust fullness.)

For shoulder ties, cut from 4-in. strips four 12-in. lengths. Fold all in half lengthwise, right sides in. Stitch edges together and across one long end on each length. Turn; press. Pin raw ends in place on wrong side on two rows of stitching that hold gathers. Try on and adjust position. Bow the ends by means of a double knot on shoulder. Turn raw ends under and whip ties in place at top of gown.

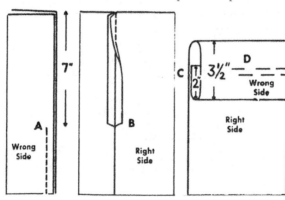

Flat-wash Nightie

▶▶▶ A JOY TO IRON, this nightie. Just run it flat through the ironer, or send it to wet-wash laundry. No fussing with ruffles or gathers—lace trim lies flat. It is comfortable to sleep in, too. Make it of cotton plissé crepe, of batiste, or of any soft, lightweight cotton, or, for winter, of cotton flannel. Buy two lengths, shoulder to floor, plus 1 in. for hem, and 2¼ yds. of Irish-type crochet lace.

Straighten ends of fabric. For ties, tear a 2-in. strip from one selvage. Clip or tear off other selvage. Fold material in half lengthwise. Pin edges together. Mark center with pin on fold (A in diagram) and on raw edges (B). Measure in from A one-third of the neck measurement, then on fold 2 in. to left of A and 6 in. to right. Mark curves and cut back and front neckline.

Measure 10 in. from B for C. Directly across on fold mark D. Measure from D one-fourth bust measurement plus 4 in. (E).

Measure 20 in. to left of corner F for G. Connect C, E, and G, making curved underarm, as shown. Cut on this line for front. Fold over on back along shoulder line (A), and cut back underarm to correspond to front.

On sleeve and neck edge turn a narrow hem, stitch to wrong side, baste lace in place under hem, and stitch. Begin at underarm seam for sleeves and on one shoulder for neck. Shape lace around curve, join in narrow seam, then overcast ends to prevent fraying.

To make center-stitched ties, turn in on both ends. Fold raw edge over a scant one-third of the width of the strip, and fold selvage over a scant one-third. Stitch through center for full length of strip. Cut tie strip in half.

Mark waistline with pin. Four in. each side of center-front make a ½-in. tuck 1½ in. long. Stitch tie ends on, as at H. Fold tuck toward side seam; stitch again, as at I.

Beginning at bottom of sleeves, French-seam underarms and sides, finishing about 12 in. above hem. Make narrow hems on these open edges. Stitch these across seam at end to prevent tearing. Turn and stitch 1-in. hem along bottom edges.

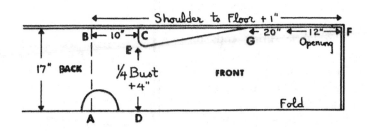

Fitted Glamour Nightgown

▶▶▶ IN THE fabric department one can usually find exquisitely dainty rayon flat crepe 40 in. wide and pretty as can be, with pink, peach, white, pale yellow, or light blue background and charming little buds or bits of bouquet.

To make the gown shown, you need two lengths of fabric, shoulder to floor. Average tall figure needs 3½ yds. Buy also 6 yds. of ⅜-in. narrow, washable satin ribbon.

Straighten the fabric, bring ends together at left, with fold at your right and selvages meeting on both sides, as diagram shows. Point C is at halfway point between corners A and B.

Measure to left of C the neck measurement less 2 in. for D, usually about 11 in. Cut through both thicknesses from C to D for neck opening. Measure straight to left of A and B a distance of one-half the armhole measurement plus 2 in. for E and F.

From E seam down to bottom edge of fabric. Do same from F. Turn cut edges of neck opening to wrong side ⅛ in. and make a rolled, slip-stitched hem. Turn selvages back on sleeve openings and slip-stitch them in position.

Gather the fullness tightly at each shoulder, making four rows of shirrings spaced ½ in. apart. Draw up fullness so that each shoulder measures 4 in.

Place four rows of elastic shirring, two above waist, as shown, two at waistline. Make two bows, each from ½ yd. of ribbon; sew each to a tiny safety pin and pin to shoulders.

At waist, make thread loops at each side seam; slip ribbon through to tie in front. Finish gown with a rolled hem at bottom.

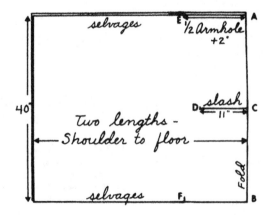

Cool Batiste Nightie

▶▶▶ THIS ONE is easy to make and to wear. You need two lengths of batiste or cotton challis, measuring from your shoulder to floor, or shorter if preferred. Three yds. is usually ample for full length.

For casing, tear off, crosswise of fabric, a strip 1½ in. wide. For shoulder drawstrings, tear off a ¾-in. strip from one selvage. If tie sash is desired, tear a 1¾-in. strip from opposite selvage.

To shape garment: Fold fabric in half lengthwise. Pin edges together for straightness. Mark center on fold A. (The diagram shows this after it has been opened out.) Slash in from fold on each side of A, one-fourth neck measurement. Make center-front opening by cutting down from slash one-half the neck measurement, as at B. Open material out, turn raw edges of neck opening to right side, and baste ⅛-in. hems. Then stitch lace over hems for a finish. Overlap lace ends at bottom of front slash, turning raw ends in and stitching across twice for security. Mark C straight out from A on edges for top of armhole opening. Measure down from C one-half the armhole measurement plus 3 in. and locate D and E. Mark points D and E on back, also. Finish armholes in same way as neck.

From casing strip, cut two strips the length of shoulder, as indicated by broken lines. Turn in raw edges, place directly over shoulder line, and make three lines of stitching, as at F.

Turn raw edge of ¾-in. strip under its selvage edge, stitch the full length of strip, and divide into four pieces. With a bodkin run one of these into each casing slot. Catch the ends of the strips at neck by stitching across two or three times, as at G. Free ends extend out, as at H, and are drawn up and tied as desired. Tie a tight knot in end of each string.

French-seam side edges of gown, leaving a 12- to 15-in. opening at bottom on each side. Make a narrow hem on both sides of each opening. Make a ½- to 1-in. hem across the bottom. If a tie sash is desired, turn raw edge under selvage (as for shoulder drawstring) and stitch. Knot ends to match drawstring. If closing at neck is desired, make a worked loop and sew a button halfway down neck opening.

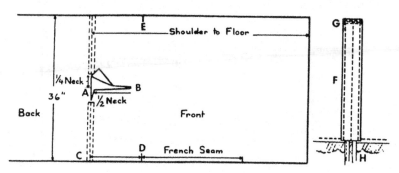

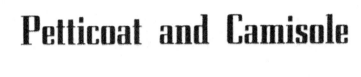

Petticoat and Camisole

▶▶▶ YOU NEED 1¾ yds. of 36-in. muslin if 5 feet 4 inches or under; 2 yds. if taller; 3 yds. of 3-in. embroidery edging, 4¼ to 4½ yds. of embroidered beading, 4 yds. of ¼-in. ribbon to lace through beading, 2 yds. of strong white string for waistline drawstring, and one spool of thread. With ruffle applied, this gives a petticoat length of approximately 31 in.

Straighten fabric at both crosswise ends by clipping through selvage and tearing. Measure from your underarm to waist, clip through selvage, and tear off this length (in diagram 9 in.) crosswise for camisole top. Tear remaining length in half crosswise. Bring selvage edges of one piece together. At one end, measure in from selvages 5¼ in. and place a pin. This represents one-fourth waist measurement less 1 in. (In this case, waist measure is 25 in.) At opposite end, measure in from fold 5¼ in.; place another pin. Mark with chalk or pencil from pin to pin and cut on this line through both thicknesses.

Measure in from selvage of remaining piece and tear off 5 in. strip. Fold remaining piece in half lengthwise. Measure in 5¼ in. from selvage, place a pin. At opposite end, measure in 5¼ in. from fold; place a pin. Draw a line pin to pin and cut on this line through both thicknesses. The narrow part of both panels and of the four gores make the waistline. Begin at top and pin gores in position, a straight edge joining each side of each panel. Stitch all edges, using French seams. Lay petticoat out and even bottom line. If beading is attached to embroidery, make a ¼-in. hem in petticoat and stitch beading just above hem. If you must gather the embroidery, do so, and join it to bottom of skirt with a French or flat-fell seam; then stitch beading in position over this.

French-seam ruffle at joining. If bust measure is larger than 33 in., add piecing from 5-in. strip to camisole. If bust is full, insert a shaped belt across front, using what is left of 5-in strip.

French-seam camisole. Turn top edge over ¼ in. and apply beading. Stitch top and bottom. Pin petticoat and camisole together at waist. Make ¾-in. lapped seam to run cord through, so that waistline can be drawn in to fit. Leave opening for cord in seam on left side. Run ribbon through beading with bodkin and finish off with bows at left side of camisole and petticoat. These may be made separate pieces by making ½-in. hems on waistline of each and drawing a cord through each.

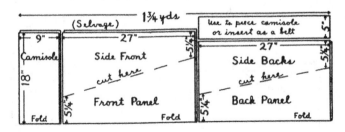

Petticoats with Dash

▶▶▶ PETTICOATS MUST always meet fashion's requirements of slim sleekness or whirling, rustling fullness. Every young woman likes a frilly, rustly, dress-up petticoat and is happy when fashion bids her wear one. The type shown is a lovely gift for any girl above fifteen years of age; it is not expensive and is ever so wearable. Make it of a favorite bright color—red, green, royal blue, or purple, or pastel if fashion approves. Buy one skirt length of 50-in. taffeta, brocade, or crepe; 2¼ yds. of lace flouncing; 2¼ yds. of narrow velvet ribbon; 1¼ yds. of beading wide enough to take your velvet ribbon; one roll of matching elastic thread. Cost will depend largely on quality of fabric and lace used.

When crinoline petticoats are in order, use the circular or semicircular skirt pattern as your guide, and cut petticoat in the same way as your outside skirt. Then skirt will fall with dress skirt and give a pleasing silhouette. Finish then as fashion decrees, with horsehair braid, ruffles, or simple hem.

To make a three-gore, flounce-trimmed petticoat: Straighten fabric. Fold in half lengthwise, with fold toward you. Following diagram, measure in from corner A along fold 7 in., or the distance from waistline to largest part of hips, for B.

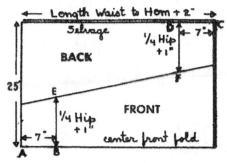

Measure same distance from upper right-hand corner (C) for D. Straight in from both B and D measure one-fourth hip measurement plus 1 in. for E and F. With yardstick touching E and F, chalk a line completely across fabric, as shown. Cut on this line, to obtain three gores.

French-seam the bias edges of the back gores together so that you have a slightly bias seam at center-back. Join the selvage edges to edges of front in same way. Clip or remove selvages if they draw up. Even the lower edge and put in a ¼-in. hem. Turn top edge over ½ in., and gather, stitching three rows ⅛ in. apart and using elastic sewing thread in bobbin.

French-seam the ends of lace flounces together; then gather top of flounce ¾ in. from edge. Pin flounce in position, seam in lace over center-back seam of skirt. Place beading over top edge of flounce, and stitch beading along top and bottom edges.

Run ribbon through beading. If lace flouncing is not available, buy lace yardage and cut ruffle to width desired, picoting or binding bottom edge, or turning and stitching it.

Smocks, Flattering and Practical

▶▶▶ IF YOU WORK at a hobby, at art or writing, or if you like to be informal at home, but not in negligee, try a smock such as the one shown. It's easy to make, to wear, and to launder. It's also easy on your purse, because you can make it out of 2½ yds. of inexpensive batiste or cotton challis. Make it of taffeta if you want it for dress-up, of rayon sheer if you want it cool for summer. Expectant mothers would find it convenient to have several in different colors and fabrics.

Take 2½ yds. of 42-in. fabric. Cut or tear off crosswise ⅔ yd. and split this piece in half lengthwise to make two sleeves. From the remaining length, tear from each selvage a 4-in. strip and cut the remaining length in half. The 4-in. strips are for the yoke and bottom of sleeves, and also for waistline tie if you want one, or to join together in a French-seam tuck to make two pockets, one for each side of the smock.

To make: First stitch the sleeves, using a French-fold seam. Begin one-fourth of armhole measurement from top. French-seam each side seam of smock, beginning one-fourth armhole measurement down from top. Join sleeves to the smock, underarms of sleeve and smock meeting, using ⅜-in. seams. Gather top of smock and sleeves all around, using elastic sewing thread in the bobbin. Put smock on to see that fullness is as you want it. Remember, smock will come to tip of your shoulders and be low, because yoke is yet to be added. If gathering line is too full, pin in fullness and then stitch gathers above first row of shirring to take up necessary amount.

Add raw edge of yoke piece to the gathered edge, making a ⅜-in. seam. Place opening of yoke to come at center-front, as detail A shows, or on left shoulder. Turn selvage edge of yoke piece over to wrong side and make a ¾-in.-wide casing through which to run a ribbon to draw up fullness (see B). If you want a low neck, make yoke shallow; if high, make casing and top hem less wide. Bottom of sleeves (C) are finished in same way as yoke. They may be any length you desire.

Make a hem in bottom, narrow or wide, according to length you want your smock. Stitch or slip-stitch this hem in place.

Dress-up Accessories

Nylon-velvet Shoulder Cape

▶▶▶ A VELVET shoulder cape is ideal for wear when you want to look "covered up" in the evening, or for afternoons when you need a little warmth in a wrap that is also attractive to look at.

Buy 1⅛ yds. of 42-in. nylon velvet (or velveteen or taffeta). Buy 5 yds. of novelty braid to finish edges and give weight to the wrap.

Lay straightened fabric out, wrong side up. Pin selvages together, fold toward you. As in diagram, mark point C one-half the distance between corners A and B. D is one-fourth neck measurement to left of C. E is one-sixth of the neck measurement plus ½ in. above C. F is ½ in. to right of C. G is 2 in. above E. Swing an arc with string and chalk, holding the string at G and swinging from A to the selvage and around to B. H is on selvage straight up from G. I and J are each 3½ in. from H. Chalk a line from both I and J in to E. Cut cape along lines A to I, I to E, E to J, J to B. Cut front opening A to D and neck curve D to E and E to F.

Seam shoulders; begin basting at E and baste down. Stitch a ⅜-in. seam. Bind

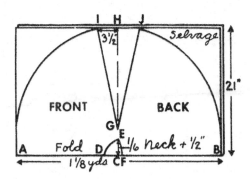

raw edges of shoulder seams with matching seam binding. Turn front edges, neck edge, and bottom edges of cape ¼ in. to right side; baste. Pin braid over the basted line; then stitch or catch braid to fabric all the way around. Take care that corners are turned neatly and that all of the raw edges are covered. Steam the edge and the shoulder seams when the edges are all nicely finished. A hook and eye at the neck completes the job.

Ribbon Accessories

cost, considering the wear and smartness it can give you.

Pleated collar and cuff set: Cut your 2 yds. of ribbon into three pieces—two ½-yd. lengths for two cuffs, one 1-yd. length for the collar. Hem the six raw crosswise ends. Begin at one end to pleat. Make pleats ¼ in. deep and ½ in apart. Pin or baste, then press these. Stitch pleats in place ½ in. from edge on both collar and cuffs. Remove bastings. Sew two snap fasteners to each for closing, one at stitching line, other at other end. If desired, a narrow velvet ribbon may be tacked over stitching line and tied in a bow at each closing.

Sachet bows: A favored trick is to put sachet in your dress decorations. For example, this bow has a little piece of cotton wrapped around two teaspoonfuls of sachet and actually enclosed inside each end of top ribbon bow.

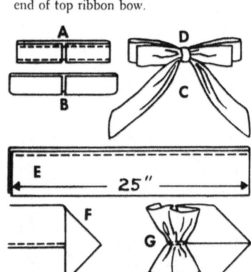

▶▶▶ JADED DRESS or basic new one can be smartened with ribbon accessories. The collar and cuff set shown, for example, is made from 2 yds. of 3-in. picot-edge striped taffeta ribbon. Set requires six snap fasteners and is most reasonable in

You need for this 1 yd. of 1½-in. striped taffeta ribbon and a safety pin about 1 in. long. Cut ribbon into four pieces, one 1 in., one 10 in., one 12 in., one 13 in. Fold 10-in. strip in half crosswise. Bring ends in to center and stitch edges, as shown at A. Insert sachet into each end of bow. Stitch across each end near center to hold bows.

Bring ends of 12-in. strip together as for 10-in. strip, as in B. Fasten ends of this together with stitches behind first bow. Fasten center of 13-in. strip behind this 12-in. strip, ends loose, as at C. With overcasting stitches draw raw edges of 1-in. strip together, thus holding securely all three pieces at center, as at D. Sew safety pin over joining of this 1-in. piece. Pull ends of 13-in. piece down and your bow is ready for wearing.

Ribbon clip-on: You need ¾ yd. of 3-in. ribbon, one button the size of a nickel, metal clip or safety pin. Cut ribbon so that you have a 2-in. piece and a 25-in. piece. Fold ribbon crosswise, bringing cut ends together. Stitch selvages on one side, as at E. Hem raw ends. Open out so that fold forms a point, as at F. Press. Fold hemmed end to wrong side 1 in. Gather from top down to within 4¾ in. of point. Draw gathers up tightly and sew, as at G. Cover button with 2-in. piece of ribbon and sew it on front directly in center of gathers. Sew clip behind gathers.

H: Buy 1¼ yds. of ribbon about 2¾ to 3 in. wide. Cut a length 4 in. longer than your neck measurement. Cut remainder into four even lengths. Fold neckband through center lengthwise and press. Lay pleats in one end of each of the four lengths and notch four ends. Stitch two of these to each end of neck band, as at H 1, concealing raw edges. Presto! You have a neckpiece that needs only a brooch to hold it in position. If desired, six 3-in. ribbon ends may be used, all worn to left side.

I: Cut off old neckline and sleeve finish of a tired dress. Face neckline and sleeves on wrong side with 1¾-in. true bias, turning ¼ in. on each edge for seams. Make a small buttonholelike opening, as in I 1, on each sleeve and front of neck. Finish these openings with buttonhole-stitch. Buy 2½ yds. of 1-in. ribbon (1¼ for neck, ⅝ for each sleeve). Run ribbon through casings, draw up to fit, finish with bows.

J: A tiny corsage and ¾ yd. of 3-in. ribbon makes this attractive neckline finish. Lay one or two pleats in neck part of ribbon and tack. Don't crease ends. Notch them as shown. Lap to fit. Sew on snap. Tack corsage to top lap as shown.

K: Belt worn out or lost? Buy waist measurement plus ¼ yd. of ribbon. Choose a ribbon 3 to 4 in. wide. Lay one or two length-wise folds in ribbon. Fold in ends and whip. Put around waist and hold in place with concealed pins or pin-on buttons.

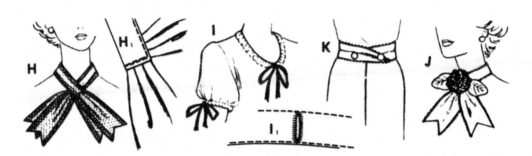

More Ribbon Accessories

▶▶▶ RIBBON IS probably the least expensive decoration you can buy for a dress or suit. It is easy to handle and easily cleanable, and it adds beauty value to whatever it is worn with, provided you plan your color and your making so that the ribbon seems to belong to the garment.

Barrel cuffs are ideal for lengthening an awkward sleeve or for adding color. Buy 2 yds. of 4-in.-wide colorful ribbon. Divide it into two even lengths. Stitch lengthwise edges of the two strips together, making a narrow seam. Cut in two equal lengths crosswise and French-seam cut edges of each. Make two rows of gathers on top and bottom edges with elastic sewing thread. Sew some gay buttons at intervals over the center seam, as shown, and you will have cuffs to slip on with a dress, blouse or suit in a jiffy.

Pleated ribbon trim: This can be used for a collar and cuff set, or worn down center-front closing of dress. Measure neckline and cuffs, or the center-front. Buy three times the measurements in 4-in.-wide ribbon. Turn one edge over 1½ in.; press this flat; then lay ribbon in 1-in. pleats, bringing the pleated edges together to form box pleats on both sides. Pin or baste these pleats. Stitch along the folded edge, remove pins or basting, and press the ribbon. Pleats will prove most accommodating on a neckline curve, a cuff, a pocket, or fabric edge of any kind. When trim is cut to specific lengths, make very narrow hem on edges.

Neckline ties: Wear these with a suit or over a plain, collarless dress. Buy 1½ yds. of 3-in.-wide ribbon. Cut off 1 in. to make the loop. Stitch the raw edges of this loop piece, using a ¼-in. seam. Turn to right side. Sew a snap on one end of this piece. Fringe ends of 1 in. of the remaining piece of ribbon. Make a 6-in. fold-back in each end of ribbon, beginning 7 in. up from fringe. Catch the three thicknesses of ribbon together at this point, gathering these across into a space 1 in. wide and making sure that stitches will hold. Sew end of loop to edge of tie where this gathering is and sew snap at other edge. When tie is put around neck, simply lap other gathered end over and snap the loop in position to hold the tie in place. An old-fashioned stickpin such as our fathers wore or a pin-on button may be used to hold ribbons together or crisscross, as you desire.

Five-point Scarf Eyeglass Case

Five-point Scarf: See what an attractive collar line this gives. It requires an 18-in. square or can be made from an attractive handkerchief.

Straighten all edges. Slash diagonally in from one corner 15 in. Make a rolled hem on all edges, including slash. Tie it in manner suggested by illustrations or to suit your requirements. Try a square in this fashion next time you make a dress. Take a square of white organdie and dress up your basic black dress.

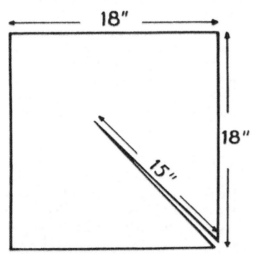

Ribbon eyeglass case: Make several of these in colors to match your clothes. Use ⅓ yd. of 2½-in. to 2¾-in. ribbon. Use a scrap of fabric or ribbon in equal amount for lining. For padding, use four cotton pads, such as you use for applying lotions. Lay them on wrong side of lining and tack them in place, as in A. Fold lining in half, pads outward, as at B, and stitch edges together. Fold ribbon strip in half, right side out. Whip or stitch selvages together on both sides. Insert padded lining B inside ribbon cover, as at C. Turn raw edges of ends of lining and of outside cover toward each other and whip together.

These cases make nice gifts, especially in white, bright red, or black for use in evening.

Beads or paillettes can be sewn on at intervals for decoration. Quilt the ribbon through padding and lining and sew sequins at each intersection of quilting.

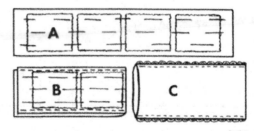

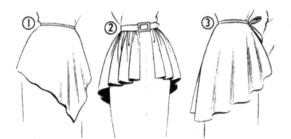

The Peplum Story

▶▶▶ IF PEPLUMS are becoming to you, try one or more of the models illustrated, made of crepe, taffeta, velvet, or even wool.

Peplum No. 1: Use ⅝ yd. of 50-in. rayon taffeta. Straighten fabric; do not fold. Following diagram No. 1, A is at 25 in. or halfway point. B, C, and D are each one-fourth waist measurement plus 2 in. from A. Swing an arc from B through D to C. F is one-third waist measurement below corner E. Chalk a line F to C. G is 3 in. below C on this line. Chalk curve G to D for waistline. Make distance from G to I same as from D to H. Chalk a curve H to I. Cut curve B to G, line G to I, I to H.

To make: In fitting, bring B and G together at right hip. Lay dart over left hip as indicated D to H. Hem or bind all edges except waistline. Stitch ribbon to waistline with ends long enough to tie in bow.

Peplum No. 2: Take 1 yd. of rayon crepe; straighten edge. Cut in two crosswise. From one piece cut three 2-in. strips lengthwise for waistband, leaving a 38-in. piece for back. Cut second piece in half lengthwise for two front pieces (each 18 by 21 in.). Seam the 18-in. raw edges of front piece to 18-in. ends of back piece. Press seams open. Turn selvages back 1½ in. for front hem. Fold in half lengthwise, seams matching, as at A in diagram No. 2. C is 12 in. down from corner B. Chalk a slightly curved line to connect with bottom edge. Cut on this line.

To make: Finish bottom with 1-in. slip-stitched hem. Miter corners. Gather top edge. Cut waistband to waist measurement plus 3 in. for overlap or use full length and make tie ends. Adjust fullness on waistband, allowing a 2- or 3-in. space between front edges. Baste and stitch gathers in position.

Peplum No. 3: Take 1 yd. of fabric and tear a 3-in. strip from one crosswise edge for belt and tie ends. Fold fabric in half lengthwise, selvages together. Measure skirt length. Following diagram No. 3, A is two-thirds of the skirt length plus 5 in. from left corner. B, C, and D are each one-sixth of the waist measurement from A. Connect these with a curve. E is directly above A on selvage. Chalk a curved line from corner F around to E and continue curve to D. Cut on curved lines B-C-D and F-E-D.

To make: Bind edge with 1-in. bias cut from corners, or use narrow bias facing. Pin peplum on. Tie a string around figure and check waistline. Some prefer a 5- to 6-in. space between back edges. Remove and stitch belt on. Tie at center-back or make a tailored bow and tack it in place, with hook and eye under it to fasten.

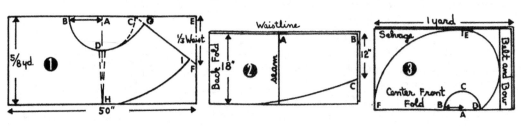

Taffeta Overdress

▶▶▶ ONE OF THE NEATEST jobs imaginable is an overdress of plaid taffeta. It is, as the drawing shows, simply a tuck-in blouse with two side aprons put into a band and tied at back.

To make it, you need 2 yds. of 42-in. rayon taffeta and 4¼ yds. of grosgrain ribbon. First, cut waistband 3 in. wide from one selvage. Now, cut off crosswise 1¼ yds. for blouse, and split remaining ¾ yd. into two lengthwise pieces 27 in. long by 19½ in. wide. Face edges and bottom of these apron pieces with ¾-in. grosgrain ribbon. Gather tops of these and pin right side of apron piece to right side of waistband 3 in. to each side of crosswise center. Sew to band. Slip-stitch raw edge down on wrong side. Hem edges and ends of ties.

To chalk out blouse: Fold blouse piece lengthwise, wrong side out, fold toward you. Measure up from corner A one-fourth bust measurement plus 5 in. for B, as in diagram. Pin top cut edge straight across at this point. D is halfway between A and corner C; E, one-fourth neck measurement to left of D; and F, 1 in. to right of D. G is one-sixth of the neck measurement plus ½ in. above D. H is one-half the armhole measurement plus 2 in. to left of D. I is one-fourth bust measurement plus 2 in. above H. J is on top cut edge above I. K is at edge of fabric straight to left of I. Draw lines K-I, I-J, curving underarm at I, as shown. L is directly above D and G. M and N are each 1½ in. from L. Draw shoulder lines from M and N to G. Fold on line D-L and cut back underarm to match front. Cut shoulder line M to G and N to G; neck curve E to G, G to F. Cut center-front line A to E. Cut a strip from top edge 2 in. wide and long enough to face both center-front edges. Cut two 3-in.-wide collar pieces from fabric cut away at underarms. It is necessary to seam them at center to make a collar as long as neck measures. Cut cuffs 3 in. wide and long enough to go around sleeves. Cut pockets to size desired, and cut top pieces for pockets 3 in. deep and as wide as pockets.

Stitch facing bands to front edge of blouse, right side of band to right side of blouse, selvage edges free. Match plaids and use a ¼-in. seam. Turn bands to wrong side, allowing each to extend ⅝ in. beyond center-front line. Button and buttonhole will hold band in position. Selvage edge, slip-stitched in place, will provide the finish.

French-seam underarms and hem bottom edge of blouse. Join collarband to neck edge and put cuffs on, concealing all raw edges inside both collar and cuffs. Make pockets and stitch in position on apron. Press all and wear over any straight skirt that harmonizes.

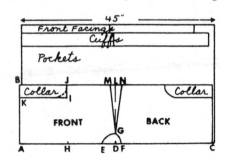

Velvet Collarette and Girdle

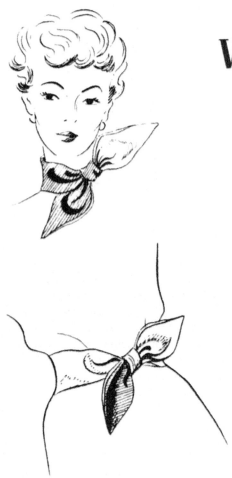

▶▶▶ WHEN FASHION says "gleam" and "glitter," then look to velvet and satin to provide the gleam, rhinestones and jewels the glitter.

Two colors of velvet ribbon make the collarette and girdle shown. One or both may be worn with a basic dress smartly and, if colors are right, becomingly.

If your dress is black, put black and American Beauty together or black and king's blue. If dress is Sanka brown, then use Sanka ribbon with deep apricot for accent. If dress is navy, then American Beauty and navy. Get your color combination right and follow these instructions for making, and you will have something you most surely will enjoy.

For girdle, buy your waist measurement plus ⅜ yd. of 4-in.-wide velvet ribbon, ¼ yd. of contrasting ribbon in the same width for ends.

Lay a true bias fold in center of the ¼-yd. length. Cut on this fold. Lay these pieces over the ends of the waist piece (A in diagram), right sides together, as at B and C. Stitch sides and across ends. Cut away ends (D and E) on waist piece. Turn the ends right side out. Turn raw edges in and gather across each turned edge, drawing fullness up, as at F.

Seam selvages of the two cut-away pieces together, as at G. Bring raw edges over folded as in H, and slip-stitch edges so that stitches do not draw. Tack this strip to one gathered end, as in H. Sew a hook and eye to ends of small strip, as shown. Put girdle on. Lap ends. Twist strip a couple of times before looping it around lapped ends, then hook it to finish closing.

Neck piece (I) is made in exactly the same way, except that you use an easy measurement here instead of a snug one, as for the waist.

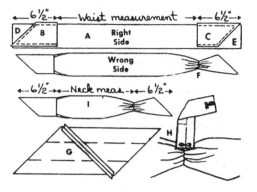

Ascot Scarf and Muff

▶▶▶ HAVE YOU WISHED for something to add color to your winter coat? This ensemble of fake fur may be just what you need. You will find it is also a very pretty accent for your spring suits. Leopard or ocelot could be used for the models sketched, because they complement so many colors.

Buy ⅝ yd. of fur fabric. Muff forms in muslin are available, ready to cover. Cost depends on size. Buy one of these, if you want a timesaver, or make your own with cotton and lining.

Straighten fabric. Lay flat face down. Chalk out muff and scarf following diagram. As scarf is reversible, you cut four lengths, shaping as indicated. Because leopard and ocelot have an up and down in the design, cut all pieces in same direction. A wide belt can be made from remainder of fabric, if desired.

Seam narrow ends of scarf pieces together. Press seams open. Decide position of opening through which one end of scarf is drawn. Mark on one side of scarf, making slash 2½ to 3 in. long. Lay 1½-in. strip right side down on right side of scarf. Stitch a round mark for slash as for a bound buttonhole. Cut between stitching lines. Draw facing strip through to wrong side and stitch around opening.

Lay scarf pieces together wrong side out. Stitch edges all around, leaving a small opening along one side through which to turn scarf. Clip corners. Press seams open. Turn right side out. Press. Whip opening closed. Cut other side of scarf through slash. Turn raw edges under and whip down. Press.

Cut lining of muff 3 in. smaller on both edges than indicated for muff fabric. Lay cotton over wrong side of lining and tack in position. Seam lengthwise edges together on wrong side.

Seam crosswise edges of muff cover together on wrong side. Press open. Turn right side out. Shirr both ends with two rows of gathers. Insert lining and cotton inside of muff cover. Draw up ends of cover to fit ends of lining. Turn raw edges in toward each other and whip together.

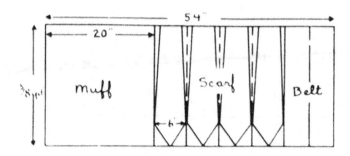

Velvet-trimmed Tricorne

▶▶▶ WHEN WORN on the head as illustrated, this pert little hat has a bicorne effect from the front view. It can be worn as a tricorne, also, with one point at front instead of back.

You need ¼ yd. of 36-in. felt, about ⅝ yd. of 1-in. grosgrain ribbon, and 1¼ yds. of velvet tubing, such as you can buy at the dime store. The hat in the sketch was made of red felt and black tubing. Velvet tubing can also be bought in brown and navy. Use this effective and easy trimming to add the velvet touch to other hats or accessories.

Lay felt out flat. Using yardstick and chalk, make a straight edge. Mark length of band, head size plus 1 in. for seam. Divide length into thirds by marking as at A and B in diagram. Measure straight in from A and B 4 in. for C and D, and measure 3 in. in from ends of band for E and F. Chalk straight lines from E to C, C to D, and D to F. Cut on chalk line. Make small notches at C and D.

To make triangle for top of hat, as at G, measure distance from C to D and mark same distance from H to I. Halfway between H and I is J. Straight in from J is K. Make lines K-H and K-I same length as H-I. Curve out each side of triangle slightly, as indicated by broken line. Round off sharp corners. Cut on curved lines.

Match notches of band to two triangle corners, bringing ends of band together at third corner of top. Stitch as in L. Stitch ends of band together, as at M. Trim to make ¼-in. seam. Turn right side out. Steam and press carefully. Stitch 1-in. grosgrain ribbon to edge of bottom of band on right side.

Turn ribbon inside. Try hat on. Decide what depth of band is most becoming in both front and back. Remove and press bottom edge. Pin tubing along seam line and slip-stitch it in position. Lap one end of velvet over other and whip for neat finish. Apply tubing to bottom edge of hat in same way.

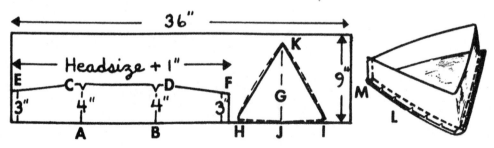

Matching Hat and Scarf

▶▶▶ WHEN LITTLE HATS are in the fashion picture, invariably you find the pillbox. Sometimes it is covered with net, with sequins, or with feathers, the smart shops making it different with an added pin, bow, or flower. But basically, it is straight pillbox—so easy to make and to wear.

Two-thirds yd. of 42-in. material is required to make the hat and scarf shown. Buy it in rayon satin or faille, or any other material preferred.

Straighten fabric and pin selvages together, wrong side up, with fold toward you.

Locate point C, as in diagram, halfway between corners A and B. D is ½ in. to left of C; E is one-fourth neck measurement to right of C. F is one-sixth of the neck measurement plus ½ in. above C. Shape neckline by connecting D, F, and E, as shown. Tie a string to a pencil, hold the string 1 in. above C, and draw the half circle from A to B. Locate G at a point on the circle directly above C. Measure 2 in. each side of G for H and I. For shoulder line, connect H and I with F.

Cut from A to H, H to F, F to I, I to B. Cut neckline D-F-E. Take a 10-in. pie plate and cut around it for top of hat. Cut headband to your head size plus 4 in. and make the band as wide as you want it. Some like to have the band only 2 in. wide finished, which means it should be cut 3 in. wide to allow for seams. If a wider band is desired, allow as much as you need, but do not make it more than 3 in. finished.

Sew the band to the circle; then fit darts at each side, one dart in the seam of the band, to bring the bottom of the band to the right measure for your head size.

Cut a sheer crepe or taffeta lining the exact size of the pillbox (circle and headband), sew band to circle, conceal all seams, and put this lining in. Cut lining for scarf also, following instructions given for cutting scarf.

Join one shoulder seam of the scarf; press open. Join one shoulder seam of lining; press open. Place lining on scarf, right sides together, with stitched shoulder seams matching, and pin completely around circle, neck, and one side of opening on other shoulder. Stitch. Turn right side out. Turn raw edges of opening in ¼ in. and close it with slip-stitches. Sew snap fasteners to this to close on shoulder.

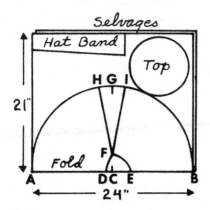

Veiling Charmers

▶▶▶ AT TOP is a glorified and glamorous catcher's mask. Buy ¾ yd. of 18-in. veiling in a fine, double mesh and 1¼ yd. of ¾-in. matching grosgrain ribbon. Interlace ribbon through one long edge of veiling. Loose ends of ribbon should be the same length at each side. To shape veil in back, make two lines of basting around sides and top of veil, as at A. Draw up tight and whip securely. Clip ribbon ends to point. Slip over face with ribbon under chin, and tie ribbon in bow at back.

To perk up a plain pillbox, as at B, buy ¾ yd. of medium-mesh veiling with fine chenille dots and 1½ yds. of matching velvet tubing. Interlace tubing through one long edge of veiling, catching it in about every fourth mesh, until loose ends are even. Gather ends of veiling to ¼ in. Lay veil over pillbox with tubing following front edge; tie bow at center-back. Tack gathered ends in place on tubing.

Almost-a-hat is shown at C. A velvet-covered bicycle clip anchors a flower-trimmed veil firmly in place. Buy ⅔ yd. of 9-in. "fishermen's net" coarse veiling, ½ yd. of matching velvet tubing, and a bicycle clip. Veil shown is trimmed with daisies, but carnations, tiny roses, or small clusters of field flowers would be equally attractive. Change about to match your dresses or as flowers lose their freshness. Insert clip in tubing. Tie a knot in ends, close to clip ends, and trim excess tubing. Interlace covered clip through one long edge of veil; tack in place 1 in. from knots. Gather short edges and tack in place just above knot. Try on veil and fasten flowers in most becoming spot by bending stems. Tack them in position if necessary.

For D, buy 1 yd. of veiling. Drape it around face and head, draw it up just above the curls at the back, pin or hold it in place; then tie with grosgrain or velvet ribbon. Make little, four-petal flowers of the ribbon. Sew three or four near the bottom edge of the veil. Use sequins or brilliants for the center of each flower.

If you like to have your hair in and under when you dine, dance, or go to the theatre, make the type of veil shown in E. Buy ¾ yd. of fine, good-quality veiling. Fit this over the head so that it comes just as you want it at the sides and front. Buy two or three bunches of artificial flowers and arrange them like a chignon or so that they will cover your hair at back. Sew the flowers to the veiling securely and in sufficiently good form so that only two large hair pins and a few small ones will be needed to keep it perfectly in place the evening through.

Mandarin Hat with Matching Belt

▶▶▶ MAKE THIS of nylon velvet, of tweed, flannel, broadcloth, or felt. You need less than 3/8 yd. of 36- or 42-in. fabric for hat and belt together, plus an equal amount of lining, and crinoline. If you wish to add the ball-fringe trimming, as in the sketch, buy an amount equal to the belt length plus the head size length of the hat.

Chalk out and cut: Take a 10-in. dinner or pie plate and chalk out a circle. Mark a 3-in. "piece of pie," as dotted lines show. Measure belt the width you want and length you need. Measure band for hat 25 in. long and 2¼ in. wide at ends, tapered to 2¾ in. at center. Cut crinoline and lining to match both band and circle.

Make the hat: Lay crinoline against wrong side of top of hat. Stitch dart in both circles on wrong side. Cut away excess fabric in dart and press seams open. Do the same to lining circle. Place wrong sides of circles together and stitch ¼ in. from edge. Place crinoline on wrong side of band and stitch together ¼ in. from edge. Place right side of lining to right side of band. Stitch along bottom edge in a ¼-in. seam. Press seam open. Join center-back seam. Place this seam exactly at seam in the crown. Stitch together, using a ¼-in. seam. Keep lining of band free. Press seam open, then fell the lining down on inside seam for a neat finish.

Apply ball fringe: Hand-sew ball fringe over the top seam all around. Make a neat joining at center-back seam. Sew one ball to top of seam in the crown, and the hat will be finished.

Make the belt: Cut the lining 1 in. narrower than belt. Place right sides of belt and lining together. Seam sides and one end with ¼-in. seam. Leave other end open for turning right side out. Turn; close open end. Sew three large hooks on one end and matching eyes opposite to make a neat, secure closing. Stitch ball fringe at top of belt, if you are long-waisted, or at bottom, if short-waisted, and in middle, if neither.

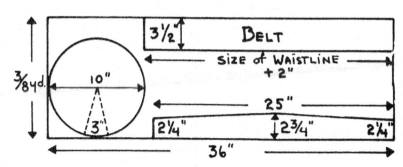

Fake Fur Pillbox, Collarette, and Muff

▶▶▶ TO MAKE THIS matched set, you need 1 yd. of 54-in. fabric and 1½ yds. of 40-in. rayon crepe or satin for lining. For muff buy wool or cotton sheet wadding.

Lay fabric flat, wrong side up. For muff, measure in on crosswise grain 18 in. and 27 in. along selvage. Cut out. Cut headband from opposite crosswise edge. Make it 1 in. longer than head size and 3½ in. deep at center, tapering to 2½ in. at ends. From lower right-hand corner, cut a circle for top of hat, using a plate for pattern.

Fold remainder of material through center lengthwise, bringing selvage and opposite edge together, wrong side out. Measure down on fold 15 in. from top edge for A (see diagram). B and C are one-sixth of the neck measurement plus ½ in. below and to right of A. D is ½ in. above A. Draw curve C to B to D. Three in. to right of B is E. Straight across from E is F. Three in. above and below F are G and H. Chalk line E-G and line E-H. Tie chalk to end of string, hold free end at E, and swing an arc from I at edge of fabric to G and from H to J. Cut both thicknesses of fabric from J to H, H to E, E to G, and G to I. Cut out neckline and cut centerfront fold C to J. Cut band collar crosswise of fabric, making this 1¾ in. wide and 1 in. longer than your neck measurement.

Cut lining of same size for all pieces and on same grain of fabric for each piece.

To make muff: Lay lining out right side down. Cover this with a pad of wool or cotton sheet wadding. Catch wadding to lining with long stitches in rows 4 in. apart, making the stitches long on the padding and as small as possible on the lining side.

Seam the 18-in. edges of muff to make tube and make a tube of padded lining. Place lining in muff, right sides together, and seam one end all around. Turn right side out and slip-stitch other ends together.

To make cape: Seam shoulders of cape; seam shoulders of lining. Place right sides of cape and lining together. Stitch centerfront and around outside edges; press seams open and turn through neck opening. Face collar with lining; stitch both ends and top edge. Trim corners and turn right side out. Pin to cape, right sides together, and stitch. Press up into position. Turn bottom edge of lining under and whip along neckline.

To make hat: Line top of hat, stitching close to edge. Stitch top edge of band around edge of circle. Stitch bottom edge of lining and band right sides together. Seam ends of band and lining. Press seams open. Turn lining inside and whip over seam edge.

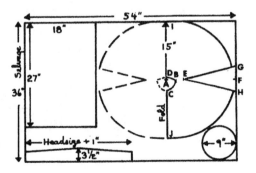

Bonnets, Visors, Sunshades

▶▶▶ CALL THEM sunshades, anything you like, but do make at least one for yourself, for your daughter, or granddaughter.

A palm-leaf fan cut in two pieces makes two visors for the two illustrated at top. A colorful 24-in. kerchief square makes two backs. In addition, you need 3 yds. of binding, one spool of thread, for two fan-visor bonnets.

The two sunbonnets illustrated below took ½ yd. of calico print, one rattan table mat, one spool of thread.

To make fan-visors: Measure down from center-top of fan 5 in. Measure up 4½ in. on each side from handle. Draw a curved line with pencil, as at A. Cut on this line to obtain two visors. Cut handle out carefully and throw away. Bind two pieces of fan on all edges. Stitch twice on curve where handle came out.

Cut the kerchief: Fold over corner on bias line, as at B. Cut on folded line. Make a narrow hem on these raw edges. Join larger piece to larger fan piece, making seam on wrong side. Draw ends back and tie, as shown.

For fabric of bonnets: Take ½ yd. of 36-in. calico. Straighten fabric. Measure and tear off one 17-in. piece. Measure and cut another piece 11 in. across, 14 in. long. Cut two casings 2 in. wide (C and D). Make four tie strings, as at E.

Curve corners of back pieces, as at F. Gather across these curved edges, side to side. Draw up to fit top of mat. Turn under raw edges of casing and stitch across each bonnet, as indicated by broken lines G and H. Hem bottoms and sides up to casing. Join two ends of longer strings in a double-stitched seam, and hem all edges. Repeat with two shorter strings.

Cut matting: A place mat of matting is about 19 by 11 in. Cut this lengthwise into two pieces—one 6 in. wide, the other 5 in. Turn up mat ends for child's bonnet 2¼ in. to 3 in., depending upon size of face. Bind the cut edge with any binding at hand, and catch this turn in to hold it securely. Join backs to matting in a seam made on wrong side. Adjust fullness so that matting comes just to top of casings. Draw ties through casing; ease back fullness so that ruffle is held smartly in back. Strings tie in a bow under chin.

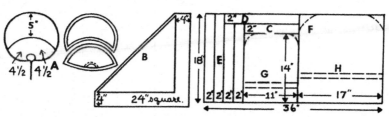

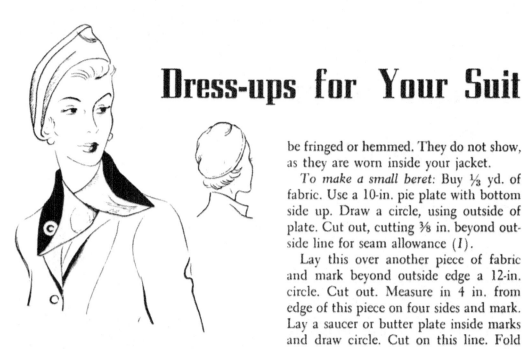

Dress-ups for Your Suit

▶▶▶ MAKE A SCARF collar of ribbon, a beret of corduroy, velveteen, velvet, or fabric, and you have two nice accessories for wear with your suit. However, either of these items may be made completely independent of the other.

Scarf collar: Buy ⅝ yd. of 3¼-in.-wide velvet ribbon, 1⅞ yds. of 6½-in. grosgrain ribbon. Beige grosgrain was used with dark-brown velvet in the model illustrated. You can use any two colors right for your suit and you. Velvet if possible should match your beret.

To make: Find center of ribbon (A in diagram). Measure 10 in. each way from center for B and C. Fold ribbon across at these points. Then turn ribbon under to make diagonal edge, as at D and E. Slip-stitch edges F and G in position. Lay a dart across back neck, as at H, tapering from ¾ in. in center to point on each side.

Place strip of velvet across back along edge from B to C and under the folded corners. Slip-stitch on inside edge, as dotted line shows. Put scarf on and lap it, as illustration shows. Use a large snap fastener, a swivel pin-on button, or pin to hold scarf in position. Ends of scarf may be fringed or hemmed. They do not show, as they are worn inside your jacket.

To make a small beret: Buy ⅓ yd. of fabric. Use a 10-in. pie plate with bottom side up. Draw a circle, using outside of plate. Cut out, cutting ⅜ in. beyond outside line for seam allowance (I).

Lay this over another piece of fabric and mark beyond outside edge a 12-in. circle. Cut out. Measure in 4 in. from edge of this piece on four sides and mark. Lay a saucer or butter plate inside marks and draw circle. Cut on this line. Fold both circles into quarters and notch outside edges.

Now lay bottom piece over top piece, right sides together. Bring edges together on sides, notches matching. Since bottom piece is larger than top, you need to lay a dart on opposite sides to take up excess on outside edge, as in J. Pin darts, tapering them to inside. Stitch and press darts flat, so that they are wedge-shaped. Darts can be stitched to right side to add a decorative note. Pin top and bottom of beret together, right sides in, and stitch ¼ in. from edge, as in K. Press seam open. From scraps left in cutting, cut a true bias facing piece 1¼ in. wide. Place right side of facing to right side of head opening in beret. Bind raw edge with this. Hem inside edge down, and your beret is complete.

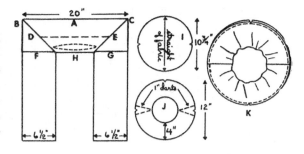

Nylon Velvet Bag

▶▶▶ THIS BAG is smart, soft, ever so right for the dress-up dress—for cocktail partying or formal evening use. Buy ¼ yd. of 42-in. nylon velvet. Buy two 6½-in. wedding-ring pull zippers, ¼ yd. of 50-in. rayon taffeta for lining, one spool of thread to match velvet.

To cut: Divide fabric into four pieces as the diagram shows—one piece 20 by 9 in.; one 18 by 9 in.; and two each 2 by 9 in.

Insert zippers: Measure 8½ in. from one end of 20-in. piece and cut straight across. Measure 4 in. from end of remaining 11½-in. piece and cut across. Rejoin these pieces with zippers to give one deep pocket, one shallow one. Open one of the zippers; place 18-in. piece of velvet over piece with zippers, velvet sides together. Stitch on sides and ends. Turn right side out through opened zipper.

Prepare the lining by cutting it exactly the size of the velvet pieces. Make two slashes in taffeta to correspond to position of zippers. Stitch lining pieces together on both sides and ends. With lining wrong side out, insert it inside velvet bag; whip the slashed taffeta edges to back of zippers, doing this as neatly as possible. Tack lining at each of the four corners, tacking it from the inside so that no stitches can show.

Make band: Join band pieces to make one. Press or steam seam open. Fold lengthwise, right sides together; seam the long edge; turn band right side out; and join ends to make a circle. Tack this to bag on zipper side 2 in. in from each edge.

Bag may be folded together and carried like an envelope, or it may be carried as by a handle, as shown.

This model is good for ribbon, for brocade, even for tweed or corduroy. Make it to match suit, dress, or coat; make it to any proportions convenient to you. The general plan may be adapted to suit any fabric or measurements.

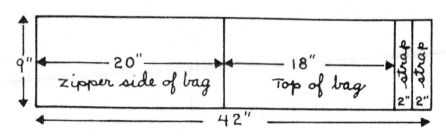

Felt Costume Bag and Belt

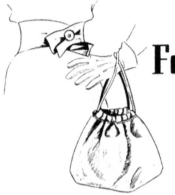

▶▶▶ FOR A BAG and matching belt, buy ½ yd. of 36-in. felt in desired color and matching thread. Lay felt on table. Mark lines with chalk as shown in diagram, using yardstick to draw all lines straight.

Draw straight lines across on both 36-in. edges. Measure a 4½-in. strip for belt and two ¾-in.-wide strips for handles, marking straight lines full width for these; cut strips off. From remaining bag piece, cut a 3½-in. pocket piece from one end. Next cut four strips, each ¾ in. wide to make the loops.

Mark center of narrow side of bag piece to help place inside pocket piece. Center pocket, as at A, about 3 in. down from top, and stitch at ends and across bottom. For lipstick pocket, make two rows of stitching in center, as at B, 1 in. apart.

Cut short straps into five even lengths, making ten loops for each side. Fold these pieces, short ends together, to make loops, as in C, and stitch them each side of bag, raw edges coming to inside.

When loops are stitched in place, turn bag wrong side out and stitch side edges (D) and bottom edges (E) together. Square corners of bag on wrong side, as in F. To do this, fold each corner and stitch across seam for a distance of 2 in. Corners may be tacked down to bottom seam. Fold long edges of a handle strip together and stitch full length. Then stitch it on fold, spacing stitching so that the two rows come an even distance from edges. Repeat with other handle strip. Beginning at side seam of bag, run one of these strips through all loops. Beginning at opposite side, run second strip through all loops so that ends are at opposite sides of bag. Now draw up these handles. Sew ends of each strip together, or sew ball buttons on each end.

Fold piece for belt in half lengthwise. Put belt on; mark where it laps. At this point at each end, stitch in from fold about 1 in., as at G, stitching twice for a distance of 3 in. Press where stitched. Put belt on and lap it at side, finishing off with a swivel pin-on button or a snap fastener. If a narrower belt is desired, turn top and bottom edges over and stitch down.

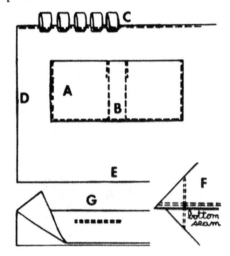

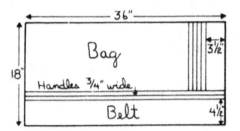

Drawstring Pouch Bag

▶▶▶ SOFT, SPACIOUS, and inexpensive, this bag made of fake fur is ideally handy to have on the seat beside you in a car, or for traveling generally.

You need ⅜ yd. of 54-in. fabric, plus the same amount of taffeta lining, plus ⅛ yd. of crinoline for stiffening and 2 yds. of ½-in. twilled tape.

Unless you prefer ribbon or military braid for drawstrings, cut strips of fake fur as indicated on diagram.

Straighten fabric. Lay flat, right side up. Chalk out front and back of bag and boxing strip (which has to be pieced), as indicated in diagram A. (Boxing strip forms sides and bottom of bag.)

Cut on chalked lines. Cut lining the same size but omit drawstrings. If desired, cut pockets to be used for change purse, mirror, etc.

Diagram B shows how to mark slashes for drawstrings. Lay both bag pieces right side down and mark accurately for these slashes on top 12-in. edge of each piece. Stitch around all vertical marks, as at C. Cut between stitching lines. Do not cut boxing, as at D, until it has been stitched in position.

Fold front and back bag pieces in half lengthwise and notch center on bottom edge. Seam together ends of the two boxing pieces, also of lining strips. Press open. Fold each strip in half and notch center on both edges.

Pin and baste one edge of fabric boxing strip around sides and bottom of one bag piece, right sides together, making ⅜-in. seam. Match notches and pin from bottom up along each side. Stitch. Pin, baste, and then stitch other edge of strip to second bag piece in same way. Clip seams on curve. Press seams toward center of boxing strip. Turn right side out.

Cut a crinoline strip 3¼ in. wide by 18 in. long. Notch center of both lengthwise edges. Center on wrong side of lining strip, notches matching. Stitch stiffening on edge, all around. If pockets are used, hem top edge, then stitch to right side of lining pieces. Pin and stitch lining together in same way as outside of bag. Press seams toward center of strip.

Insert lining inside bag, wrong sides together. Pin. Stitch bag and lining together around points for drawstring slashes. Cut between stitching lines. Overcast or buttonhole edges of slashes. Turn top edges of bag in toward each other. Stitch all around top a scant ¼ in. from edge to prevent slipping.

For fabric drawstrings, center a piece of ½-in. tape on wrong side of each strip the full length. Baste. Fold edges of fabric over tape, turning top edge under. Stitch through center.

For ribbon or twilled-tape drawstrings, select color desired. Stitch two 2-yd. lengths on top of each other, stitching along both edges. Cut in half for two strings.

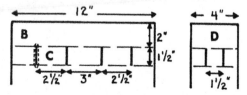

Shirred Evening Bag

▶▶▶ MAKE OF ⅓ yd. of 50-in. taffeta, all one color. Also needed: ⅛ yd. 35-in. buckram; one 8-in. dress or wedding-ring zipper; one spool matching thread; 5 yds. elastic thread; ½ yd. matching-color ribbon ¼ in. wide. Bag measures 8½ by 4¾ in.

Measure off 17 in. of buckram; cut in half. Bring two 8½-in. edges of these pieces together and stitch in lapped seam. Cut two pieces of fabric 8½ by 9½ in. Put one over buckram and stitch around all four sides. For pockets, cut 2 in. from 8½-in. edge of other piece and discard this. Seam 8½-in. edges together, as at A in diagram; turn right side out. Center this on crosswise line of buckram-covered piece; stitch across bottom; stitch up and down ¾ in. each side of center, as at B, to form lipstick pocket.

Put zipper in. Fold bag, buckram side out, and pin zipper tape along top edges, as at C; baste. Using cording foot, stitch fastener in place. To strengthen bag at ends, stitch twice across ends of bag and through ends of fastener tapes (D).

Place pin at halfway point of ribbon length and pin this to seam at one end of bag. Pin free ends of ribbon to other end seam.

Wind bobbin by hand with elastic thread and put it in machine as you would any other thread. Lengthen stitch to make 8 to 10 stitches per inch; and shirr remaining piece of fabric. Since fabric must be stitched on right side, carefully mark rows for shirring by placing a pin ½ in. from each edge; and other pins 1 in. apart. Mark opposite edge of fabric in same way. Stitch across fabric, from one pin to another, keeping lines straight, until all rows are complete. This done, fold fabric right side in; stitch twice across each end (E) to catch ends of shirring threads securely.

Turn shirred pouch right side out and bring it up over buckram-and-lining foundation. Baste ribbon along top of shirred pouch on right side, taking a seam's width from pouch and a scant ⅛ in. from ribbon. Stitch; remove basting. Turn ribbon up all the way around with stitched edge inside, then catch free edge of it to fastener tape with short, neat slip-stitches. Tuck ribbon ends in and whip them in place.

Aprons

Circular Dress-up Apron

▶▶▶ THIS DESIGN is ideal for rayon taffeta or organdie. Decorate it with bows, flowers, or pockets.

It requires ¾ yd. of 36- to 40-in. fabric.

Measure down on the selvage 4½ in., clip selvage, and tear or cut off this crosswise strip to make your waist band (A in diagram). Fold apron piece through center lengthwise and pin selvages together.

Measure along fold to a depth of one-fourth waist measurement plus 1 in. to locate B. Measure up from fold one-third of the waist measurement, plus 2 in. (C).

Draw curve B to C. To do this, tie a string to a pencil, place pencil at B; then about 2 in. beyond edge of fabric hold other end of string (D). Make curve by swinging pencil from B to C. Draw similar curve from E to F, testing correctness of second curve by a practice swing or two to find the correct point at which to hold string.

When narrower fabric is used, the distance from C to F will be narrower. Cut on curved lines for waistline and bottom edge.

Make notch G 6 in. from C. Make a line of gathers from G to B on both sides of apron, using a long machine stitch. Draw up bobbin thread so that shirring measures 4 in. Make ¼-in. hem on side and bottom edges.

Center band at center of waistline, right sides together. Pin and stitch from one side of apron to the other.

Fold one tie end in half, wrong side out, and stitch edges together and across ends, stitching from G to H as in detail. Repeat with other tie end. Turn tie ends inside out. Turn under raw edge of band and whip.

Piece I can be used for pockets.

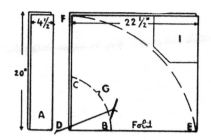

Lace Shoulderette and Matching Apron

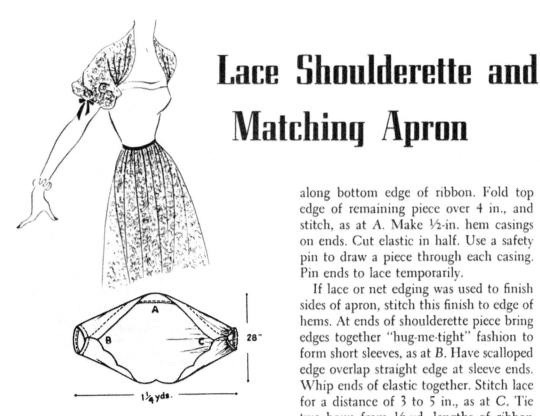

▶▶▶ PERHAPS NOTHING dresses up one's dress or lifts one's spirits more than lovely lace accessories, such as the apron and shoulderette shown here. Made of lace, they are suitable in white, for the girl graduate, in black or brilliant color for the sophisticate. Both are as easy to make as A B C.

Buy 2¾ yds. of lace, preferably with a scallop and in the usual width of 28 in.; 2 yds. of velvet ribbon for apron waistline and ties and ½ yd. for each sleeve (total 3 yds.) of ½-in. width. Measure around arm above elbow. You need double this measurement of very narrow, matching elastic.

Cut off 1½ yds. of lace for apron piece. Hem side edges of this, or stitch a narrow lace or net edging over the cut edge to finish. Gather the top edge of apron so that it measures one-half your waist measurement or slightly less. Center 2-yd. piece of velvet ribbon at top edge of apron. Stitch from one side of apron to the other along bottom edge of ribbon. Fold top edge of remaining piece over 4 in., and stitch, as at A. Make ½-in. hem casings on ends. Cut elastic in half. Use a safety pin to draw a piece through each casing. Pin ends to lace temporarily.

If lace or net edging was used to finish sides of apron, stitch this finish to edge of hems. At ends of shoulderette piece bring edges together "hug-me-tight" fashion to form short sleeves, as at B. Have scalloped edge overlap straight edge at sleeve ends. Whip ends of elastic together. Stitch lace for a distance of 3 to 5 in., as at C. Tie two bows from ½-yd. lengths of ribbon and tack one to each sleeve as a finish.

Crisp, Lace-edged Apron

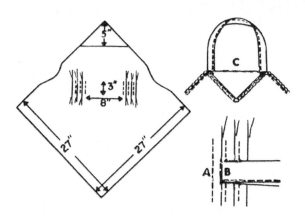
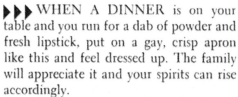

▶▶▶ WHEN A DINNER is on your table and you run for a dab of powder and fresh lipstick, put on a gay, crisp apron like this and feel dressed up. The family will appreciate it and your spirits can rise accordingly.

To make, all you need is ¾ yd. of 36-in. fabric—cotton dimity, dotted Swiss, or organdie, etc., and 3¼ yds. of narrow lace.

Straighten your fabric. Tear one 3-in. string from each selvage. Tear another string 2 in. wide for halter. Make a narrow hem ⅛ in. all the way around on apron piece and on one side and one end of each string. Stitch lace over the hem on all four sides of apron.

Hold apron up to you; turn bib down 5 in. and pin; tie a string around figure to mark waistline. On each side of front at waistline lay three ½-in. tucks, beginning first of each group of tucks 4 in. from center-front line. Place each tuck on true bias, as shown. Stitch them 3 in. long—1½ in. above and 1½ in. below waistline.

Fold strings lengthwise, right side out. Slip raw end under first tuck on each side of front panel, as at A. Stitch in place, as at B. Turn lengthwise edges of halter inside and stitch. Join behind turned-over bib, as at C.

This type of apron will take embroidery nicely, or other decoration: a spray, for example, on right lower half, or appliqué on bib and halfway between points on lower right-hand side. Style it to suit your individuality. Make aprons of this type for gifts or for your church bazaar. They cost little and are sure to please and to prove becoming.

Variations: Halter may be omitted, if desired, and halter piece used to make a neckband with button on one end and buttonhole on other. Make bound buttonhole in top point of apron and button apron on neckband, as in D. Or omit neckband and button apron to collar of your dress.

Instead of lace, a narrow bias ruffle may be added to all edges or to bottom half only.

Side-pleated Braid-trimmed Apron

▶▶▶ THIS ATTRACTIVE but simple-to-make apron can be made of any washable, reversible cotton.

Buy ¾ yd. of 36-in. cotton and 1¼ yds. harmonizing novelty braid. Straighten fabric. Measure and tear off, as indicated in diagram, a 6-in. crosswise strip for pockets and strings. Cut 6½ in. off 6-in. strip for pocket piece. Tear remaining strip in half crosswise to make two 3-in. strings. Then tear off a 3-in. lengthwise strip from one selvage edge for waistband.

Turn a 2-in. bottom hem on a 33-in. edge. Crease. Turn hem to wrong side and stitch across ends, as at A. Turn hem back to right side and clip away edge at end, as at B. Finish side edges above bottom hem, using a ⅛-in. hem. Stitch braid on, as at C, placing bottom of braid over hemline so as to catch it in stitching. Turn braid ends under. Stitch across ends and along top edge of braid.

Turn ½-in. hem on top of pocket to right side. Place braid over this and stitch both edges of braid.

Mark center-front of apron. Lay seven ½-in. pleats at each side of center-front, beginning 2 in. from center and spacing pleats 1 in. apart. Pin them in place. Then stitch across top of all pleats to hold them.

Mark center-front of band, place it to center-front of apron, right side of band to wrong side of apron. Stitch. Hem sides and one end of strings. Fold each string in half lengthwise. Fold a tuck in string and place string at each end of band. Stitch as at D. Fold band to right side of apron, turning edge under and stitching across strings and along bottom edge of band.

Pin pocket in place 6 in. in from side edge and 6 in. down from band on right-hand side of apron. Turn raw edges under and stitch, stitching back at top edge on both sides to reinforce the pockets.

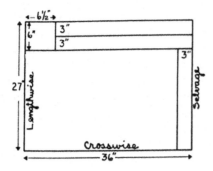

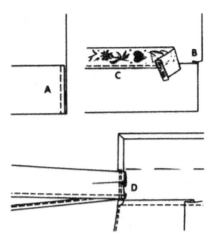

To the Back with Aprons

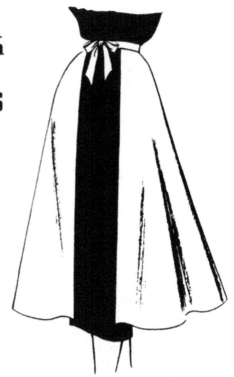

▶▶▶ A TWIST on the dress-up apron, is to wear it in the back, as the illustration shows. This is a neat trick for refurbishing a skirt that shows signs of wear in the back.

Buy one skirt length (waist to hem) plus about 9 in. of 42- to 50-in.-wide taffeta or faille. Just be sure that fabric looks same on both sides. Straighten your fabric and measure off two crosswise strips each 3 in. wide. Join them together crosswise to make one long strip. This is to serve as both a waistline belt and ties for center-front.

See how easy it is to mark and cut. Simply measure 7 in. to right of corner A for B, as in diagram. C is one-half the hip measurement straight up from B. Starting with D at upper right-hand corner, repeat this procedure to locate E and F. With a yardstick, chalk a line through F and C, from one crosswise edge of fabric to the opposite edge. Cut on this line.

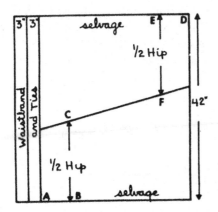

Stitch a seam in center-back by placing these two bias edges together, points C and F meeting. Press seam open.

Put the apron on, bringing center-back seam to waistline at center-back. Tie a cord around figure at waist. You may need to shape waistline slightly. Adjust skirt at waistline; then chalk under tape all around to determine amount to be cut away.

Turn center-front edges back and under to make width of panel desired. Pin these back; then decide length of skirt. When the hem is turned, front will be correct, but the back, because it is bias, will need to be shaped evenly. First slip-stitch bottom hem, then front hems.

Place waistband seam at center-back seam, right sides together. Stitch to waistline. Fold band and ties in half, turning raw edges inside. Stitch all around to finish.

If waist is small in proportion to hips, use pleats or darts at side fronts to control any excess fullness.

Plastic Cover-up Apron

▶▶▶ THIS DESIGN, made of plastic in the sketch, is also practical for percale or denim. You need 1⅛ yds. of 36-in. plastic for the average figure, plus 7 yds. of bias binding.

Measure shoulder width from tip of one to tip of other (about 16 in.). Cut this width from one 36-in. edge for bib. Cut a 2½-in. strip from same side for waistband.

Fold remaining piece in half lengthwise, with fold toward you. A in diagram is lower left corner. B is 5 in. above A. C is upper right corner. D is 9 in. down from C. Connect B and D. Cut on this line. Notch corner A to mark center-front.

Fold bib piece in half lengthwise, with fold toward you. E is lower left-hand corner. F is a shoulder-to-waist length to right of E on fold; G is same distance to right of F. H and I are 5 in. in from E and G. J is straight above F. Connect H-J and J-I.

K is one-fourth neck measurement above F; L is same distance to left of F; M is 1 in. to right of F. Mark neckline curve as shown. Notch at E to mark center-front.

Cut from H through J to I, rounding point at J slightly. Cut out neckline. Cut fold from M to G for back opening.

Bring the narrow ends of side skirt gores together with narrow ends of front gore, matching B to D on each side. Bind these edges together with binding on right side. Bind outside edge, starting at one upper corner, continuing down, across bottom, and up to other corner. Bind outside edges of bib and both back center edges from M to G. Bind neckline, leaving 8-in. ends on both sides for ties.

Cut waistband to waist measurement plus 3 in. Fold in half and notch center on top and bottom edges. If top of skirt is larger than waistband, gather it to fit.

Match center-front notches of bib and waistband. Pin together. Bring edges of back bib section and back ends of waistband together and pin top of apron to bottom of waistband, matching center-front notches. Bind bib to waistband, starting at center-back and continuing around front and back to center-back. Do not cut off binding, but continue binding apron to waistband. A binding loop and button can be used at back of waistband.

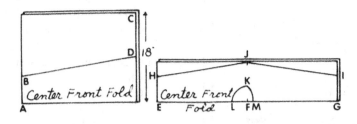

House-cleaning Apron

▶▶▶ AT LEAST once a week we need to wear an apron like the one shown, when the house gets a thorough cleaning. Pockets save time, since you can pick up and put into them various little things to be put in their places later, use them to carry your cleaning cloths, window cleaner, polish—so many things.

Make this from 1 yd. of 32-in. denim, drill, or sail cloth, plus 6 yds. of contrasting twill tape for ties and finishing.

First, if fabric has a right and wrong side, tear off straight across, selvage to selvage, a 9-in. piece for pockets. If fabric is same on both sides, as sail cloth, for example, turn pocket piece up on fabric 9 in. Lay the straightened fabric out, right side in, selvages together, fold toward you.

To chalk out: Point B in diagram is 4 in. above corner A. D is 9 in. to left of corner C. Draw underarm curve to connect B and D. Cut on this curve through both thicknesses. (With a little padding, a nice, sturdy potholder can be made from the cutout corner, or, if you wish, this piece can be used for a chest pocket for eyeglasses.)

To make: Stitch one side of tape to wrong side of fabric across bib (line A-B), and across top of pocket piece. Turn to right side and stitch flat, concealing raw edges.

Pin, then stitch pockets, simply by dividing bottom of apron into four even pockets. Bind the selvage edges of apron with tape, catching pocket edges in. Stitch this part twice, so that pockets will hold in hard use.

Take a 3-yd. piece of tape and place a pin at the 1½-yd. point. Put apron on and, with this tape piece centered at back of neck, adjust apron to a comfortable position on your body, pinning tape at sides of bib top so that neck is comfortable. Remove apron and stitch tape on underarm curve, beginning at point B. Put tape on as a binding on underarm curves, easing it on so that it will not be tight. Allow ends to extend to make ties. These should be long enough to cross and tie at center-front, thus holding apron in position and keeping it out of your way when you work.

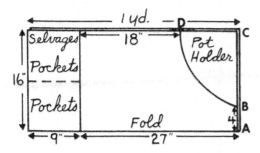

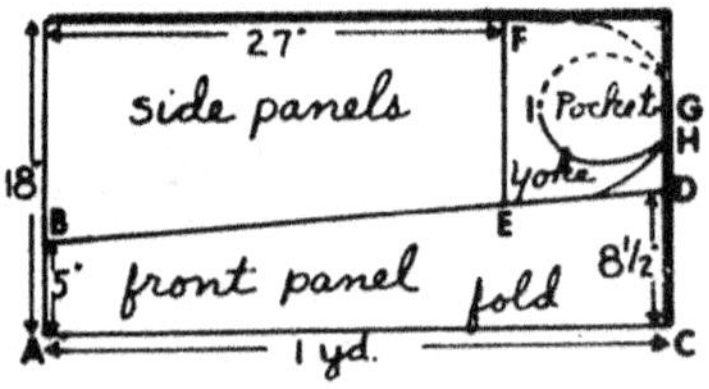

Cover-up Aprons

▶▶▶ YOU WILL FIND these aprons so easy to make and economical in material that you will want to make several.

Top left: Take a square 36 by 36 in. and fold it lengthwise through center, fold toward you. Following the diagram, point B is 5 in. above corner A. D is 8½ in. above corner C. Draw a line B to D. E is 9 in. to left of D on line B-D. F is directly above E on edges. Cut lines B-D and E-F.

Now make yoke and pockets. Fold material for these together lengthwise through center and cut as diagram shows. On fold line measure down from G 2 in. for H and draw a curve from H to side line, as shown. For pockets, measure 7 in. to left of G for I. Draw curve from I to H, to make pockets about 7 by 7 in. Cut from H around through I. This gives you yoke and pocket pieces cut out together.

With right sides of yoke pieces together, stitch twice all around neck edge, using a ⅛-in. seam. Clip corners; turn right side out. Rounded corners make binding easier.

Join straight edges of yoke to center of front panel of apron at line A-B of diagram, making ⅛-in. seam to right side and covering seam with flat bias binding. Bind top of pocket. Stitch pocket to raw edge of side panels, about 4 in. down from top (or narrower) end. Cover bottom and side edges of pocket with flat bias binding. Sew bias to top edge of side panels, allowing bias to extend ½ yd. beyond selvages for ties. Stitch ties twice for strength.

Place side pieces to front panel, wrong sides and raw edges together. Stitch in a ⅛-in. seam. Bind this seam, beginning at bottom of apron and continuing to point H of yoke. Let binding extend 9 in. beyond H for a tie. Bind opposite side in

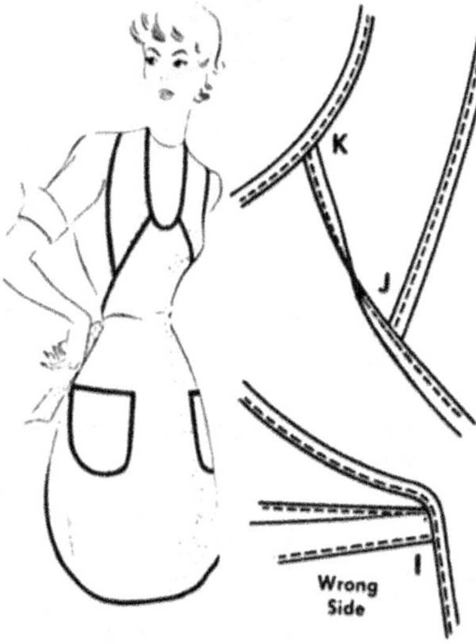

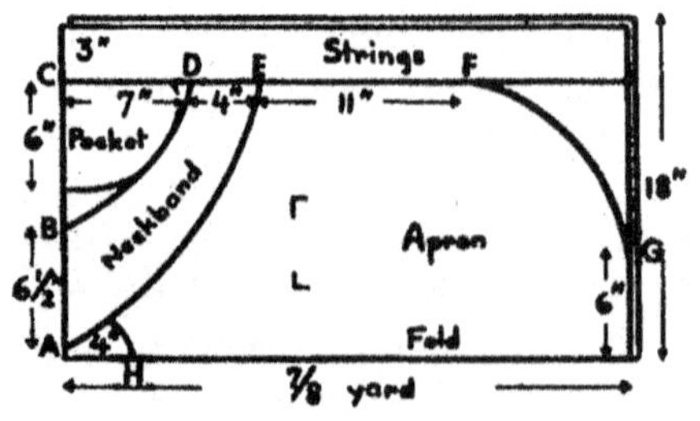

from One Yard or Less

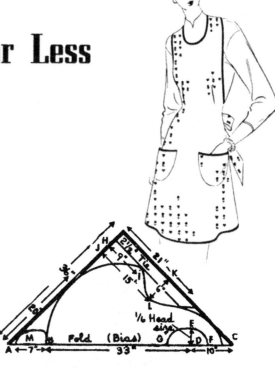

same way. Use a ⅜-in. hem to finish.

Below left: A recent survey among housewives shows that this apron is the one purchased most often at church bazaars, in stores, and from pattern books. It requires only ⅞ yd. of percale or gingham and 5 yds. of binding.

Straighten both ends of fabric. Tear 3-in. tie strings from each selvage edge. Fold fabric in half lengthwise. Locate point A ½ in. from fold, as in diagram. Place B 6½ in. in from A. Measure 7 in. to right of corner C for D. Place E 4 in. from D and F 11 in. beyond E. Measure in 6 in. up from fold along bottom edge (G). Measure 4 in. to right of A for H. Draw curved lines from A to E, F to G. Connect H with curve, as shown, for front neckline. For neckband, draw curve from B to D. Shape pockets, cutting along curved lines.

Seam narrow ends of neckband together and bind outside edge of this piece. Bind pockets. Hem raw side edges and one end of tie strings. Lay raw end of each tie string in three folds and stitch one to each side of apron on wrong side. Stitch neckband ends to side edges of apron. Bind outside edges of apron, binding over ends of ties, as in I, and over ends of neckband, as at J. Bind inside edge of neckline, beginning at seam in back, as at K. Locate pockets at convenient position for you and stitch. Tall girls may need 1 full yd. of material to make the distance E to F 15½ in., instead of 11 in.

Top right: Several features recommend this. It is inexpensive, requiring only 1 yd. of 36-in. percale; it is easy to make, flattering to wear, and it irons easily.

Straighten fabric; fold on a true bias line, as in the diagram, with fold next to you. Place point B 7 in. to right of corner A. D is 10 in. to left of corner C. E and F are each one-sixth of head size from D. G is one-third head size to left of D. Draw a curve from G through E to F.

Chalk off ties 21 in. long at shortest point, and 2½ in. wide, as diagram shows. Measure in on line where tie was marked off from H for I 9 in. away. L is 15 in. from J on left edge and 6 in. from K on right edge. Mark curve from fold B to edge of fabric, then to I. Mark underarm curve from I to L up to edge and around to fold 2 in. to left of C. Cut out apron; then cut out neckline. Mark a pocket as at M. Cut out. Lay this over piece cut from neck and cut second pocket of same size.

Bind pockets across top. Bind neckline, overlapping edges on left shoulder.

Hem strings on sides and pointed end. Pin string to wrong side at each corner I. Bind entire outside edge, beginning where one string is joined. Put on apron. Pin pockets in position. Remove apron and stitch pockets, double-stitching top edges.

Mother-and-daughter

▶▶▶ A HAPPY FASHION, this—for mother and daughter to wear garments of the same type of fabric and in the same color. The two aprons here can be made from 2 yds. of fabric and be lovely as can be and good for many, many partnership wearings. Checked gingham, dotted swiss, sateen—so many fabrics are appropriate.

Straighten fabric. Measure on selvage 27 in. for mother's apron. Tear across. Next, measure and tear off 18 in. for daughter's. Remaining square makes scarves and pockets. Tear tie strings and waist bands off lengthwise edges of two apron pieces, as in A and B, making each strip 3 in. wide.

Aprons and Scarves

Fold scarf square diagonally, as in C. Cut on folded line for mother's scarf. On remaining half of square, turn another fold 8 in. deep on true bias; cut on this fold line (D). The small triangular piece becomes child's scarf. Bias piece cut out from center makes pockets for both aprons in proportions shown. Fold scarves in half to form triangles. Cut in on fold from bias edge 8 in. and 5 in. as at E and F. When scarves are worn, these corners roll back to make revers.

To make scarves and aprons: Hem all edges of both scarves, using a narrow machine hem. Hem strings, also side edges of both aprons. Put a 1-in. hem in bottom of child's apron, 1¾-in. in mother's. Gather top edges of both aprons into a space equal to 2 in. less than one-half the waist measurement. Place right side of waistband to wrong side of apron and stitch in place. Turn band to right side, insert strings in ends, as at G, and stitch band and across ends.

Hem top edge of pockets, using a 1-in. hem on mother's, ⅝-in. on daughter's. Turn sides and bottom edges under. Stitch in place on apron, and, presto! both aprons are finished and need only pressing to be ready to wear. Illustration shows how ends of scarves are tucked inside waistband of apron.

Make buttonholes in front of waistband and sew buttons to the scarf to hold the points of scarf becomingly.

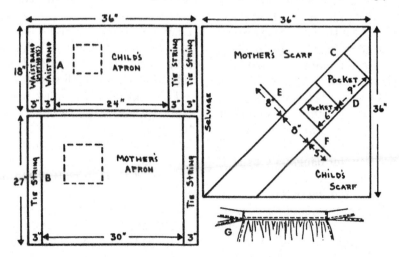

Ruffled Aprons for Mother and Daughter

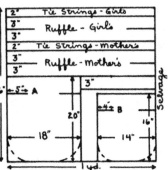
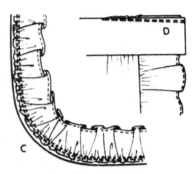

▶▶▶ THESE MATCHING APRONS are decorative, as well as practical and economical.

For two aprons, you need 1 yd. of 36-in. cotton fabric. Fast-color percales, ginghams, organdies, voiles—all are suitable. For larger aprons, buy 1⅛ yds. of 42-in. fabric and follow the proportions on the diagram, but make aprons wider, strings slightly longer, and bands each ½ in. wider.

Straighten fabric. Tear off crosswise, full width, two 2-in. strips for tie strings and four 3-in. strips for ruffles. Remainder of fabric is used for the two aprons, allowing for a strip 18 in. long by 3 in. to add to length of ruffle for mother's apron. Cut aprons following measurements indicated in diagram. Cut pockets from scraps. Fold each apron in half lengthwise. Round bottom corners. Notch center-front at bottom edge. Slash in from outside edges of each apron—4 in. for daughter's, as at B; 5 in. for mother's, as at A.

Make a row of shirring on bottom edge of each slash. Knot threads at inside point to prevent pulling out. Seam ruffle lengths together, two lengths for girl, two and one-half for mother. Press seams open.

Make narrow machine hems along one edge of each ruffle and both edges of tie strips. Make ½-in. hems in both ends of tie strips. Cut each strip in half for two strings.

Gather both ruffles. Pin center of ruffle to center-front of apron, wrong sides together. Draw up ruffle to fit outside edge of apron from slash on one side around to slash on other side. Pin. Full gathers on curves, as at C. Stitch. Trim to ⅛-in. seam. Turn ruffle to right side and conceal edges in French-seam turn. Press. Draw up gathers in slash so that outside edge of ruffle is even with edge of apron. Fold along slash and stitch from wrong side, as at D. Stitch all slashes alike.

Fold top hems to wrong side, turning raw edge under and bringing edge down to cover raw edges of side slashes. Pin. Turn in ends of hem at sides of apron. Fold ends of tie strings in half, right side out. Insert these in ends of top hem and pin. Stitch hem from side to side and twice across ends to make tie strings secure. Hem top of pockets. Turn edges under and stitch in position. Press.

Father-and-son Work Aprons

▶▶▶ FATHER AND SON will find it jolly to have work aprons alike, especially when they are *really* made for work, sized for comfort, easy to put on, and have convenient pockets for tools. The two shown can be made from 2 yds. of 32-in. denim or sailcloth. The dimensions for the man's apron are average. The boy's can be made shorter or longer, to suit his height.

Straighten both ends of fabric. Measure along selvage and tear off crosswise for man's apron 11 in. for pockets, 27 in. for apron, two 3-in. tie strips. Remainder makes boy's apron. Tear off each selvage edge a 2-in. and 3-in. lengthwise strip. (One 3-in. strip is for man's neckband.) Then tear off an 8-in. crosswise piece for pockets.

Fold apron pieces in half lengthwise. Mark and cut underarms as diagram shows. Cut upper pockets A and B.

Fold neckband and tie-string strips in half lengthwise, right side in, and stitch full length and across one end. Turn right side out and press.

French-seam pocket piece to bottom of apron. Make 1-in. hem along top of pocket. Turn pocket to wrong side of apron and stitch sides to sides of apron. Turn pocket to right side; clip selvages at top. Turn side edges of apron to wrong side and stitch. Continue with narrow hem on underarm curves.

Make 1-in. hem along top edge of apron, turning ¼ in., then 1 in. to wrong side, and crease. Insert raw end of neckband under hem edge on each side of bib. Stitch hem in position; then stitch hem ends and across top edge to secure ends of neckband.

Stitch ends of ties to sides of apron.

Hem top of small pockets. Turn under three sides and stitch in position. Divide bottom pocket by stitching from bottom up and back, following measurements in detail.

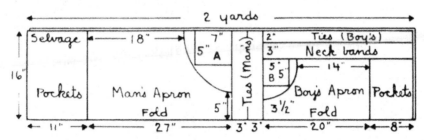

Heart-shaped Apron

▶▶▶ A HEART-SHAPED apron has quite obviously a bit of sentiment about it that disguises its practical, domestic, easy-to-iron character. This attractive apron is made from ¾ yd. of 40-in. gingham, with a package of bias tape and matching thread for finishing.

To cut: Straighten fabric. Tear off two crosswise strips 2 in. wide for band and strings. Place fold of apron piece next to you, as in the diagram. Measure up from point A 13½ in. to B. Measure to right of B 16 in.; place C. Draw a curved line from C to corner D for bottom of apron.

Place E 3¼ in. above B. Measure across 9½ in. to locate F. Draw a curved line for the bottom of pocket, as shown. Chalk straight from G down 5 in. to H. Shape the bib as shown, by slanting line to I, then curving around end rather deeply. Cut out apron after it is chalked on fabric. Cut B through C to D for apron part. Then cut pocket and bib.

To make: Seam selvages of the bib pieces together on right side, using a ⅛-in. seam. Clip selvages at intervals of about 1 in. along their full length. Press seam open and cover it with seam binding. Notch a point at top center of each heart curve. Then notch waist about 2 in. from center-front on each side. Stitch bias binding from notch to notch.

Hem tops of pockets, turning ¼ in.; then 1½ in. Bind edges of pockets. Bind outside edge of apron and sides and top of heart bib. Gather waistline of apron for band. Seam two selvages of strips together. Place this seam at center of waistline; stitch band in position, using ¼-in. seam. Turn raw edges and ends of band in all the way and stitch them.

Turn bottom of bib over ¼ in. on right side; stitch this behind waistband, centering bib at center-front of apron. Pin pockets in position, as shown in sketch, and stitch them in place, turning and stitching back about 1 in. at top of each so that edges cannot pull out.

Sew small safety pins under the side bands at top of bib to pin to your dress, or use two decorative scatter pins.

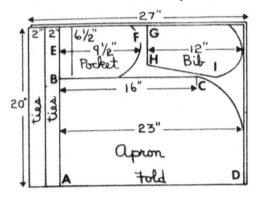

Apron for Home Chef or Carpenter

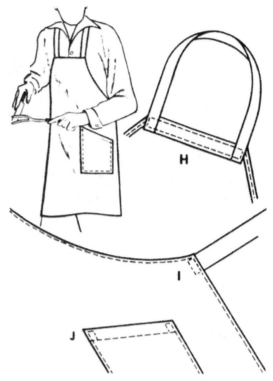

▶▶▶ FOR THE MAN who likes to help with the steak or with Sunday-night suppers, this can be made in a dark-colored percale, navy, forest green, or burgundy. For a work apron, a heavy fabric such as denim or Indian Head can be used.

Take 1¼ yds. of fabric. For apron ties, tear two strips crosswise, each 3 in. wide, as at A and B in diagram. Fold fabric in half, lengthwise. Measure down on fold 2½ in. and in 8 in., for halter, as at C. Measure in 5 in. from fold and place a pin, as at D. Measure along selvage 12 in. and place a pin, as at E. Draw a curved line for underarm from D to E.

For pocket, measure in from selvage 8 in. and in from end 8 in. Place pins. Mark for top hem, as at F. Cut pockets, G, underarm curve, and halter, C.

Use 8 in. from strip A to piece halter strip C, making it 24 in. long and an even 2½ in. wide. Make both tiestrings (A and B) the same length. Fold strings and halter lengthwise, wrong side out; stitch ¼-in. seam. Press seam open, turn right side out. Press.

Make ¼-in. hems on sides and curves and 1-in. bottom hem. Make 1-in. hem at top of apron. Pin ends of halter strap under edge of hem. Stitch hem along top and bottom edge, forming box at each end, as at H, to secure halter. Stitch tiestrings at apron sides, as at I. Turn top hems of pockets to wrong side and stitch. Turn raw edges under ¼ in. on three sides. Pin in position on apron (see dotted lines on diagram). Stitch around pocket, reinforcing top corners, as at J. Press, and apron is ready to wear and give good service.

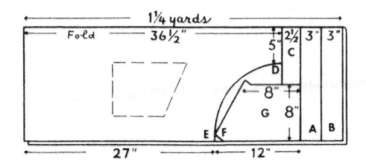

Four Pretty Aprons

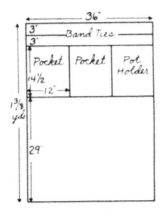

▶▶▶ MAKE ALL or one of these lovely aprons. You will be delighted, and the cost, considering their beauty, will surprise you.

A is made from 1⅜ yds. of 36-in. plaid-printed percale, B needs 1¼ yds. of star-studded cotton, C is made of 1 yd. of organdie and ⅜ yd. of cotton lace, and D takes 1 yd. of 36-in. cotton and a pretty motif cut out of drapery remnant.

To cut A: Straighten both crosswise ends of fabric. Tear from one crosswise end two 3-in. strips for waistband and ties. Next, for pockets, tear off a crosswise strip 14½ in. wide. Divide this into three 12-in.-wide strips, as diagram shows. Two of these make the large side pockets; the third one can be used to cover a worn washcloth and make a very nice potholder.

To cut B: Tear off two 3-in. crosswise waistband ties. Tear off one 10-in. crosswise strip. Divide this pocket piece lengthwise into three equal pieces. A hem 2 in. deep is made in the top of two pieces.

The only difference between aprons A and B is that A has deep pockets. These may be shaped at top or not as you wish. B has two less-deep pockets each side.

These are made by stitching lengthwise of the apron through the center of B pockets after the pocket is in place.

Gather waistline into a space 14 to 16 in. wide. Stitch band on from wrong side; turn it over to the front, and stitch down. Continue stitching to end of ties, thus concealing all raw edges. A 2-in. hem is put in the bottom of each apron.

Apron C is made in same way as A and B, with these exceptions: Make a 1-in. hem in lace across top. Turn edge of lace under and stitch to each side. Stitch lace lengthwise to divide it into three pockets as shown. Make two rows of stitching in each of the panel lines. Turn hem to right side to catch bottom edge of lace inside hem when it is stitched.

Make D in same way as B except for pocket. Appliquéing is not difficult. Cut carefully, turn edges back evenly, and baste neatly. Apply motif by hand or by machine. The machine zigzag attachment is ideal for doing appliqué work. If you wish, hand-hem top of appliqué piece and leave top open to serve as a pocket.

Clothespin Apron

▶▶▶ EVERY HOUSEWIFE needs a sturdy, convenient clothespin apron—one with a big pocket in front and adequate strings that can tie securely around waist.

Buy 1 yd. of 31-in. fast-color drill or sailcloth. Tear a 4-in. strip off one selvage edge to use for waistband and ties.

Straighten ends and fold apron piece through center lengthwise. Following the diagram, from corner A measure in 11 in. for B and down 11 in. for C. Swing an arc from B to C, using a pencil tied to a string and holding the string end at A. Cut on this line through two thicknesses.

Make a ⅜-in. hem on each of these curves, clipping seam ¼ in. every ½ in. all around curve, as at D. Then make second stitching for strength, as at E.

Fold apron in half crosswise, as in F. French-seam side edges together from corners up. Make a ¼-in. hem from pocket corner to waistline on each side. Stitch top center edges together, stitching ⅛ in. from edge.

Apply waistband and ties. Tear waistband piece into two 2-in. lengthwise strips. Seam two ends together. Mark center of apron waistline. Lay five ¼-in. pleats on each side of center of apron, as at G and H. With right side of band to wrong side of apron, match seam in band to center-front of apron. Stitch in place. Bring over to right side of apron and turn in raw edges of ties and band. Stitch full length from one end to other. Turn tie ends inside and stitch across twice.

Make a pot holder by seaming together two curved pieces that were cut from apron, stitching on curve and one straight side, as in I. Turn inside out. Line with a pad of flat cotton or flannelette. Turn in edges of open side. Stitch this; then stitch across pad, as at J, to hold padding in place. A small metal or plastic ring can be sewn to corner for hanging.

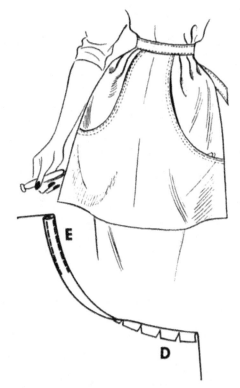

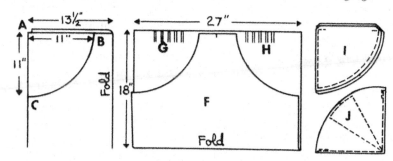

Special Pocket Aprons

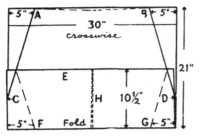
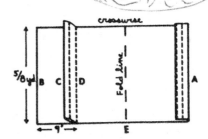

▶▶▶ *Two-pocket Apron:* Seven-eighths yd. of any firm fabric—butcher linen, denim, sailcloth, chintz, percale—and 2 yds. of rick rack are needed to make this.

Straighten fabric at each end. For band and strings tear a 2½-in. strip from each selvage edge. Fold one-third of length (10½ in.) up on apron for pocket section. Pin. Measure in 5 in. from each side on top edge (A and B in diagram). Mark halfway down on each side of pocket section, C and D. Draw and cut on lines A to C, B to D. Turn ⅛-in. hem to right side along top of pocket (E). Pin rick rack over this and stitch, keeping free of apron. Turn pocket to wrong side; stitch from top of pocket to C and D, then down to fold, on each side. Turn right side out.

Turn side edges over, making ⅛-in. hem on right side. Finish by stitching rick rack over these hems from A down to top of pocket and diagonally down on pocket to F, then B to G. Turn under bottom ends of rick rack. Pivot and stitch back an inch or more.

At center-front stitch pocket to apron, as at H. Stitch up and back. Fold apron through center lengthwise. Place a pin ½ in. down from top on fold. Cut from pin to edge, as shown by broken line.

Gather apron across top to slightly less than half the waist measurement. Seam ends of two 2½-in. strips together. Press seam open. Place seam at center-front of waistline, right side of band against wrong side of apron, with selvage along gathered edge. Stitch length of apron. Turn in all raw edges and stitch band its full length, thus making tie ends.

Sewing or Knitting Apron: Buy ⅝ yd. of 50-in. rayon taffeta or faille. Straighten fabric. Tear off two 3-in.-wide strips from one end. Make a ¼-in. hem on both crosswise edges the full length of piece. Make a ¼-in. turn and a 3-in. hem across one lengthwise edge, as at A in diagram. Stitch again 1¼ in. away to form a casing.

Measure in from opposite end B 12 in. and crease straight across, as at C. Stitch 3 in. from this fold, as at D, forming a tuck. Stitch again 1¼ in. away for casing. Place A over C, line E being bottom. Stitch both sides, starting at fold E, going up to bottom of casing, and returning to fold E. Turn inside out and press.

Join two ends of waistband pieces. Gather top of apron (B), so that it measures 16 to 18 in. across. Center waistband at center-front of apron. Stitch it in position with a ⅜-in. seam. Fold band in half lengthwise, turn in all raw edges, and stitch full length and across ends.

Use 3½ yds. of cord or narrow ribbon for drawstrings. Cut in half. Insert both lengths through casings. Knot or sew ends together. Draw up, one from either end. When not in use, top of apron is tucked inside bag and strings are drawn up.

Clothes for Children

Baby Wrapper and Jacket

▶▶▶ WHEN YOU are "expecting," everything you see for a baby will interest you, and you will come to "time" with lots of lovely things that Baby may wear only on special occasions. But seven days a week your little one will need simple canton flannel wrappers like the long one shown. Use the kimono jacket over dresses for warmth and softness.

Both garments shown can be cut from 1⅜ yds. double-faced canton flannel. Use white, lightest blue, or baby pink. Straighten fabric. For ties, tear two 1-in. strips from one end. Fold fabric lengthwise with one selvage edge in 12 in., and pin. Cut full length along selvage to obtain two pieces, one 24 in. wide for wrapper, and one 12 in. wide for jacket, as shown in diagram.

Fold wider piece and mark center of fold A. Directly above, mark B on edge. For neck curve, C is 1¼ in. to right of A; D is ¾ in. to left, and E 2 in. above. Cut neck as shown.

For sleeves, measure to right of B 5¼ in. for F. Straight down 3¾ in. mark G. Draw line F to G, then G to corner H.

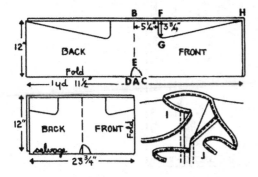

Curve underarm. Cut on this line. Fold front over on line A-B and cut back to match front.

To cut jacket: Fold 12-in. length in half crosswise, with selvages toward you. Pin. Mark crosswise center and lay A-B line of wrapper directly over this line. Pin wrapper to jacket piece, front and back lines true. Cut neck, sleeves, and underarm in same way as for wrapper.

Slash fold on bottom of jacket. Slash fold of wrapper from C to edge for center-front line.

Begin making both garments by French-seaming underarms. Overlap selvages at center-back of jacket and stitch.

Finish edges of sleeves, center-front, and bottom with plain ¼-in. hem, making first a ⅛-in. turn.

Find center of each 1-in. strip. Place a center to center back of each neckline on wrong side. Baste, then stitch around necklines. Turn raw edges in full length of each strip and stitch, as in I, concealing neckline seam. Cut 6 in. off each end. Attach these strips about 5 in. down from neck, as at J, for second ties. Turn in and whip ends.

Receiving Blanket

▶▶▶EVERY NEW BABY needs not one, but four, six, or eight of these, and, of course, at least one especially pretty one. Make this of medium-weight (fleeced) Canton flannel.

Even cut edges. Trim selvages off so that they won't tighten after washing. Turn all edges over to the wrong side ¾ in., stitching each corner diagonally as at A. Clip away the surplus fabric. Press seams open.

Turn hem to right side. Press it on all edges, keeping ¾-in. turn even. Cover the raw edge with a decorative braid or with flat bias binding. The braid shown in the illustration has tiny pink and blue ducks on a white background.

Place braid ½ in. from outside edge. Stitch on. Make first stitching on the outside edge of the braid so as to catch the hem. Miter corners neatly. Make second row of stitching along inside edge of braid to hold braid securely, taking care to ease braid on so that it will not appear tight in any place. Final stitching should make each corner appear as in B.

Make a bowknot of braid, as in C, for one corner. Make it 6 in. wide from edge to edge of bow and 4 in. deep. By careful planning, you can stitch this bow in place without interrupting your stitching line. Press all four edges of the blanket, also bow. Fold blanket with bow corner up.

You can make a narrow hem and crochet a picot edge around such a blanket or you can bind with washable ribbon.

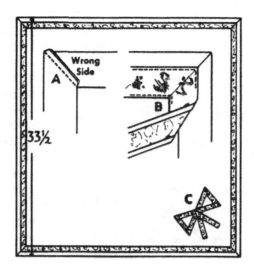

Carriage Cover and Pillow Case

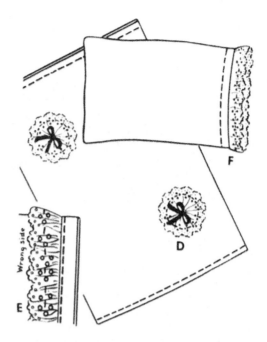

▶▶▶ WHEN BABY goes out, he must be dressed up. A washable cover with matching pillow cover can be a real addition to a carriage. They are easy to make and to launder. Use white, pink, or blue, as baby requires. You will need 1¼ yds. of lightweight piqué, 2½ yds. of 2½-in. embroidery, and 1 yd. of ¼-in. baby ribbon.

To make: Straighten your fabric. Cut off 14 in. crosswise for the pillow case. The remaining length is for the cover. Fold larger piece lengthwise of fabric, wrong side out. Stitch across one end, as at A in diagram, and seam the selvages together. Turn right side out. Press. Turn raw edge of open end in 1¼ in. and stitch together 1 in. from edge. Fold smaller piece lengthwise, and French-seam raw edges (*B* and *C*) together.

Cut embroidery into three lengths, two ½-yd. pieces for the rosettes and the remainder for pillow ruffle. Gather top edge of the three pieces. Seam the end of each ½-yd. piece to make two circles. Draw up fullness in each and catch raw edges together on wrong side. Make two bows each from a ½ yd. of ribbon and tack to center of rosettes, as at *D*. Tack rosettes in position as indicated on diagram.

French-seam ends of the 1½-yd. ruffle together. Draw up fullness until ruffle measures same width as pillow case. Turn 1-in. hem to wrong side of pillow case. Stitch ruffle to the hem of the pillow case all the way around. Before stitching hem, raw edge of ruffle may be caught under selvage and ruffle and hem stitched at one time, as in *E*. Turn pillow case to right side. Smooth ruffle out along edge, as at *F*. Press. This finishes both the cover and pillow case. Both are attractive and easy to launder. The rosettes on robe should be removed for washing and ironing, then tacked back in position.

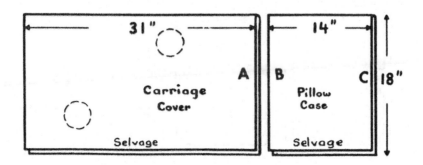

Bibs for Babies

▶▶▶ A WARDROBE OF bibs should be at least nine in number. They should be of absorbent cotton fabric, completely washable, requiring no ironing, and be simple enough for a clean one for each feeding or meal. Bibs are useful from the first day to the age of three years, when tots have a way of deciding suddenly that they have outgrown them.

A bib should be long enough to come down over the lap of the child to catch any food that falls or dribbles. This length has an added advantage in that the apron part can be used as a napkin to wipe the mouth when meal is finished.

In every chain store and many drug stores you can buy the flour-sack type of unbleached-muslin dish towels. They measure approximately 18 by 36 in. Take three of the largest ones for bibs. Fold each into three sections, each 12 by 18 in., as in A. Cut on folds. Take a tea cup and mark a half circle in the top center of each piece, as at B. Cut on neck. Round corners, as at C, if desired.

Hem all edges, except neckline, with a ¼-in. hem. On neck edge, to prevent pulling out, turn raw edge ⅛ in. and stitch length of curve. Cut matching-color twill tape into ¾-yd. lengths. Place crosswise center of one length to center of neck curve. Stitch tape on curve. Then turn tape over seam and stitch again, as at D, so that it will hold securely.

If a set of bibs is to be given as a gift, put baby's initial in one corner, as illustrated. If desired, the edge can be bound with contrasting bias tape. Do not embroider "Baby," because well-made bibs last beyond baby days.

Some like to take little terry guest towels, cut half circle at one end for neck, bind neckline with tape, and make bibs of these. Such bibs are lovely, indeed, and only slightly more expensive than the dish-towel type.

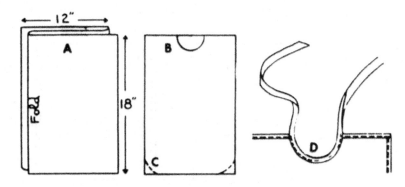

Baby-carriage Cover of Ribbon

▶▶▶ THIS CARRIAGE COVER can appear to be worth several times its cost. Time of making shouldn't count, because it is so pleasant and easy to do.

Buy at five-and-ten-cent store 15 yds. of baby pink ribbon 1½ in. wide, and 14 yds. of same kind of ribbon in baby blue. Buy 4 yds. of pink or blue of the same ribbon for binding. Buy ¾ yd. each of rayon crepe and canton flannel for lining and interlining.

Fold a sheet and put it on table so that you'll have a nice, clean surface to work on. Place lining right side down on this. Lay the canton flannel over this, and pin selvages at one end together. Cut edges of lining and interlining so that both measure 24 in. wide and 34 in. long. Stretch both straight with grain, and press both smooth.

Cut your 14-yd. length of ribbon into 19 pieces, each 26 in. long. Cut 15-yd. piece to make 15 pieces, each 36 in. long. Lay these 15 pieces out lengthwise, right side up, over the canton flannel. Pin each to selvage at top of cover. Now take one of the short lengths of ribbon and pin end of it to top left-hand corner at side so that this strip can be woven in crosswise of the lengths you've just pinned in place. Weave this length through, then repeat. Pin as you work, and keep each piece of ribbon exactly the width of ribbon from its neighboring piece. Weave and pin, making sure that there is no crowding of ribbon and no gap between ribbons at any point. When all the short pieces are woven into the long ones, replace pins with bastings on all outside edges. Stitch all around cover ¼ in. from edges, catching through all thicknesses of ribbon, interlining and lining. Turn edges up close to the stitching.

Press the 4-yd. length of ribbon lengthwise just off center so that woven edge of one side comes inside woven edge of the other. Beginning at one corner of cover, baste widest edge of this ribbon to wrong side of the cover ⅜ in. in from cover edge. Miter each corner as you come to it. Turn the top edge of the ribbon over on the cover on right side and baste it all the way around. At joining turn raw end of ribbon in and cover the beginning end. Whip ribbon together at this joining. Stitch all around cover, close to edge of ribbon from right side. This will catch both edges of ribbons in the one stitching. Pin each corner carefully so that you will have a nice miter. Remove bastings and press the binding, using a cool iron and a cloth or tissue paper over ribbon.

Child's Dress— Easy to Make and Wash

▶▶▶ EVERY MOTHER knows how practical lightweight seersucker or plissé crepe is, especially for summer wear. Buy it in light pastels or white. You can wash it as often as necessary, but you need not iron it. Use 1 to 1¼ yds. for a dress.

Take child's chest measurement straight around body. Fold fabric lengthwise. Measure from fold to selvage ½ chest measurement plus 3 in. as at A in diagram. (This allows for fullness.) Pin edges together at both ends. Place a pin on selvage halfway between ends (B) and a corresponding pin on fold (C). Measure neck measurement less 2 in. on each side of B, on selvage. Measure 3 in. in from selvage at each point. Draw lines D and E, then F and G, for underarms. Cut on these lines, including sleeve edge between D and E. Measure from C one-half the neck measurement. Draw a half circle with C as center, and cut out neckline. Slash down 4 in. from neckline on back fold for neck opening (H). Mark for 1-in. bias strips, as at I, and cut. Gather dress around neck by using a long stitch and your machine gathering foot. Make three to seven rows ⅝ in. apart. Draw up bobbin threads to make a complete flat circle, as shown in J. Take embroidery floss, and overcast each row of machine gathering, as at K. Stitch bias binding on right side around neckline and along edges of back opening, extending each end of binding 9 in. beyond neck opening for ties. Turn to wrong side. Turn raw edge of binding under and baste. Stitch, keeping close to edge of binding on right side. Gather edge of sleeves, placing most gathers in center of sleeve; bind edge in the same way as neckline. French-seam underarms.

Put dress on child and mark hem length. Put in hem. Remember, short dresses are cutest.

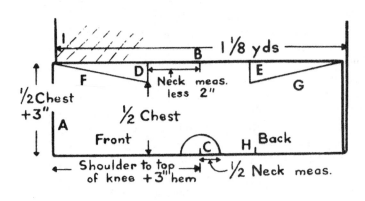
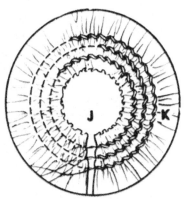

Dress for Small-fry Cinderellas

▶▶▶ A RUFFLED FROCK for youngsters is a delight when ironing is not a bugaboo. This little tot's frock makes laundering ever so easy. Ruffle at bottom may be of self-fabric or embroidery edging. You need ½ yd. of 36-in. cotton and 2 yds. of ruffling. Buy ¾ yd. of cotton if ruffle is of same fabric as dress.

Straighten fabric. Tear off two 4½-in. ruffles crosswise. Fold material lengthwise. For arm openings place mark at halfway point, or 9 in. from fold, as at A in diagram. Two inches away on either side of A place B and C. Measure in from B and C 2½ in. for D and E. Measure in from A 5 in. for F. Draw a curve from D through F to E, and cut on this curved line. Bind the cut edges of these arm openings, or hem, using narrow rolled hems.

Beginning 1 in. below corner G, seam selvage edges together all the way down.

Join ruffle strips; hem bottom edge, and gather top edge. Join to bottom of dress, using a French-seam turn, as at H. Make a ⅝-in. hem casing along top edge of dress, through which you can run a drawstring of ribbon or tape to draw up and tie in a bow at center-back. This drawstring allows dress to be opened out flat for ironing. For a girl over three years of age, simply make this dress longer. A tie sash at the waistline is desirable for taller tots. This can be of ribbon or make it from a ¼-yd. crosswise strip of extra fabric. Use any pretty print of percale, lawn, cotton, challis, or gingham.

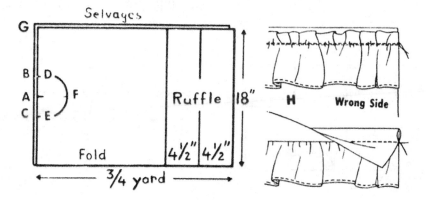

Youngster's Blouse

▶▶▶ THIS BLOUSE is easy to slip into, easy to iron, right for wear under jumpers, with suspender skirts, or with separates. The same pattern can be used to cut several blouses. Use any washable cottons in plain, bright colors, that match or contrast happily with the jumper or skirt.

Buy a length of 36-in. cotton that is twice the measurement from the shoulder to the waist plus 8 in. A yard is ample for older teen-agers and more than enough for youngsters. In addition you need 2 yds. of lace edging ½ in. wide.

Straighten fabric at both ends. Pin selvages together, wrong side out, and lay fold next to you, as in diagram. B is at a distance equal to length from shoulder to waist plus 4 in. to right of corner A. C is 3 in. left of B, and D is 2 in. to right. E is on selvage directly above B, and F is the armhole measure less 1 in. to left of E (9 in. in the diagram). G is directly opposite F on fold. Measure up from G, one-fourth breast measurement, plus 4 in. for H. I is straight to left of H. Fold back of blouse under on line B-E and cut back underarm as you cut front, making a curve at underarm H in cutting I to F. J is one-half neck measurement above B. Cut neckline C to J to D.

French-seam sleeves and underarms. Make a casing at bottom of sleeves and at neckline by stitching bias binding along edges on wrong side. At left side of neckline and top of sleeves cut small openings in right side of casings to insert cord or ribbon, and buttonhole edges of these openings. Whip lace to edges of neckline and sleeves as at K. Join lace on neckline at left shoulder and on sleeves at underarm seam. With a slim bodkin, run ribbon or cord through sleeve and neck casings, ready to draw up fullness.

Put blouse on; ease fullness on cord at neck and sleeves. Pin a tape around waistline, adjust waistline fullness evenly all around, and chalk a line below tape. Remove blouse. From wrong side of blouse, stitch top edge of bias binding to chalked waistline; then stitch bottom edge. Run a cord through this casing to draw up waistline fullness. Make cords or ribbons long enough to open out for blouse to be ironed flat. Finish blouse by hemming lower edge.

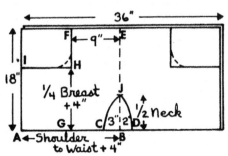
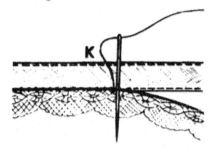

Middy Blouse

▶▶▶ LITTLE GIRLS of three to ten like middy blouses. They are easy to wear; they have handy, big pockets; they enhance any simple skirt; and when it's cold, they can go over a dress nicely.

For this type of blouse, 36-in. corduroy or broadcloth is a good fabric choice. For the blouse itself, you need one length, shoulder to waistline, plus 5 in. For sleeves and pockets, allow an additional half yard for a little girl of three to four, ¾ yd. for age five to six, and 1 yd. for size seven or larger.

Straighten fabric. Tear off length for blouse. Fold this lengthwise, bringing selvages together in center, as at A in diagram. B is lower left-hand corner. C is one-half the armhole measurement plus 2 in. to right of B. Chalk a line straight up from C. D is one-fourth breast measurement plus 1 in. from C. F is one-fourth breast measurement plus 2 in. from E. Measure above B and to the right of B one-sixth of the neck measurement plus ½ in. G is 1 in. to right of A. Chalk neck and shoulder lines and front underarm from selvage to D and over to F. Round underarm. Cut front neckline and shoulder to G. Cut from F through underarm curve to selvage.

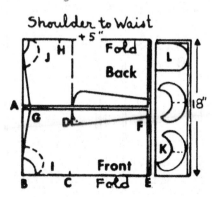

Fold front over back section along selvage edges, matching folds. Cut back to match front, except neckline. Cut back neckline down only ½ in. Cut between selvages to separate back and front.

Mark Peter Pan collar around neckline as at I and J. Lay tissue paper over outline, trace collar, and cut out. Lay this pattern on folded fabric, shoulder edges together as at K. Mark for half of collar. Cut four collar pieces. Mark for pockets as at L, if desired. Slash from neck down center-back fold about 5 in. for neck opening, as at H.

French-seam shoulder and underarms together, clipping underarm curve after first stitching. Bind or face back neck opening. Make ½-in. hems in bottom of sleeves. Make 1-in. hem on bottom edge.

Lay right sides of two collar pieces together. Stitch around outside edge, clipping curves. Press seams open. Turn right side out. Press. Make second half of collar in same way.

Turn ½-in. hems in top of pockets. Turn pocket edges on three sides and stitch in position on blouse.

Stitch collar to neckline and finish with bias facing. Use worked loop and button at center-back to close.

Child's Jumper and Blouse

▶▶▶ BLOUSE AND JUMPER are easy to make and will give good service.

For a six-year-old you need ⅜ yd. of 54-in. striped tubular jersey and ½ yd. of plain. Add from ⅛ to ¼ yd. to each measurement for a larger size, and reduce by ⅛ yd. for a smaller.

Lay fabric flat with one fold each of blouse and skirt pieces toward you, as diagram shows.

Blouse: A is lower left-hand corner. At center of fold is B. Chalk a line straight across from B to opposite fold. C is one-fourth breast measurement plus 1½ in. in from B. From C chalk a line straight across to D on right edge. E and F are one-sixth of the neck measurement plus ½ in. from A. Measure from E length of shoulder plus length of sleeve desired and mark G. Straight across from G on line from B is H. I is one-half the hand measurement plus 1 in. to left of H. Connect H and I; I and E; E and F.

Cut out front, rounding underarm, as shown. Lay front over back piece, folds together, and cut out back to match front except for neckline. Curve back neck down ½ in. Cut back fold from neckline down 3 or 4 in. for neck closing. From scraps, cut pockets for jumper. The pockets can be pieced if necessary.

French-seam shoulders and underarms. Turn ½-in. hem in bottom edge. Bind or face neck, back opening, and bottom of sleeves. Tack a ribbon bow at front neckline.

Jumper: J is at center of fold. Chalk a line straight in from J a distance of one-fourth breast measurement plus 2 in. for K. Through K, chalk a line straight across from edge to edge. L and M are one-fourth neck measurement plus ½ in. to left and above J. N is 1 in. to right of J. O is width of shoulder from M. P and Q are one-half the armhole measurement from K. Cut bodice off along line K. Cut out neck and armhole. Cut two 1-in. binding strips (R) from skirt piece.

French-seam skirt and underarms of bodice. Gather top of skirt to fit bottom of bodice. Put on bodice. Tie a tape around waistline. Pin skirt along this line, matching skirt seam to left underarm seam. Make a placket on left side if jumper is fitted at waistline. Mark skirt length. Remove garment.

Stitch waistline. Trim seam to ½ in. Turn seam up on wrong side and topstitch from right side. Bind neck and armholes. Turn and stitch bottom hem. Turn and stitch hem in pockets, turn three remaining edges under, and stitch to jumper.

This blouse and jumper can also be made of cotton percale or gingham.

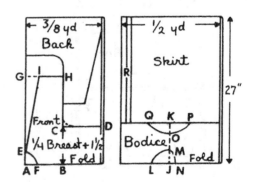

Wool Jumper for School

▶▶▶ A JUMPER made of a soft woolen in a becoming color is a boon to mother and daughter, as it can go on quickly over a blouse, sweater, or too-small dress. Besides, such a jumper costs very little. Fabric length needed is equal to the measurement from underarm to hem, plus 3 in. for hem. From ⅝ to ¾ yd. of 54- or 60-in. woolen or the rayon like wool is ample for girls six to eight years of age. This jumper provides an excellent make-over of mama's old skirts, if they are thoroughly cleaned, carefully ripped, and cut completely anew.

Straighten the fabric. For bodice, use measurement from close up underarm to slightly below waistline, allowing 1 in. for hem at top. Tear this bodice piece off crosswise of fabric. Larger piece is for skirt. From the bodice piece measure and cut off on crosswise grain a piece equal to the chest measurement plus 2 in. (Take this measurement around body, close up under the arms.) From remainder of the piece, cut four 4-in. lengthwise strips for shoulder straps. Use remainder of strip for one or two pockets.

Stitch side seams of both bodice and skirt. Press seams open. To avoid bulk, stitch seam binding to top of bodice, top of skirt hem, and top of pocket, turn 1-in. hem at top of bodice and pocket, and slip-stitch. Gather top of skirt, using two rows of gathering. Draw up threads to correspond to bottom of bodice. Baste bodice and skirt together, matching seams at left underarm.

For each strap, join ends of two 4-in. strips. Fold strips in half lengthwise, right side in. Make a tube by stitching lengthwise raw edges together. Press seam open. Turn right side out, placing seam in center of each strap. Press. Turn edges of pocket to wrong side; press.

Put jumper on. Since it slips over the head easily, no placket is needed. Pin straps in position. Bring them a little closer together in the back than in the front, so that they will stay on shoulders. Pin pocket in position and turn hem. Keep it short—skirts that are too long are awkward for little girls.

Sew straps to hem of bodice so that no stitches show on right side. Slip-stitch pocket, catching seam turn only; make secure stitches at top corners of pocket to prevent pulling off. Finish skirt hem. Press jumper, and it is ready for wear. As a child grows taller, hem may be let down and a ribbon belt inserted at the waistline to give needed length.

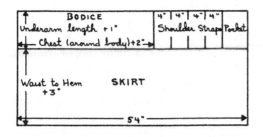

Pleated Skirt

▶▶▶ FOR ANY pleated skirt, choose a fabric firm enough to hold the pleat lines, not only when you make them but during wearing. Many cottons, light and medium-weight woolens, silks, and some rayons, especially taffeta, pleat beautifully.

For pleats all around a skirt, provide material enough for three times the hip measurement. For example, a 36-in. hip requires 108 in., or 3 yds., in skirt width. For a 37- to 41-in. hip measurement, skirt can be paneled at front and back, so that 3 yds. will do. If 40-in. fabric is used, you may need to tear a strip from one width.

Straighten your fabric. Measure and tear or cut each skirt length plus a 1½- to 2¼-in. hem allowance. Join three widths together, using two seams. (One seam is left open until pleats are in.) Use plain pressed-open seams. Put hem in the bottom.

Have material pleated at a pleater's or at your local sewing center; or use a ready-made canvas pleater—the kind now available at notions departments; or lay pleats one at a time, pinning, basting, pressing as you proceed.

Child's skirt illustrated was made for a 26-in. hip and had a 15-in. finished length. It required ½ yd. of 54-in. fabric and had panels at front, back, and sides to allow enough material with 1-in. pleats to go around figure.

First, put in a 1¾-in. hem. Bring selvage edges together. Make a notch at top end of fold, indicating center-front. Fold again and notch each side halfway between center fold and selvages. Divide each between-panel space into as many 1-in. pleats as space allows (usually three or four), planning pleats so that top of skirt, after pleats are laid, will equal waist measurement. Pin pleats in; press. Baste across top to hold them together until you join them to band. One inch at top of pleats was allowed to come up inside band to be dropped down later as child grows.

After pleating is done, seam selvages at center-back. Begin at bottom of hem and stitch up to within 5 in. of top.

Usually in straightening your fabric, you will have enough material to make a waistband. If not enough, line band with plain muslin or ribbon.

Cut band to size of waist plus 2 in. for overlap. Turn edges of band in. Stitch pleated top to band, right side of band to wrong side of skirt. Use a narrow seam and a long stitch. Bring band over to right side of skirt and stitch, completely concealing seam. Button-and-buttonhole is best as closing for this type of skirt.

Circular Skirts for Wee Ladies

▶▶▶ FOR SCHOOL, for dancing, or for skating, circular skirts delight little girls. The skirt may be lined or faced with fabric to match the bloomers that are worn underneath.

Velveteen or a cotton print makes a perfect skirt, and sateen, so shining and silky, makes perfect lining and bloomers. Buy a good bloomer pattern or use an old pair that fits well as a guide in cutting new ones.

You need 1 yd. of 36-in. fabric, plus the same amount of lining fabric. Fold fabric in half lengthwise. Lay fold toward you.

As in diagram, A is halfway on fold. Measure to left of A one-sixth of the waist measurement for B. C is the same distance in from A. Tie end of string to chalk or pencil. Hold other end at A and mark a curve from B through C to D. Measure from B a distance of the desired length of skirt for E. Keep it short, because that's the way this type of skirt looks best. With chalk and string again, mark a curve from E to F and around to G. Cut on both curved lines. Mark 2-in. strips for waistband and shoulder straps, as indicated on both corners. Cut and seam lengths together. Press seams open. Cut lining exactly like the outside. Lay skirt and facing on flat surface, right sides together, and pin carefully. Stitch lower edge of two skirts together. Press seam open. Turn right side out.

Cut from waistline down on center-back or on left side to make placket about 6 in. deep. Slip-stitch two thicknesses of fabric together on each side of placket opening, reinforcing end of opening to prevent tearing. Stitch a narrow belt on. Fasten with button and buttonhole or large hook and eye.

Line shoulder straps. Make shoulder straps about 2 in. longer than needed. Extra length can be tucked under belt in back to be let out as child grows.

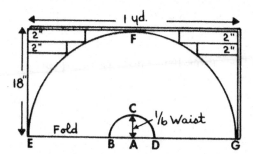

Bow Drawstring Dress

▶▶▶ YOUR LITTLE LADY, be she one or eight, will delight in this full-skirted, bow-tied dress—and you will love the way the drawstring allows it to open flat for easy ironing. This dress will grow along with the child for some time, too. Simply tie bows shorter and eventually drop hem.

You need to buy a pretty 36-in. cotton twice length from close up at underarm to knee. One yard is right for a two- to three year-old. Buy 3 yds. of white twill tape for drawstring and one spool of matching thread.

Tear from one selvage a 4-in. strip. For pockets, cut two 4¼-in. pieces from one end of this strip. Make ¾-in. hems on one crosswise edge of each pocket piece. For shoulder ties, tear remaining 4-in. strip in half lengthwise. Make a narrow hem on all edges and ends of both strips. Cut strips in half crosswise, thus making two ties for each shoulder.

Cut dress piece in two crosswise. Seam selvages together, beginning seam 4 in. below top edge to allow for casing opening. French-seam the other lengthwise edges.

Turn a 1½-in. hem on top edge, as at A. Place tie strings under edge of hem 6½ in. from each seam, as at B, C, D, and E. Stitch them in place. Make second row of stitching through center of hem to make heading. Draw tape through casing with safety pin or bodkin. Put dress on. Tie shoulder bows. Draw up tape to fit comfortably around body. Make a double bow of long tape and tuck this inside dress at underarm. Adjust fullness. Pin pockets in position. Pin hem to a becoming length—never too long. Remove dress. Make hem an even width all way around. Stitch, using a long stitch so that hem may be let down when needed. Drawstring will adjust for fuller chest size. Turn raw edges of pockets in, and clip corners at bottom. Place straight with lengthwise grain of dress, or diagonally, as shown. Stitch pockets in position, stitching twice across each hem and to prevent tearing out.

For tall girls, buy 4 in. extra in length, and tear two 2-in. crosswise strips off for a tie-belt sash for waistline.

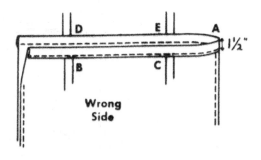

Little Girls' Two-toned Dress

▶▶▶ ANY LITTLE GIRL will be delighted to wear this two-toned dress with full skirt and puffed sleeves. A variety of effects can be obtained depending on the colors and patterns combined.

Of 36-in. printed cotton, buy one length, shoulder to waist, plus one length, waist to hem, plus 3 in. for hem. Of plain cotton, buy one length, waist to hem, plus 3 in. for hem. Average needed for seven-year-old is 1⅜ yds.

Straighten fabric. Tear a 6-in. lengthwise strip from one selvage of printed fabric for sleeves. From remaining piece tear a piece equal to length from shoulder to waist plus 1 in. for waist. Fold in half lengthwise, then fold in half again. Crease folds sharply and pin layers together. Lay double fold toward you, as in diagram.

A is lower left-hand corner. B is one-sixth of the neck measurement plus 1 in. from A. C is one-half the armhole measurement plus 1 in. to right of A. Chalk a line straight across to opposite edges. D is one-fourth breast measurement plus 1 in. above C. E is one-sixth of the neck measurement plus 1 in. from A. F is shoulder length from E. Taper shoulder from E to F, as shown. Chalk armhole curve from F to D and make underarm straight from D to edge of fabric (G).

Mark neckline E-B, but do not cut. Cut shoulder E-F, armhole F-D, and underarm D-G. Separate waist pieces. Fold front (one with marked neckline) on crease. Cut neckline. Back neckline can be curved down slightly at center-back. Slash down 3 in. at back of neck for opening.

Fold sleeve piece into quarters crosswise. Lay selvage toward you, folds at your left, as at H. I is upper left-hand corner; J, upper right. K is 2 in. below J. Chalk curve from I to K. Cut on this line. Cut lengthwise fold to separate two sleeves.

Seam sleeves together. Make ½-in. hems on selvage edges, leaving opening at underarm for inserting elastic. Make two rows of shirring on top of sleeves.

Seam shoulders and underarms of waist. Bind neckline and back neck opening. Draw up sleeve shirring to fit armhole. Pin in with sleeve seam matching underarm seam. Stitch. Draw elastic through sleeve casings and pin ends together.

Lay out and cut skirt sections as shown in diagram. Pin narrow ends of skirt sections together for waistline, bringing lengthwise edges of side gores to bias edges of front and back panels. This brings bias edges at side seams. Stitch six seams. Gather waistline and adjust to size of waist. Baste, then stitch waist and skirt together.

Put on dress. Check size of elastic in sleeves. Even bottom of skirt. Mark hem. Remove dress. Put in hem. Whip ends of elastic together. Use button and worked loop to fasten back closing.

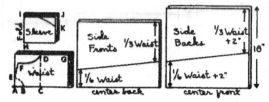

Big-and-little-sister Pinafores

▶▶▶ USE FINE GINGHAM or calico for this pretty pinafore. You need two lengths, waistline to hemline, plus 3 in. for hem, plus ½ yd.

Divide ½ yd. as shown in diagram, first tearing two tie strings from lengthwise edges, then marking other pieces. Make waistband strip equal to size of waist plus 4 in. Make shoulder bands 3 in. wide and same length as from front waist over shoulder to back waist. (Piece one shoulder band.) Fold shoulder and waistbands in half lengthwise, turn in edges ¼ in., and press. Mark center of each band. Hem one edge and both ends of each shoulder ruffle. Hem raw edges and one end of each tie string.

Turn ½-in. hems to right side on top of bib and pockets. Pin braid over raw edge and stitch.

Cut skirt fabric into two lengths. Bring selvages on one length together. Slash in 4 in. on fold for lapped placket. Turn and stitch narrow hem on under edge (A). Turn under ½-in. hem on top side (B) and pin; lap bottom and stitch from right side, stitching twice across bottom end, C.

Seam skirt lengths together. Hem, using a long stitch. Stitch braid ¼ in. above this stitching so that hem can be dropped easily when necessary. Gather top edge to fit waistband. Gather shoulder-ruffle pieces to one-third the length of shoulder bands. Gather bottom edge of bib. Turn in ends of waistband; pin, baste, and stitch it to skirt. Place center of gathered edge of shoulder ruffle at center of shoulder band; pin and baste ruffle between turned edges. Stitch edges together from one end of band to other end, thus stitching ruffles in position.

Turn side edges of bib to right side ¼ in. Lay ends of shoulder strap over bib. Pin and stitch, as at D. Pin center of bib to center-front of waistband. Turn raw edge ¼ in. and stitch waistband to bottom of bib, E.

Put on pinafore. Lap waistband. Pin back ends of shoulder straps in position under band. Pin pockets on. Remove pinafore. Make fold in raw ends of ties, as at F, and lay on waistband (G). Stitch them in place, stitching back ends of shoulder straps at same time. To close placket, use button and buttonhole.

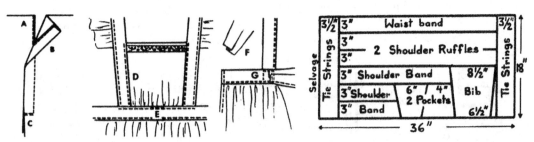

Cover-up Apron

▶▶▶ WHEN LITTLE LADIES go to school or to kindergarten, they play with paints, clay, and paper, and sometimes their dresses are soiled too quickly for good appearance or for mother's comfort.

A little cover-up apron that takes only ¾ yd. of 36-in. calico is the answer for the four- to seven-year-olds, and if color is gay and becoming, such an apron will make a hit with wearer as well as with teacher.

Straighten fabric. Tear off 3-in. crosswise strip for tie strings. Tear 24-in. piece in half lengthwise. Bring lengthwise edges together. Place folds of both pieces toward you. Following the diagram, measure to left of meeting point A 2½ in. for B, to right of A 4 in. for C. D and E are 3½ in. above A. F and G are both 2 in. on edge from corners opposite A. Draw back neck and shoulder lines from B through D to F; front, from C through E to G.

For H measure to right from A a distance equal to the center-front measurement from neck to waist. I is same distance on back fold to left of A. J is straight up from H 6½ in. K is 7 in. above I. Cut from G through J to right-hand corner. Cut from F through K to left-hand corner. Round the corners as shown.

To make pocket, take two pieces cut out for neckline and join together. Lay wrong side of front piece to right side of back piece and seam as at L. Fold top piece over 1 in. above the ¼-in. joining seam, as at M. Bring this over to right side. Turn edges under and stitch, as at N. Clip off points. Turn raw edges in ¼ in. around pocket. Baste in position; stitch as shown.

French-seam shoulder seams. Tear tie strip in half. Hem sides and one end of both 18-in. strips with narrow hem. Fold raw ends in half and pin one on either side of front at waistline, stitching in position with the binding of outside edge. Using bias binding, bind neck edge, then outside edge of apron all the way around. Tie string ends in bow at back.

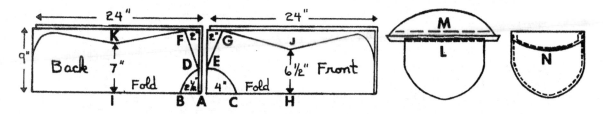

Play Smock

▶▶▶ CHILDREN LIKE to dress up—but when dressed up, they do not like to have to forego play for fear of soiling a good dress. This smock is perfect when the little lady is ready and waiting to go visiting or waiting for company at home but insists on playing in the meantime. It is good also for paint and clay dabbling, since it protects and still looks attractive.

Make it of 36-in.-width fabric—muslin, or plain percale, cotton, or broadcloth. You need twice the length from shoulder to hem, less 4 in. and ¼ yd. of colorful plaid or check for trimming.

Straighten fabric. Fold in half lengthwise. Following the diagram, make A at halfway point in length. Measure from collarbone at back neck down over shoulder to wrist for shoulder and sleeve length; then fold fabric so that selvage is this same measurement above A. Directly above A is B.

C is one-half the armhole measurement plus 2 in. to left of A. Chalk a line straight above C to selvage. Measure in from C on this line a distance of one-fourth chest measurement plus 2 in. for D. E is one-fourth chest measurement plus 4 in. above F. Connect D and E. Curve underarm, drawing line straight out to selvage, as diagram shows.

G is one-fourth neck measurement to left of A. One-fourth neck measurement plus 1½ in. above A is H. I is 1 in. to right of A. Chalk neckline curves and cut out neckline. Round corner E and cut toward D, rounding underarm; then cut up to selvage. Cut along selvage to B. Fold front over back on line A-B, and cut back sleeve and underarm to match front. Slash center-back fold 6 in. from I to J for back neck opening.

From plaid or checked fabric, cut off two pockets, making them 5 by 4½ in. Finish top of each pocket with a 2-in. bias band. Turn in three edges ¼ in. and stitch pockets in position. Cut remaining plaid or checked fabric in true bias strips 1¼ in. wide. Stitch these together, using ¼-in. seams. Press all seams open.

French-seam underarms, clipping first seam around curves. Gather neck and bottom of sleeves. Bind all edges with the bias—first back neck opening, then neckline, extending bias 5 in. at top on each side to use for ties. Finish bottom of smock and sleeves in the same way.

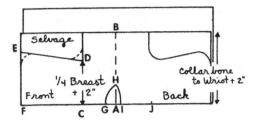

A Special Apron for Crayons

▶▶▶ IMAGINE THE JOY of a little girl of two to eight with a very special apron made to hold her crayons, small drawing pads, hanky. Use ½ yd. of plain cotton, 1½ yds. rick rack.

Straighten fabric. For waist and neck ties, tear from one selvage edge five 2-in. strips. Tear a 4-in. strip from other selvage. For pocket cut 5 in. off this strip; for bib, two 6½-in. pieces.

Overlap selvages of these 6½-in. pieces; stitch. On one 6½-in. edge of bib and on one 4-in. edge of pocket piece turn ¼ in., then turn a ¾-in. hem. Lay rick rack over turned hems and stitch it and hem with one stitching. Stitch rick rack over lapped seam in bib and another row halfway between it and first row.

Turn ⅛-in. hem on one 22-in. edge of apron piece; stitch rick rack over hem. Turn this edge back 3½ in. on apron, rick rack side down, and make ¼-in. seam at each end. Turn right side out; press turned edges. On each side edge of apron, from rick rack up, turn ⅛-in. hem to wrong side. Stitch, beginning at bottom of apron and continuing to top.

For crayon pockets, measure in 6¼ in. from each side edge; place pin. Using pins, divide space A into nine 1-in. slots,

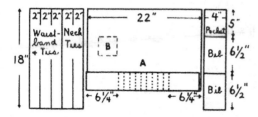

as in diagram. Stitch these, beginning at rick rack line, stitching down to bottom, across to next pin, then up, lifting edge of rick rack as you approach it. Stitch back on same line, across bottom, and up again until all are stitched. Turn under edges of pocket piece. Stitch on, as at B. Gather top edge of apron to measure 12 in. Join three 2-in. strips together for waistband and tie strings. Fold in half lengthwise and stitch to top of apron, enclosing all raw edges. Fold two 2-in. strips in half lengthwise and turn in edges. With ends even with bottom of bib, stitch one over each side of bib. Continue stitching up and across ends of neck ties. These bands tie together at center-back of neck.

Turn bottom edge of bib to right side. Lay waistband over bib, matching centers. Pin and stitch across twice. Fill slots and pockets with colorful crayons and a writing pad.

Cowboy Bolero and Chaps or Skirt

▶▶▶ IF YOU WANT to "sit pretty" with young folk, make this gay set. For a boy from four to eight years old, you need: ¾ yd. of 52-in. fake fur—pony or calfskin; ¼ yd. 36-in. contrasting felt for trim; ⅜ yd. matching lining; 2 yds. twilled tape; and ten bright buttons about the size of a nickel.

The boleros for a cowboy and a cowgirl are cut the same. Instructions for making the skirt follow.

Chaps: Measure on crosswise edge one-half the waist measurement plus 18 in. Cut this off the full length of piece. Fold larger piece in half lengthwise with fold toward you. As in diagram, B is at a distance equal to the waist-to-ankle measurement less 2 in. to right of corner A. Chalk a line straight up from B for C. D is depth of crotch plus 1½ in. from A. E is 2 in. above A; F is one-half the waist measurement above E. G is 1½ in. to right of E. Three inches to right of D and 1 in. from fold is H. J is one-half the waist measurement plus 2 in. above B. Connect F, G, D, and H with curves as shown; with a straight line, connect H and B. Nine inches to left of C is I. Connect F and I with broken line as shown and mark two scallops above it. Chalk a line straight across from F to J. Round corner above J, as shown, and continue line down to 1 in. to left of B. Make a notch 2 in. above J. Cut out. Cut a 2-in.-wide strip for waistband, measured to size of waist plus 2 in.

Seam chaps together from G to D. Press seam open. Finish inside leg and bottom edges to notches with ½-in. hems to wrong side. Turn outside leg edges to right side ½ in. and stitch. Lap fringe over this edge ⅜ in. and stitch. Trim

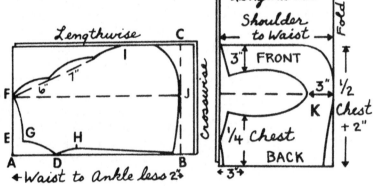

fringed edges to shape, as illustrated. Center waistband at center seam of chaps, allowing ends to extend on each side. Stitch band in position. Use lining fabric to face waistband, and lap it in back with button and buttonhole.

Cut eight 7-in. lengths of tape. On wrong side sew a length 2 in. below either side of crotch and one 6 in. above lower edge on either side. Directly opposite these tapes sew another pair on line F-J on each chap. If preferred hammer-on snaps may be used on these edges.

Make fringe as described for skirt.

Bolero: Cut paper pattern as indicated in diagram K. Fold remaining fabric in half crosswise. Lay center-back of pattern along lengthwise edges. Cut out bolero. Seam together center-back edges and shoulder seams. Press open. Line completely or bind edges with contrasting bias binding.

Mark and cut cuffs from scraps. Line, or finish with bias binding.

The streamer decorations are made of circles of felt the size of a silver dollar with ⅝-in.-wide streamers of felt. A bright button holds all together in the center.

To make a cowgirl skirt, you need 1 yd. of 36-in. felt in a bright red, green, royal blue, orange, or brown; ⅜ yd. velveteen or corduroy for bolero in a harmonizing or contrasting color; ¼ yd. of 36-in. felt for fringes; ⅜ yd. lining fabric; and eight of the brightest imitation jewel buttons you can find.

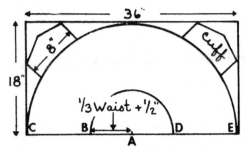

Skirt: Lay felt flat. As in diagram, A is at center of one 36-in. edge. B is one-third of the waist measurement plus ½ in. to left of A; C is the length from waist to hem from B. Keep skirt short, and remember that fringe is added to bottom edge. Tie chalk on a string. With one end of string held at A, chalk an arc from B around to D, and another from C around to E. Cut on these two curves. From piece cut out at waistline, cut 2-in.-wide strips. Lap ends of strips together and stitch for waistband. Cut two cuffs from corner pieces, as indicated. Pink ends and top edge of cuffs. Seam ends of skirt together, starting 4 in. below top edge for back opening.

Fit skirt. Pin pleat in center-front to take up any excess in waistline. Check length and decide on depth of fringe desired. Remove skirt. Stitch waistband to right side of waistline. Face waistband with lining fabric or stitch to 1¼-in. grosgrain ribbon. Use large hook and eye to close.

Fringe: Cut strips for fringe from 2 to 3 in. wide. Pink one edge. Slash other edge to within ½ in. of pinked edge, as in F. Lap top edge of fringe over bottom edge of skirt and stitch ¼ in. from edge.

Ruffled Nightie for Your Fairy Princess

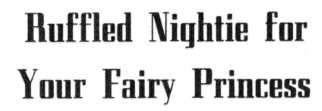

▶▶▶ COTTON CHALLIS or batiste, ribbon and lace, and a little time and ingenuity on your part will make a lovely nightie like this.

Take the child's measurement from shoulder to floor and buy twice this length in 36-in. wide, soft, inexpensive batiste, challis, or muslin, and four times this length of lace edging. Cut from each selvage edge a strip 2½ in. wide. Stitch the lace to the selvage edges of both strips. Cut one strip in half crosswise to make two armhole ruffles. The long one you use for the neck. Gather the three ruffles and make each into a circle ready to apply to the nightdress.

Fold fabric in half crosswise and French-seam the underarms, beginning 8 in. down from the fold and stopping 8 in. from the bottom. Turn a ¼-in. hem on each of the 8-in. open edges at the bottom, and make a ¾-in. hem across the bottom of each piece. Cut on fold, beginning 3 in. in from one edge and cutting to within 3 in. of the other, as diagram shows. Gather the top, front and back, and sew the gathered neck ruffle on over the gathered top. Sew the sleeve ruffles into the armholes, and cover the seam joining of all ruffles with a matching-color bias binding applied as a facing.

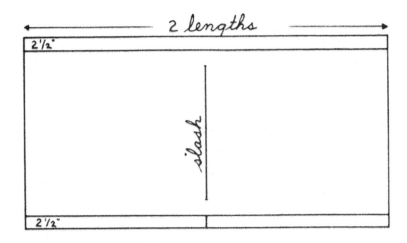

Nightdress—Big or Little

▶▶▶ THE MODEL illustrated was made for an eight-year-old. It required two lengths, shoulder to floor, of 36-in. flannelette. This amount is right for three to twelve years. Buy 4 yds. of ¼-in. ribbon for drawstrings. For adults, buy two lengths plus ½ to 1 yd. for short or long sleeves.

To make for a child: Straighten fabric. Tear or cut in half crosswise. Cut from each selvage edge of one piece a 4-in. strip (A and B in diagram) for yoke and extensions of sleeves. For sleeves, cut from remaining piece a lengthwise strip 9 in. wide (C).

Divide strip B crosswise into three equal parts. Seam one to strip A, selvages meeting, for yoke. Two remaining pieces are joined to sleeves. Divide sleeve piece C crosswise into four equal parts. Lay selvage edges together and stitch to make two sleeves. French-seam one side of each sleeve. Stitch other side halfway of seam, leaving opening for armhole, as at D.

Lay two body pieces together and French-seam sides, leaving armhole opening of same depth (E) as in sleeves. French-seam sleeves to body. Mark center-back and center-front at top edge of nightdress. Using two rows ¼ in. apart, gather top of nightdress and bottom of sleeves.

Hem both ends of sleeve pieces and yoke. Turn selvage edges over on all three, and stitch first on selvage, then halfway between selvage and fold to provide casing for ribbon.

Fold sleeve extensions to find center. Divide yoke into four sections, marking each division with pins. Place wrong side of yoke to wrong side of nightdress, with hemmed edges meeting at center-front. Distribute fullness evenly. Top sleeve seams should meet one-fourth mark in yoke sections. Stitch yoke on, making a narrow seam. Trim if necessary. Turn and make a French seam. Apply pieces to sleeves in same way, hems meeting at outside sleeve seams.

Put in 1-in. bottom hem. Cut off ribbon two ¾-yd. pieces for sleeves. Remaining 2½ yds. is for neck. Use a bodkin to draw ribbon through casing. Secure ribbon at center-back and underarm sleeve seams, so that it will not pull out.

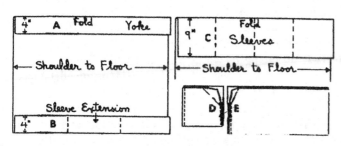

Little Girl's Robe

▶▶▶ FOR THE ROBE shown here, made of 36-in. corduroy, you need double the length from shoulder to floor. Average amount needed for 6-year-old is 1¾ yds.

Straighten fabric. Fold fabric in half lengthwise, wrong side out. Pin edges together. Lay fold toward you, as in diagram. A is lower left-hand corner. B is at halfway point on fold. Straight across from B is C. D is 1 in. to left of C; E is 1 in. to right of B.

Chalk shoulder line D-E. F is one-half armhole measurement plus 2 in. to left of E. Chalk straight line across from F to locate G. H is one-fourth breast measurement plus 2 in. in from F. I is one-half breast measurement from A. J is 2 in. to right of G. Connect I-H and H-J. Curve underarm at H. K is one-sixth of neck measurement plus ½ in. from E. L is length of shoulder and arm from K. Chalk neck curve as shown. Chalk line straight from L to line J-H.

Cut out back, cutting from E to L; B to K for back neck; from L to line J-H; along underarm, rounding at H, to I.

Chalk a line 2 in. from selvages, straight across as at M. Lay back over front section, center-back in line with center-front, shoulder lines matching. Cut underarm and sleeves to match back. Remove back.

N is one-sixth of the neck measurement plus ½ in. to right of L on center-front line. O is one-sixth of the neck measurement below center-front line. Chalk and cut curve, continuing across facing as shown.

Outline a 2-in. front collar, as at P, and back Q. Trace and cut out a collar pattern on paper from these outlines. Lay collar pieces together, overlapping shoulder edges a seam's width. Cut a half collar pattern. Lay center-back line on fold, and cut top and bottom collar pieces, as R shows, allowing for seams. Lay right sides of collar together. Stitch outside edges. Clip seams. Turn right side out and press.

Seam shoulders and underarms. Fold front facings back 1 in. and pin. Put on robe, tie tape around waist, and mark for 2-in.-wide side openings. Rip both side seams 2 in. at this waistline point. Put tape around waist through openings and across front. Check sleeve length. Mark hem length. Pin collar in position.

Turn and stitch hems on bottom and sleeves. Turn top part of front facings to right side; stitch across facings at neckline. Clip corners; trim seam. Turn facings back to position; stitch from neckline to hem.

Baste collar around neckline on right side, center-back matching. Pin bias facing over basting. Stitch around neckline through all thicknesses. Clip seam. Turn facing to wrong side and whip down.

Cut pockets from scraps. Hem top edge. Turn three sides under and stitch.

Make tie belt from 2-in. strip as long as desired; insert in underarm openings so that back hangs loose. Tie across front.

Little Girl's Accessories

▶▶▶ A SURE-ENOUGH muff, a neckpiece cozy and warm to cuddle her chin, a pillbox hat in her size—these delight a young lady. And what could be more appropriate for a gift? You can make all three articles of fake fur, with rayon satin lining and padding very reasonably. Where could you find anything else to give so much pleasure, usefulness and downright value?

Buy ⅜ yd. of 52-in. imitation krimmer in grey or white, the same amount of lining and one sheet, approximately 18 by 30 in., of sheet wadding.

Straighten fabric. Lay it flat, wrong side up. Chalk out muff, scarf, and pillbox, as diagram shows. Measure carefully so that your proportions will be correct. These are good average dimensions. Scarf can be made longer, if necessary.

Scarf: Cut three thicknesses of padding in same shape as outside, minus seam allowance. Center padding on wrong side of lining and tack or stitch it to lining. Stitch across lining and padding at intervals to hold together, as in A.

Lay right sides of fake fur and lining together; seam, leaving an opening large enough to turn scarf right side out. Clip seams at intervals of 2 in.; cut away surplus at corners. Turn right side out and close opening with slip-stitches. Make a little strap of the fur fabric and whip it to right side of one edge of scarf, as shown in illustration.

Muff: Cut lining for muff 2½ in. narrower and 2 in. shorter, or 11 by 16 in. Cut muff padding ½ in. smaller than lining all around.

Center padding on wrong side of lining. Tack or stitch it to lining.

Seam 11-in. edges of lining together; also the 13½-in. edges of fur fabric, thus forming two tubes. Gather each end of fur tube. Insert lining tube inside fur tube, wrong sides together. Draw up gathers to size of lining tube. Turn ends in toward each other and slip-stitch together.

Pillbox: Stitch hatband to circle. Notch seam. Press seam open. Turn right side out. Stitch lining pieces in same way. Press. Insert lining inside hat, wrong sides together. Turn bottom edges in toward each other and slip-stitch together.

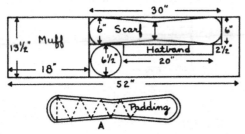

Bretelles— Over-shoulder Suspenders

▶▶▶ LITTLE GIRLS like to be dressed up, and they are usually especially fond of ribbon. The bretelles shown, pleated or plain, can do wonders for a basic dress and for the spirit of any little lady.

Six yards of 2-in. ribbon will make a lovely pleated set, while 2¼ yds. will usually make a plain set for a girl four to seven years of age. Add ½ to 1 yd. more ribbon for older girls.

To make pleated bretelles: Cut three times the waist measurement for sash. For example, if waist is 24 in., cut off 2 yds. For shoulder pieces (which should reach from waistline to waistline over shoulder when pleated), cut remaining piece of ribbon in half. Lay ¼-in. pleats in one shoulder piece, as in A, pinning each pleat and creasing it as you proceed. (If you should run short of ribbon in these shoulder pieces, last four pleats may be omitted in back and the ribbon left plain to gain needed length.) Lay pleated ribbon on tissue paper and stitch in from one edge one-fourth of the ribbon's width or in line with a stripe, if ribbon has one. Pleat and stitch second shoulder piece, making sure that pleats run in same direction as in first. Press.

Pin sash ribbon around waistline with bow ends even. Locate on waistline, on each side of center-front and center-back, position for pleated ruffles—not too far to side lest they fall off shoulders. Place pin at these points.

Stitch shoulder pieces to points located on waistband ribbon, placing wrong side of ribbon to wrong side of waistband piece, as in B. Turn shoulder piece up, as in C. From right side, stitch close to edge of waistband across pleating, as at D, to hold securely. Tie all thread ends, and your set of pleated bretelles is ready to don over shoulders and the belt to tie in a nice bow at center-back.

For plain bretelles: Cut ribbon into four lengths—two long enough to go over shoulder plus 1 in. at each end for casing and two to make bars across chest and back, usually 4 to 5 in. each.

Place ribbon over shoulders. Pin bar ribbons in place at a becoming point for the child. Join bars to edge of ribbon in same way pleated bretelles are joined. Make a ⅛-in. turn, then a ⅜-in. hem in ends of each shoulder piece. Run a cord or elastic through this that can fasten comfortably around waist under skirt belt and hold bretelles nicely in position.

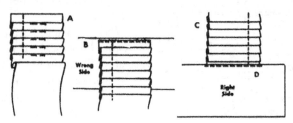

Ranch-branded Suede Cloth Slipover

▶▶▶ THE SOFT, suedelike fabric of the original shown here was stamped with ranch brands in bright colors. Fabric is 52 in. wide. You need only ½ to ⅝ yd., depending on boy's size. This slipover can also be made in fake fur pony. You need one length, shoulder to waist, plus 6 in.

Straighten fabric. Fold lengthwise edges toward center, as at A in diagram, wrong side out. B is lower left-hand corner. C is one-half armhole measurement plus 3 in. to right of B. Chalk a line from C to opposite fold. D is one-fourth chest measurement plus 1 in. from C. E is one-fourth chest measurement plus 2 in. from corner F. G is one-sixth neck measurement plus ½ in. from B. H is one-sixth of the neck measurement to right of B. I is 1 in. to right of A. Chalk neck and shoulder lines; front underarm from selvage to D, curving underarm, and over to E. Cut front neckline H-G and shoulder line G-I. Cut from E through underarm curve to selvage.

Fold front over back section along selvage edges, matching folds. Cut back to match front, except neckline. Cut back neck down ½ in., as at J. Cut between selvages to separate back and front.

Mark center-front fold from H to C with basting. Chalk out front facing on a scrap as at K, making it 4 in. wide and 2 in. longer than distance from H to C. Lay facing over center-front basting line, right side of facing to wrong side of shirt. Stitch center-front to within 2 in. of bottom, as at L. Cut between stitching lines. Turn facing to right side. Turn under edges, clipping corners, and top-stitch edge, as at M. Reinforce point with whipping stitches.

Measure neckline. Cut a straight collar of this length plus seams and 2 in. wide. Piece, if necessary. Fold collar in half lengthwise, wrong side out; stitch across ends. Turn right side out. Press. Stitch one edge of collar to right side of neckline; turn in other edge and stitch it in place. French-seam shoulders and underarms, clipping underarm curves after first stitching. Make ½-in. to 1-in. hems on bottom of sleeves and shirt. Cut and apply pocket, if desired.

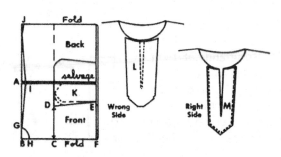

Ribbon Bows for Little Girls

▶▶▶ MOST LITTLE GIRLS can wear some kind of hair bow—if not for school, then surely for dress-up.

The four bows shown here are easy to make and require a minimum of ribbon for nice bows. Each is put together in a slightly different way.

Bowknot 1: Buy ⅓ yd. of 1-in. velvet ribbon. Cut off 1 in. for center piece. Fold the remaining 11 in. zigzag, as at A. Stitch across the center. Draw ribbon together. Fold in raw edges of 1-in. piece; wrap it around center of bow, as at B; whip together on underside. Slip a bobby pin underneath and you have a bow that is decidedly attractive.

Flat bow 2: Buy ¾ yd. of 2-in. moiré or taffeta ribbon. Cut it in three lengths 14 in., 12 in. and 1 in. Bring ends of 14-in. length together in center, as in C, and stitch, as in D. Fold and stitch 12-in. length in the same way. Draw each together at center. Place shorter length over longer, and fold 1-in. piece around both at center, as in E. Tack securely underneath, then sew to a plain barrette.

Folded bow 3: Buy 1 yd. of 1½-in. checked ribbon. Cut off 1 in. for center piece. Divide the 35-in. piece into three even lengths. Bring ends of one length together at center. Fold loop ends into points, and stitch across, as at F. Do this for all three lengths, and press loop ends flat. Draw up center of each bow, as in G, winding thread around tightly. Overlap the three, as in H, and fold the 1-in. piece over all three at center to make a swirl. Sew securely. Sew to narrow barrette.

Band bow 4: Buy 1⅛ yds. of 1-in. novelty ribbon, and ⅛ yd. of ¼-in.-wide elastic. Cut ribbon into three lengths, 1 in. for center piece, 23 in. for bow, 16½ in. for band. Fold ribbon as in I, three loops with one end on each side. Stitch through center and draw thread up. Lay bow on ribbon band about 2 in. to side of center. Fold 1-in. piece around bow and band, as in J, sewing ends together on under side. Sew an end of elastic to an end of ribbon and bandeau is ready to wear.

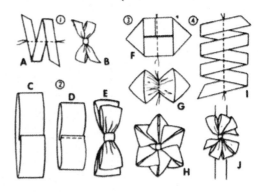

218

Home Furnishings

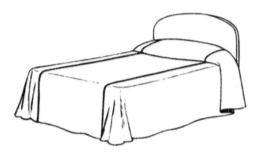

Flanged-edge Pillows

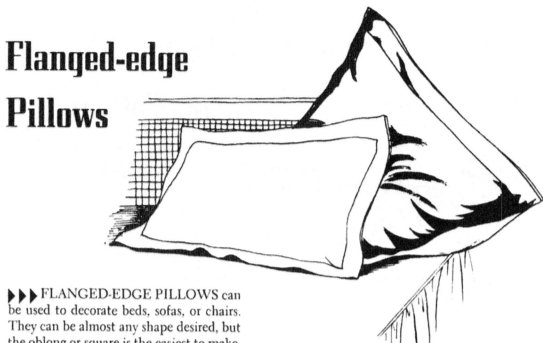

▶▶▶ FLANGED-EDGE PILLOWS can be used to decorate beds, sofas, or chairs. They can be almost any shape desired, but the oblong or square is the easiest to make. Some have a flange 1 in. wide, others as much as 6 or 8 in. The one shown here is planned for a 2-in. flange. The same method holds in making, no matter how large a flange you make.

Velveteen is an ideal material. Fabric to match your slip covers, felt, corduroy, or any favored fabric may be used, as you choose.

Measure the length and width of your pillow. Add 1 in. to each measurement for seams and ease. Allow for desired flange width, bearing in mind that the same amount must be allowed for each side and each end.

Tear or cut tops straight with grain of fabric. Lay two pieces with right sides together. Seam all around edges, leaving one end open to the width of your pillows, as at A. Clip off seam allowance at each corner to avoid bulk, as shown at B. Press seam open.

Turn cover right side out. Square out corners neatly. Press edges. Slip pillow inside and center it. Pin up close to pillow all around, as dotted line shows in C. Baste; with zipper foot stitch close to pillow, pivoting at each corner so that turn will be nicely squared.

Turn seam edge in, and slip-stitch opening together so that edges look the same all around.

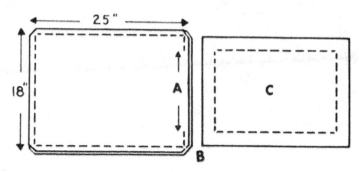

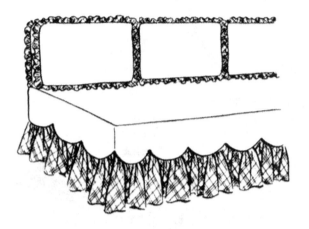

Daybed Cover of Felt and Chintz

▶▶▶ MAKE THE COVER of any color of felt that is right for your color scheme. Choose a chintz, gingham, or plastic fabric that is pretty with the felt, preferably in a check, plaid, or small floral design.

Cut felt to fit your pillows. Make a double bias ruffle of chintz 1¾ in. wide finished, to go around the pillows. This means that you cut ruffling 4¼ in. wide and use ⅜-in. seams. Gather the ruffle; stitch it to one pillow top, as shown. Lay second pillow piece over this and stitch again. Leave an opening large enough to insert pillow easily. Slip-stitch the closing after pillow is in place. If pillows are box-shaped, as in the daybed sketched, make two ruffles and insert one between each pillow piece and boxing strip, stitching in same manner as for single ruffled edge. Chintz flounce is of one thickness, finished with a 1½-in. hem. Hem flounce first. Then gather opposite edge; sew this edge to a 2-in.-wide muslin band or tape. Catch this tape neatly to the box spring of the daybed so that bed looks nice even when felt cover is removed.

Use edge of a dessert plate to shape the scallops. Measure and be sure scallops are right in size and depth so that you have all scallops complete across front and at ends.

Top and valance may be of one piece, corners mitered; or you can add valance, using a seam to join it to spread.

Edge of scallops in felt needs no finishing. If made of fabric, they should be lined, faced, or bound.

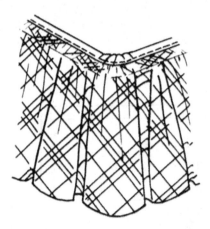
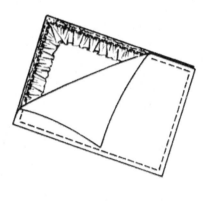

New Dress-up Tops for Beds

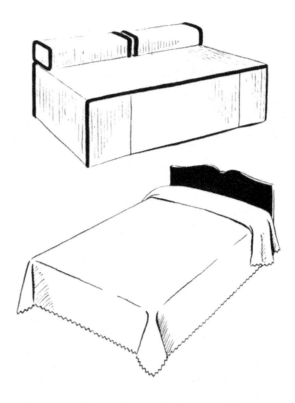

▶▶▶ VERY OFTEN a box spring and mattress without headboard are used in den, hall bedroom, even living room, and the idea is to make such a bed look as little like a bedroom piece as possible. The box cover in the illustration, made of a nubby rayon and cotton fabric, has bulk. Trimmed with moss fringe or cording, this fabric makes a substantial top. It is also ideal for covering the square box bolsters.

Lay the top piece on the bed right side down and lengthwise. Smooth it, cut it to fit top. Front and sides are cut crosswise of fabric so that grain runs lengthwise when on the couch. This means piecing the fabric as shown. When pin-fitting is done, mark seam line, both sides, with pencil or chalk. Remove cover, open seam, insert trimming, close again, and baste. Then stitch three thicknesses together. It is good to finish back of such a top exactly like front so that it can be reversed to save wear. Use a zipper at one corner to allow top to be slipped over bed easily. Finish bottom edge with ½-in. hem or with trimming.

Bolsters may be round or square. Use one piece to cover, unless you have strips left from top and can satisfactorily use them. Fit each bolster as carefully as you do top. Insert trimming in same way. Use a zipper at one edge on bottom to get bolster in and out, or slip-stitch seam together. The latter fastening is practical, since bolsters are for ornament only and covers need not be removed.

Regular beds with headboards can be covered with 72-in. felt, with an allowance of at least 1¼ yds. to cover pillows bolster-fashion. All edges can be pinked. Felt can also be trimmed with a double taffeta ruffle on two sides and one end, or with braid or fringe trim on the ends. If fabric is used, split one width through center lengthwise and add half of a split width to each side of a full width. This avoids having a seam down the center. Fabric may have a 1-in. hem on edges or be finished with cording, fringe, braid, or a ruffle of self or contrasting fabric. Corners may be left square, or rounded.

If a top is to have a lining, make top and lining the same size. Place right sides together. Stitch all around except for a 2-ft. opening on top edge. Press all seams open; clip surplus away at corners. Turn top right side out. Stitch ¾ in. from edge all around to hold lining in position.

Lace-trimmed Blanket Covers

▶▶▶LOVELY lace-trimmed blanket covers are a delight to own. They make the bed pretty even when its spread has been put aside for the night. In addition, such covers protect the blanket and are especially useful for those who read newspapers in bed. Printer's ink does come off, and covers are easier to launder than are blankets.

Make your cover of rayon challis, cotton challis, satin, or crepe. Choose a fabric that does not muss easily, that will not slide, but is firm enough in weave to stay straight on the bed, and one that lace or embroidery can flatter. Blanket covers should be pretty or else just a sheet type of spread such as hospitals use.

For a 33- or 36-in. single bed, use two lengths of 36-in. fabric (measure from head to foot, then from foot to within about 6 in. of floor) and two lengths of insertion and three of lace.

For a double bed use three lengths of 36-in. fabric or two of 50-in.; two lengths of insertion and three of lace.

When using two lengths of fabric, split one of these in half lengthwise and use it on either side of the full-width length. If selvages are tight, remove on all edges.

Make scant ¼-in. lengthwise hems on four edges where insertion will be stitched. Lap edge of insertion over turned edge and stitch as at A, starting all stitching from top end.

Pin lace along foot and side edges of cover ¼ to ⅜ in. from edge, wrong side of lace to right of fabric. Miter corners of lace as at B. Stitch along top edge of lace.

Turn cover to wrong side, turn fabric over, and stitch again along edge of lace, as in C. Trim off excess fabric, as at D. Finish top end of cover with 1-in. hem all the way across.

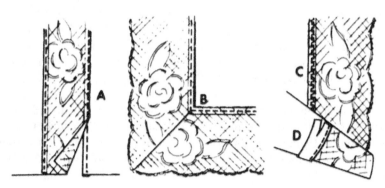

Summer Bedspread

▶▶▶ BEDSPREADS FOR SUMMER may be made of many types of fabric—printed cotton, plissé crepe, seersucker, organdie, dotted swiss, chintz, taffeta. Their cost is reasonable, considering how attractive they can be. With just a few measurements, they can be cut to fit any size of bed.

For type of spread illustrated, you need two lengths of fabric, measured from floor at foot to headboard, plus ½ yd. for cord covering and 1 yd. extra for each length for sham or pillow cover that is cut in one with spread. This will total approximately 8 yds. of fabric. You will need also 24 ft. of cord ¼ in. in diameter.

Select fabric 40 in. wide if bed is twin or three-quarter size. Try to choose a fabric 50 in. wide for bed 4 ft. 6 in. or wider; otherwise, you need three lengths of fabric.

If you are making a spread for a twin bed 3 ft. 3 in. wide and using fabric 40 in. wide, cut off ½ yd. for cord covering, then cut or tear 7½-yd. length in half crosswise, making two 3¾-yd. lengths. Cut one of these lengths in half lengthwise. Place narrow lengths with right sides together. Round off two corners, A.

Cutting bias for cording: Fold corners of ½-yd. piece on true bias (B). Crease and cut on fold. Mark and cut 24 ft. of true bias 1½ in. wide (C). Join strips together (D). Cover cord, using cording or zipper foot and longest machine stitch (E). Allow underside to extend ⅛ in. beyond top (F). This is called "seam blending" and is done to even thicknesses.

Stitch cording on right side of each side of center panel (G). (Remove selvage if it is tight before stitching cord to edges.)

Lay side pieces over cording—right sides together. Begin at the curved end in each case. Pin, then baste, full length of seams. It is important to baste so that one side cannot be tighter or looser than another. Stitch as at H.

Finish top edge with a ⅜-in. hem. Make a plain hem on two sides and across bottom. Before hemming bottom, make machine gathers ⅛ in. from edge on round corners, and ease in fullness (I). Put hem in with long slip-stitches or machine stitch.

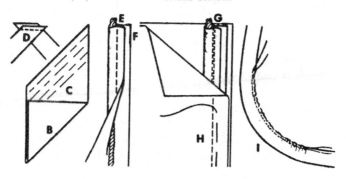

Bedroom Ensemble

▶▶▶ WHEN DRESSING UP your bedroom, make it gay with color. Chintz is lovely for this purpose, but if you find it beyond your pocketbook level, flowered percale will give you a pleasing result. Many a farmhouse has been made gay and charming with the printed fabric of feed bags. The necessity for economy need not discourage you.

The room illustrated took 20 yds. of printed cotton, 10 yds. of plain, and 6 of quilted, plus a pair of sheer glass curtains.

To make the spread, measure width and length of bed and buy enough quilted fabric for this. If bed is double, two lengths will be necessary. Split one width and seam these half widths to one whole width, thus paneling the center. Seam may be brought to right side and bound or covered with a band of the plain fabric. For bed flounce, allow twice two bed lengths and one width. Cut fabric crosswise so that flouncing extends from top of mattress (with blankets on) to floor. Stitch selvage edges together, making a ⅜-in. seam. Press seams open. A 1½-in. blind-stitched or machine-stitched hem should be used in the bottom. Top edge should be gathered and sewn to top piece, either with a cording or in a plain seam.

Measure front and sides of dressing table and buy double this amount in flowered material. Measure the skirt to come from top of dressing table to floor. This will allow you to turn 1¼ in. over at top and gather 1 in. on turned edge to make a heading as shown. To the bottom, add a 2-in. band to match bed flounce.

Draperies are straight and unlined. A 1½-in. hem, or a 2-in. band is used at bottom. Buckram pleating is stitched to the top edge so that pleats will be made and evenly spaced when rod is slipped through the buckram.

Cabin or Cottage Dress-up

▶▶▶ WHEN VACATION TIME comes, many women want to dress up the family's cabin or cottage—make it more homelike and give it eye-appeal. There is a rayon fabric that is ideal for the purpose. It comes in lovely colors of plaids and checks, is firm enough to require no lining, distinctive enough to be really good looking, and practical enough to serve for many summers.

To make a bedspread or daybed cover: Measure width and length of top of bed. You need approximately 2 yds. for top, 5 yds. for gathered flounce if it is to go all around, only 4 yds. if you use the ruffle on two sides and one end. This makes 18-in. flounce with 1-in. hems and allows one-half of additional length for fullness.

Stitch flounce lengths together, leaving selvage as seam finish. Clip seams (A) before turning and stitching hems (B). Gather top of flounce, using ruffler or stitching with a long stitch and drawing up bobbin thread. To fit top piece: Pin flounce to cover, wrong sides together, and stitch (C). Trim seam edges. Pin and baste bias binding over seam and stitch (D).

Ruffled sham: Finished sham should measure the same width as bed. Make center section about 27 in. long by 24 in. wide. Make ruffle 5 in. wide and one-and-one-half times the measurement of all four sides (about 3 yds.). Make narrow machine hem on edge of ruffle. Gather top of ruffle. Pin and baste shirred edge to sham piece, fulling gathers at corners (E) to prevent cupping. Finish in same manner as cover above. Sham is laid over a flat pillow.

Window trim: Use a double rod for this: drapery on inside rod and valance on outside. Use one width for each side of window, making the length to sill or floor, whichever is most appropriate. Make 1-in. hems on sides and bottom. Turn top, making casing of width needed to go on rod easily. Make valance one-and-one-half or two times window width. Make depth about one-sixth of drapery length plus heading, casing, and hem. Make 1-in. side and bottom hems. Turn top hem (F) and stitch. Divide in half and stitch to make casing and heading (G).

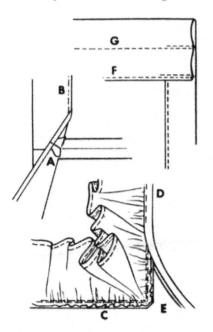

Dressing Tables

▶▶▶ THERE ARE almost as many ways to make a dressing table as there are ideas for covering them. The way shown here is ever so simple. You need a board as long and as deep as your space allows—one 40 in. long and 12 in. wide is ideal. A board 36 by 10 in. is a possibility, and if space warrants one, 60 by 8 in. can be made attractive.

Buy ½-in. pine lumber cut to size desired. Buy two sturdy metal brackets with enough screw holes to allow you to fasten board securely to the wall. Fasten shelf over brackets, as in A. Hang a mirror above this, or screw a piece of plate mirror above it. For covering for board, use fabric to match the skirt, or paint the board, or cover it with plastic or a pastel-color oilcloth. A glass cut to fit board and placed over fabric matching the skirt is best of all.

Make the skirt: Measure from wall to corner of shelf, across front of shelf to next corner, then to wall. If this is, say, 64 in., then provide approximately twice as much fabric for skirt width, or 128 in. Length should be as long as from top of shelf to floor, plus allowance for casing and hems. The allowance in the model was 3½ in.—1¼ in. at top and 2¼ in. at bottom. Make 1-in. hems at center-front opening. Make hems of desired depth on top and bottom of your dressing-table skirt. For the casing, stitch between hem and top edge, as shown in B. Run a cord through casing. Draw up cord so that fullness will appear as in C. Knot each end of cord and insert tacks, as at D. Bring casing around shelf, wall to wall, and tack it in place. Use long tacks with small heads so that you can conceal them in folds of gathers.

Some like to use two shelves—one 7 in. below first for toiletries. If you cover a table, proceed exactly as described for a shelf. If table sits away from wall, make skirt to go all the way around.

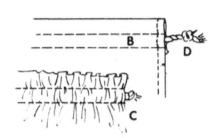

Dress up Your Windows

▶▶▶ WHEN YOU WANT all possible light from your windows, consider using the sheer fabrics. Nylon is straight and easy to handle in sewing, hanging, and washing. Use the pastel colors to make your room cheerful.

Fabrics are not too expensive. There are ranges to suit every pocketbook. Draperies and curtains do not require a great deal of sewing skill—rather, they need planning in color, design, and textures to be right for your windows, accurate measurements and straight cutting and stitching.

Privacy, view, light, and sunshine influence the dressing of windows.

The three windows shown represent: A, cottage curtains, especially suitable when light is desired in the room; B, a style for both light and view; C, a type of curtain to use when privacy is the essential.

Organdie, dotted swiss, lawn, ninon, nylon sheers—all are suitable for A. They may be white, cream, tan, or pastel. Light-green dotted swiss is very pretty with cream or butter-colored walls. White is always safe. For single windows, buy widest fabric in drapery department. Cut your ruffles on a true bias. Cut selvages off. French-seam widths as you join them. Hem edge by machine, using hemmer foot. Use two rods and narrow heading. Tiebacks may be of fabric lined with crinoline or two thicknesses of organdie. Sew ivory or plastic rings at ends to hook on edge of frame.

The type of ruffling shown in B can be bought ready-made, or you can make it of two 4-in.-wide bias ruffles or embroidery—the two ruffles stitched in center of a piece of twill tape. Stitch a decorative braid or lace or embroidery insertion over raw, gathered edges of ruffles; hem raw edges at bottom to make a neat finish. Tack the ruffled piece in place on outside edge of your window frame, laying pleats at the corners to square out nicely.

For privacy, as in C, use a sheer nylon or ninon for glass curtains. Make these full enough so that light can come in but no one can see in. Curtains should measure two and one-half to three times as wide as length of window rod to provide necessary fullness. Use a traverse rod and pulley equipment for the lined drapery so that it can be drawn to center to close when light is on in the room. Any good drapery department can provide you with equipment for traverse curtains and show you how to assemble them.

If valance is covered with the drapery fabric, cut this so that design runs up and down, rather than across. Make a piece to fit, allowing 2 in. to tuck in at top, at ends, and underneath. If seams are necessary, cut selvages off and press seam open. Sometimes a padding of two thicknesses of old sheet stretched over valance board first, gives a smoother finish. Stretch and tack the top securely so that there is no wrinkle, edge, or tack showing.

Dress up

▶▶▶ IF YOU WANT to dress up your table to make it different from every day, or if you want to please the family, make one or more of the items shown here.

Petticoat doilies: Make a set of base doilies with embroidery ruffles, and novelty or plain color place mats to go over them. For variety, use a quilt block made according to a pieced design. Use a color or print to harmonize with the dishes that will be used, and you will have a set that is far more attractive than you would believe possible at so low a cost. Petticoats can be used several times before they need washing; place mats wash quickly and easily.

Base doilies should be of plain bleached muslin 18 by 12 in. You can get six out of 1 yd. by careful cutting on lengthwise and crosswise grains. Each doily requires 1 yd. of 2½-in. ungathered embroidery edging.

Make a ⅛-in. hem on 18-in. edge of each muslin doily. Cut edging in half crosswise. Make a narrow hand hem in each end of each piece. Gather ruffles. Sew one to each 12-in. end, putting these on in a flat-fell seam, as shown in A.

One-color place mat: Plain-colored mats should be cut 13 in. on width and 19 in. on length and be finished with a narrow, rolled hem. If preferred, a narrow hem may be turned to right side and narrow rick rack stitched over hem, one stitching holding hem and rick rack. Take care in doing this that rick rack is basted on easily so that it cannot draw tight.

Quilt piece block: Make as carefully as if you were making it for a treasure quilt. Use narrow, even seams; make perfect corners. Turn outside edges of basket motif under and appliqué this to a piece of plain fabric, as shown. At ends, add band of fabric to match motif. Finished doily is ½ in. larger on ends and sides than is base doily. Make a lightweight lining of same size as pieced doily. Place right sides together; stitch two sides and one end; turn right side out; square corners. Close open end and your doily is ready for use over its petticoat.

Everyday dining: If there are children and laundry is a problem, buy a pretty piece of chintz, cretonne, or percale—one with colors that will flatter your dishes. Hem the ends and the sides if selvages are marked, using ¼-in. hems. Buy a length of clear plastic cloth to go over this colorful base. All you need do is wipe the plastic carefully after each meal with a damp cloth, then a dry cloth. Thus with little effort you can have a nice partylike cloth

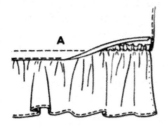

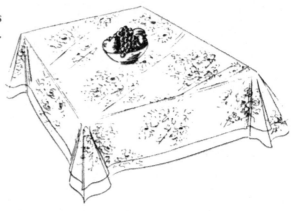

Your Table

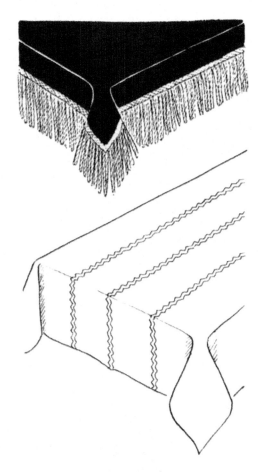

with no laundry. You and your family are sure to enjoy it.

If your table surface is nice, buy remnants of pretty, colorful fabrics and make place mats 13 by 18 in. Make a narrow hem on all four edges of each, doing this by hand or machine; or stitch rick rack on all edges. Ease the rick rack on so that it cannot tighten; just let points peep out a scant ¼ in. Cut a clear plastic fabric mat for use over each colorful woven fabric mat. If you have damask cloths that are worn thin or faded, tint them a pretty color. The plastic fabric will subdue the color somewhat. In this way, get a new color scheme that harmonizes with your dishes or glassware.

Valued linens that require too much time to iron can also be used under plastic.

A little precaution in cutting plastic is to "true" edges with a yardstick, marking a line with pencil, then pinking or cutting on the pencil line. Some like to make the plastic more festive by putting a 2½-in. pinked ruffle of plastic fabric all around the cloth, gathering ½ in. from top edge to provide a heading.

Holiday dining: There was a time not so long ago when a damask cloth was as necessary for the table on Thanksgiving and Christmas as a white uniform is to a registered nurse. Today it is the fashion—and a gay one—to buy turkey red, or Christmas green, or bright blue percale, and make a special cloth to fit your table. Use your silence cloth underneath, just as though the new cloth were expensive damask. Percale is 36 in. wide, and for an oblong table you need two widths plus 3 in. more overhang at each end than you have at sides. This 3 in. is for hems, shrinkage, etc.

Cut the fabric into two equal lengths, and join two sides by making a ¼-in. seam, or lap the selvage edges, using the machine edge stitcher to hold the two together. Put hems in, making a ¼-in. turn and a 1¼-in. hem. Some like to add fringe or braid to the outside edges. Or, instead of fringe, stitch on three lines of rick rack—one over the center seam and one 6 in. away on either side to panel the center.

You will find this type of cloth a good investment. You can use it at New Year's, Halloween, for February birthday parties —in so many ways. Less expensive than damask and easier to launder, it will last for years and years and provide good cheer with each use. You will find, also, that such a cloth will help to enhance the color of your centerpiece, your decorations, even the china.

Colorful Felt for Girl's or Boy's Room

▶▶▶ FELT IS so easy to use and is colorful, practical, and reasonably inexpensive. Many things can be done with it in a minimum of time to brighten a room and make it more pleasing. It is especially suitable for a dormitory room.

A *felt cover over a table* makes a pleasing surface on which to spread out books and work. It is as handy at home as at school.

A *bedspread of felt* is ideal, especially if a room is small and the bed serves to seat guests, or if the student is a lounger. Buy 72-in. width in a length long enough for bed plus necessary overhang at bottom —usually 2½ yds. will do.

Felt-covered pillows are as practical as they are attractive and are ever so easy to make. For example, cut two squares 3 in. larger on all sides than pillow. Make a diagonal slot at 3-in. line on each corner of one piece. Sew buttons to correspond on other square, and button your cover on. Lacking buttons, punch two holes 1 in. apart in both squares at each corner. Pull a gayly-colored cord through, and tie in a bow on each corner.

Streamers for snapshots: Every young person has treasured snaps or pictures of his idols of the moment that he likes to have on display at all times. Strips of 3-in.-wide felt, topped with 1½-in.-wide bows of felt, make an ideal resting place for many types of pictures and clippings. These can be pinned, pasted, or clipped on and are easy to replace. The streamers can be as decorative as they are convenient. Two such streamers about 33 in. long make a pleasing gift for any young person going away to school.

Bedspread can be of one color felt, pillows and streamers of another. Buy suitable colors, and pink edges of all pieces, if possible, to add that extra decorative note.

Gifts You Can Make

Santa's Stockings

▶▶▶ HANGING UP the stocking is a happy custom, one that appeals to big and little children at Christmas. Big, bulky stockings are especially useful when Santa has miscellaneous sizes and shapes of stocking presents.

Three giant and two wee stockings can be made out of 1 yd. of 36-in. red felt. (Use green or white or blue felt if you prefer.) They are so easy to make and they last for years. Some like to put an initial on, so that each stocking is at once identifiable. This can be done with rick rack, braid, press-on initials, or letters cut from felt or embroidered on with yarn or floss.

To chalk out: Fold square yard in half as diagram shows. Measure in from corner A 10½ in. for B and down 11 in. for C. E is 9 in. to right of corner D, and F is 4 in. from E. G is 7 in. above E and 9 in. to right of C. Chalk a line straight up from F for about 5 in. Chalk a line from A to bottom of stocking 1 in. to right of D. Connect B and G; then make a curve from G to line F and around to E. Curve corner D as shown. Make nice, round, jolly-looking curves; then cut out first stocking. Place this on remaining felt and chalk two remaining large ones. Two small stockings can be cut as indicated on diagram. These are ideal for hanging on the tree with pennies, with a new dollar bill, or with tiny candies—gum drops or lollipops.

You can use pinking shears to cut all edges. Stitch stockings from right side ¼ in. from edge. Stitch back for 2 in. on each at points A and B to prevent seam from ripping. From scraps, cut hangers ½ in. wide and 3 in. long. Fold them in half to form loops, and stitch to back seam of each stocking.

Before stitching stockings, add sequins, beads, pearls, even glistening buttons, for sparkle. After stitching, apply cotton or fur to the tops, or use a ruffle of taffeta or ribbon—anything to make them gay and decorative and welcomed as gifts.

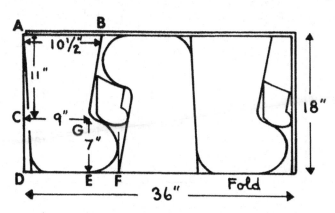

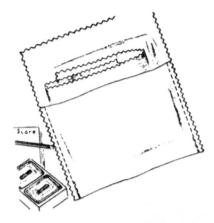

Card-play Cover

▶▶▶ WHEN YOU TRAVEL, go picnicking, or play cards at the beach, a card-play cover is convenient. The bands prevent melds or tricks from blowing away. It is easy to fold up into its own case, which provides room also for cards, score pad, and pencil.

It makes a perfect gift for a man going on a fishing or hunting trip. Make one and see how practical it is; your next Christmas-gift problem for the men on your list will be solved.

Buy 1 yd. of 36-in. felt for cover, ¼ yd. in contrasting color for bands—say dark brown with bands of turquoise.

Half a yard of 36-in. clear plastic fabric will make the case. Buy thread to match both colors of felt. Use darker on bottom and lighter on top.

Straighten edges of square yard by drawing lines with ruler and chalk. Pink along these lines. (Plain cut edges can be used, if preferred.) Cut 30 in. off ¼-yd. piece. Divide 9-in. edge into four parts; draw straight chalk lines down 30-in. strip. Pink edges and along chalk lines so that you have four even strips pinked on both edges, and along ends. Cut off a small square (about 2¼ in.) from each strip.

Measure in 7 in. from all sides of 36-in. square piece and lay strips on these lines, overlapping ends 3 in., as at A. Pin, keeping strips in even square. Stitch ends in position, as indicated, starting each corner as at B, stitching around ends of two strips and back to B. Divide center section of each strip (C to D) into seven even sections (2½ in.); mark with chalk. Stitch across bands, as in E to make pockets for tricks or melds. Pin one small 2¼-in. square near each corner, as at F. Stitch close to edges.

For plastic holder, fold one 18-in. edge over 14 in.; stitch edges together on each side, as in G. (Stitching over paper helps to keep stitching line straight.) Pink seams, continuing around top edges (H). Top folds down to make envelope effect. For ease in carrying, fold card cover into thirds, both ways.

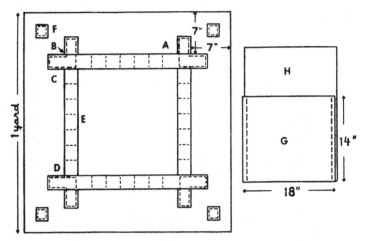

Bean Bags

▶▶▶ HERE IS SOMETHING for youngsters to throw that won't harm either windows or heads. Toy bean bags, like the cat shown, are popular with most children, especially when you let them help make their own. A quarter yard of 36-in. felt makes two bags, and you will need about ⅔ cup of beans per bag.

Use a 6½-in. plate to draw around for body, a 3¼-in. cup of glass for head. Cut two circles of each size for each bag, as in A. Cutting each piece individually, pink all edges, if possible. Use scraps for ears, feet, and tail. On one small circle design eyes, nose, and mouth with chalk, turning corners of mouth up for good cheer. With contrasting thread, stitch around features five or six times.

Pin two large circles together. Fold small squares diagonally in half and pink, as in B. Insert these two folded pieces for feet between edges at C. Five inches from feet insert tail at D. Pin in place. Put a pin 3 in. from feet at E, another pin 1½ in. from first one, F. Stitch edges together (⅜-in. seams), stitching from F around circle to E, leaving 1½-in. small opening, as shown. Fill with dried beans. Place pins 1½ in. from opening to hold beans out of way while stitching on head.

Pin two small circles together. Insert two ears between edges above eyes, G.

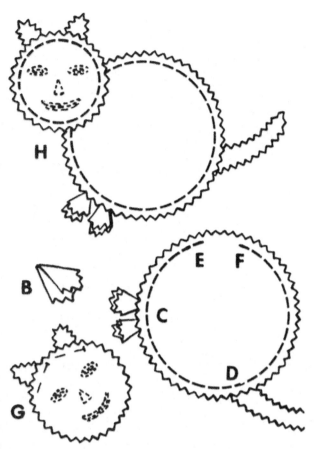

Insert edges of body between edges of head, overlapping 1 in. or more. Pin. (A few beans can be put inside head.) Stitch completely around head, as in H, and bean bag is finished.

Make the second toy in same way, or arrange feet and tail differently for another position, or make an owl face and omit tail.

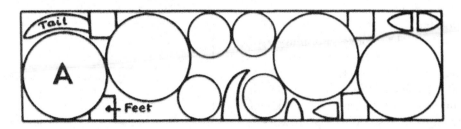

Glove and

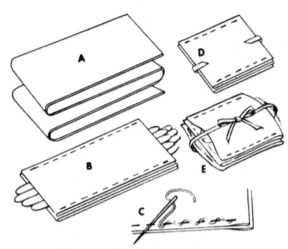

▶▶▶ *Glove case:* These cases are easy to make and can be used for dresser drawer or suitcase. Buy 2⅔ yds. of 5½-in. rayon ribbon in your favorite color.

Stitch cut ends together, using a ⅜-in. seam, with seam on wrong side of ribbon. Press seam open.

Fold piece right side out into one long strip of two thicknesses of ribbon. Pin edges together to keep them even. Fold in four even folds, as in A. Pin selvage edges together on each side so that you have three pockets for gloves, two at one end and one at the other.

With buttonhole twist in matching or contrasting color, sew edges of each side together with a long running-stitch, as in B. Make stitches about ⅜ in. long and sew through all thicknesses. Start and finish with a back-stitch to prevent ends from pulling apart. Do not draw thread too tight.

For decoration, you can go back over each stitch with an overcast-stitch to make a twisted running-stitch, as in C. If desired, an initial or name may be embroidered on ribbon before sides are sewn together. This in dark 6½-in. ribbon makes an ideal gift for a man.

Stocking case: Buy 1⅓ yds. of same ribbon as used for glove case, plus ½ yd. narrow ribbon for tie ends. This case is folded and sewed in the same way as glove case, but will be shorter in length, about 6 in. Cut tie-end ribbon in half. Using small back- or whipping stitches, sew one 9-in. length on fold at each end of case, as in D. Bring ends up and tie in bow, as in E.

Next time you give stockings as a gift, add that "special touch" by inserting them in a case like this, that you have made yourself. Either of these cases may be made very nicely of strips of fabric—all seams concealed, of course.

Ribbon stocking holder: An envelope folder can be quickly and easily made of 5¾-in. rayon-satin ribbon. For a three-pocket holder, buy 1⅔ yds. ribbon. Be sure it has selvage, not cut edges. The holder sketched was made of pale blue satin, trimmed with a pair of ribbon garters.

Join ends of ribbon with ⅜-in. seam. Clip corners of seam. Press. Fold ribbon so that seam is 9 in. to right of left-hand fold, as in diagram. Crease fold at both ends. Baste selvage edges together. From right to left, place six pins 4 in. apart on upper and lower edges.

To make pockets: Bring A to C, folding on B. Baste together, as at H. Stitch across both ends of pocket, as at I. Bring C to E, folding on D. Baste together, as at J. Stitch across both ends, as at K. Fold

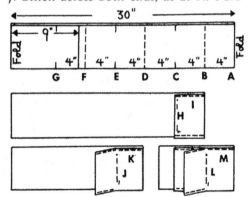

Stocking Protectors

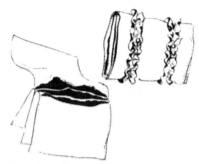

first pocket back over second. Bring E to meet G, folding on F. Baste together, as at L. Stitch across both ends, as at M. Stitch from G to left-hand fold on both edges. Leave thread ends long enough so that they can be threaded into needle and all ends fastened under folds of pockets. Edges may be finished with featherstitching, or lazy-daisy motifs may be embroidered on the cover.

A pair of garters can be made and used to go around the stocking case. For each garter, use 10-in. piece of ¼-in. elastic and 15 in. of ⅝-in. ribbon. Pin one end of ribbon and elastic together, centering elastic under ribbon. Pin opposite end of elastic to ribbon 1½ in. from end. Pin ribbon and elastic every 2 or 3 in. so that fullness will be even. Stitch together, using long stitch and stretching elastic as you stitch. Overlap ends, keeping long end of ribbon on top. Sew ends together. A pearl, small flower, or rosette of lace may be used for decoration.

Bags for stockings: We all know that hangnails, rings, and everyday handling play havoc with our nylon stockings, even when we are reasonably cautious.

The newest trick in protection is this: Buy ½ yd. of cheesecloth at your drugstore or favorite five-and-ten. Fold this, selvages at top, and stitch the sides up to within 2 in. of selvages. Make a 1-in. hem in each top or selvage edge, stitching back on each end of these hems so that they will not pull out. Cut two lengths of white wrapping cord or tape, each three times as long as your hems. Lace one cord through both hems from right-hand side, other from left-hand side. Tie a knot in each cord where ends meet, as diagram shows. Then, as you draw cord from each side of bag, fullness will come in evenly and easily.

Put your stockings in the bag, draw the cords, and wash them in lukewarm, mild suds. Rinse twice, squeeze excess water out, then hang bag up, stockings inside for drying. If you wish your stockings to look like new when dry, instead of leaving them to dry in the bag, carefully smooth them out on a bath towel. The towel will not be soiled, because the stockings are clean. When they are dry, fold them carefully, and put them in small plastic bags so that no harm can come to them in your dresser drawer, such as in catching them on the drawer as it is closed or catching on your rings when you reach for another pair.

To make the plastic bags, buy ¼ yd. of clear plastic. This will enable you to see the stockings you want to wear. Cut the bags 9 in. square. Fold through center, seam sides, and gather tops with two rows of elastic sewing thread. Bags such as these are a great convenience in traveling and will definitely protect your stockings. Try a set and you'll be making them for gifts and selling the idea to your friends. Nylons cost money and are fragile, but we can easily protect and save them with these bags.

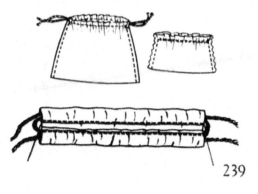

Shoe Covers

▶▶▶ WHENEVER YOU TRAVEL, extra shoes must go along. Very often you don't care to take a bag expressly for shoes, but you do want to have your shoes covered. Three kinds of shoe cases are suggested here. Many types of fabric are suitable, but it is an advantage to be able to see the shoe inside the case. Visibility can be achieved by using either old stockings or clear plastic fabric. Size of shoe cases can vary for individual needs, but the average for women's shoes is 7½ in. wide by 15 in. long; for men's, 9 by 18 in. In cases for masculine use, the darker shades of tape or binding are preferable—navy, dark brown, green, wine, or grey.

Stocking shoe covers: Cut off the feet above the ankle of stockings. Stitch twice across cut ends. Turn right side out and use these for covers. Runs do not interfere with efficiency. Such covers are handy, washable, and readily packable.

Drawstring shoe bags: Men have shown a preference for the type of cover that can be closed at the top. A square yard of clear plastic or fabric will make four average-sized shoe bags (for two pairs of shoes). Turn 1-in. hems on two opposite edges, as at A. Fold in half by bringing hems together. Divide into four sections and mark with pins or chalk, as at B. Stitch ½ in. away on both sides of these marks, as at C, stitching from fold to edge of crosswise hem but not across hems. Seam ends together (D). Cut between stitching lines with pinking shears, as at E, or, if preferred, cut a plain edge. Cut two ½-yd. pieces of cord or twilled tape for each shoe case. Use a safety pin to draw a piece of tape through the casing at top of bag. Sew or tie ends of tape together. Insert a second tape in same way. Draw up opening by pulling a loop of tape on each side, as at F.

Women like this shoe bag for its convenience. The loops make it easy to hang shoes up. Some people like to hang shoes for a special dress on the hanger with dress, especially when away from home.

Bound shoe bags: Use bias binding or ribbon to finish these cases. About 1¼ yd. is needed per case. Cut squares of plastic, as at G. Fold in half lengthwise, and round off corners (H). Make 1½-in. loop at one end of binding. Start at top with loop, as at I, and bind edges together.

Total cost of such covers is very small, when you use inexpensive, lightweight plastic fabric and cotton bias for binding. A set of three pairs of these makes a welcome going-away gift.

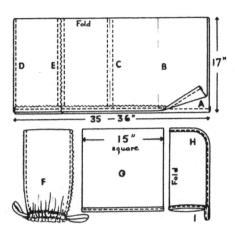

Sailcloth Handy Bag

▶▶▶ BUY UPHOLSTERY-WEIGHT sailcloth. This fabric is bright in color and firm enough to hold its shape. Royal blue with white tape trim was used for the model illustrated. You need one spool of matching thread and ¾ yd. of 32-in. fabric.

Straighten crosswise edges by tearing. Lengthwise, your piece measures 26 in.

To make a bag 13 in. deep: Measure on one selvage 13 in. plus 3 in. for hem. Tear crosswise on this line. For pocket, measure in from selvage 12 in. and tear lengthwise, as at A. For strap handles, tear remaining piece into four 2½- by 20-in. strips.

For straps lap two selvage ends ¼ in. and stitch along both selvage edges. This gives you two 39½-in. strips. Fold each strip lengthwise. Stitch a ¼-in. seam. Press seam open and turn inside out, centering seam, as in B.

Make 1-in. hem turn on one 12-in. edge of pocket piece. Place folded tape under hem so that ⅛ in. of tape shows, as at C; stitch hem. Turn one 32-in. edge of bag piece over ¼ in., then 2¾ in. for hem. Place folded twill tape under this and stitch to within ½ in. of each selvage. On one side, as at D, mark exact position of pocket with pins. Lay a 1-in. fold on each side so that pocket measures 6¾ in. plus ½ in. on each side to go under the straps (see E). To conceal pocket seam, bring pocket down and stitch bottom of pocket to bag, stitching through folds on both sides. When pocket is lifted back into position, the seam is inside it. Stitch sides of pocket.

Begin at bottom of bag, pin straps on, forming loops at top, as at F and G. Stitch straps as shown, stitching up, along each edge of handle and down other side. When both handles are securely in place, lap selvage edges of bag at sides ¼ in. and stitch up and back, making a lapped seam. Fold right sides of bag together. Begin at lapped seam; stitch across bottom, pivot, and return. To make box corners at each side of bag: Fold the corner into a point. Make a 2-in. stitching across the point, as in H. Stitch this twice. When bag is right side out, you have a 2-in. flat or "standing" bottom. Press and clip all thread ends.

Smaller or larger versions may be made for sewing bags, school or shopping carryalls, bag for golf-ball practice, art portfolios. Simply make the proportions to fit your needs, measure carefully, sew neatly and securely as suggested, and a good result is yours.

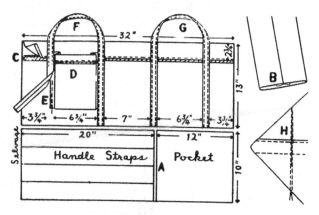

A Rucksack Carryall

▶▶▶ MAKE ONE of these handy, time-saving carryalls, and every friend who sees this attractive and practical rucksack will want one.

Buy 1⅜ yds. of 36-in. cotton rep, drill, or plain-colored bed ticking.

For the rucksack, tear crosswise of the fabric a perfect square, measured from width. Tear a 13-in. piece from one end of smaller strip for base pocket. Tear off a 19- by 13½-in. strip for over-arm handle. The remaining 4-in. strip may be used for small inside pockets if desired.

Make a ¼-in. turn and then a ⅜-in. turn for a center-stitched hem all around the large square of fabric which forms rucksack. Stitch. For base pocket, make a ¼-in. hem turn on three raw edges of small square. Center this small square on *wrong* side of big square at right angles to corners. Stitch on three turned edges, as broken lines indicate at A. With razor blade cut from firm cardboard or corrugated board a square ½ in. smaller than finished pocket. This slips into bottom pocket when carryall is used as in B. If a soft effect is desired, as in C, the cardboard can be removed.

Faced slash: Mark rucksack square for three 2¼-in. slashes (see D, E, F). Note direction each slash takes in each corner. Cut three 3½-in. strips of twill tape. Lay one of these on right side of slash, as at G, marking ends of slash with pins. Stitch as shown and cut between stitching. Turn tape to wrong side and stitch around the slot twice, as in H, for firmness and neatness.

Make handle by folding strip of fabric crosswise, right side in, 19-in. edges together. Pin. Taper ends so that they measure 4 in., as at I and J, and full width at center (K). Stitch on two sides and across one end. Turn right side out. Turn in raw ends of open end; pin. Place two ends across unslashed corner, as at L, and stitch across handle three or four times to hold securely.

Now for magic! See the attractive form it takes! Lay rucksack right side down. Bring corner with handle toward center, and pull handle through slot D, then slot F, then E. Now open rucksack up again, pack it full, then close it—and you will be delighted with this practical carryall.

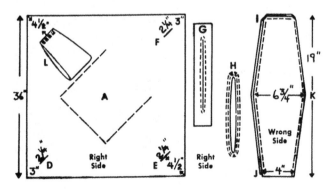

Make Your Own Carpet Bag

▶▶▶ A BAG THAT opens up wide is easy to carry—is a real convenience for knitting, sewing, for baby things, for shopping, for books, and for many, many other uses. Originally such bags were sturdy and made of carpet fabric, and some had handles of wrought iron. Today practically every art-needle shop, every five-and-dime, carries wooden handles. You need, besides a pair of handles, 1/3 yd. of 40-in. fabric, one spool of thread, and six buttons.

For straps, cut a 3-in. strip from each selvage edge. For bag, bring 12-in. edges together, right side in; seam lengthwise edges, as at A, then across bottom, as at B. Double-stitch seams. To box each bottom corner, fold flat and stitch across twice, 2½ in. from point, as at C; then bring points over on bottom seam and tack them securely in position, as at D. Turn bag right side out.

Turn selvage edge over raw edge of each of 3-in. strips. Stitch through center, as at E. Cut each strip into three straps.

Turn a ½-in. hem to wrong side around top of bag. On one side of bag, pin one strap at center of top edge, and one strap 2 in. to either side of center straps, as in F. Repeat on opposite side. Stitch top hem, catching ends of straps in place under hem edge. Pull straps to right side through slot in handles. Turn corners of each strap under diagonally, to make points, catching with secure stitches. Sew a button on right side of each point, sewing through strap and bag and sewing firmly so that handles will be secure and bag will look nice enough to be carried anywhere and serve you conveniently years on end. Top corners can be folded in and pressed, if desired. Large wooden or plastic knitting needles may be used for handles if preferred. If used, omit straps and make hem large enough to insert knitting needle along each side, points of needles opposite each other.

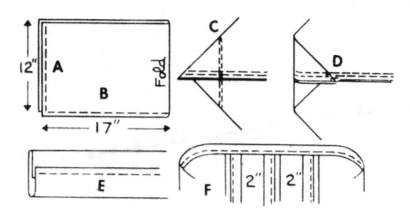

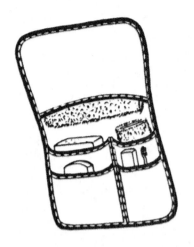

Traveling Bath Kit

▶▶▶ WITH THIS WATERPROOF plastic kit for bath needs, you can travel without worries about wet or damp wash cloths in your suitcase. Large pocket holds towel. Smaller pockets are for washcloth, soap holder, nail brush, toothbrush in its holder, and tooth paste. Tuck in a shower cap, and you're equipped for hotel or motel.

Buy 1/3 yd. of 36-in. plastic and one 3-yd. package of contrasting cotton bias binding. The kit sketched was white opaque plastic with medium-blue binding.

Cut a 5½- by 12-in. piece off one end. Fold longer piece in half crosswise. To shape, 1 in. from each edge of fold trim off ¾ in., as at A and B; then taper each edge to a distance of 7 in. from fold, as at C and D. Open out and fold lengthwise. Trim one end from 1 in. in on fold to nothing at corners, as at E. Bind this end and opposite end with bias binding. Then bind one long edge of 5½-in. piece.

Fold ends of larger piece to within 1 in. of either side of center fold, as in F. Even raw edges and pin so that pockets are fuller on top than on underside. On side G, 3 in. from left-hand fold, stitch in 6½ in. from top edge to form under pocket for soap holder. Lay 5½-in. strip over side G, raw edge even with fold. Pin at sides to hold. Round four corners, as shown. Baste kit all around edges.

Fold a 7¼-in. strip of bias in half and lay it straight across left side 5 in. from bottom edge, as at H. Pin in position so that section I has ½ in. fullness at pocket top. Turn this bias under pocket at top, and stitch the strip in place, stitching along both edges.

On outside of kit, stitch a piece of bias over center fold from J to K. Bind all around outer edges.

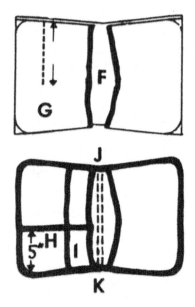

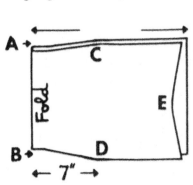

Shirt or Blouse Traveling Case

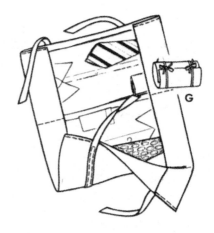

▶▶▶ A FABRIC traveling case to hold shirts or blouses in a suitcase is a convenience. This case is easy to pack, protects, is easy to open and close, makes an ideal gift. It can be monogrammed to make it especially attractive. Two fabrics are used—one for outside, one for lining. Moiré or Roman stripe faille is ideal for outside and satin for inside or use brown, black, or gray with flesh lining, or navy with light blue or flesh. Each piece should be 31 in. long and 29 in. wide. If you buy 40-in. fabric, a glove case can be made from leftover material. You will need 3 yds. of ¾-in. rayon ribbon, also.

Cut ribbon in half. Center each piece on right side of dark fabric 8 in. from lengthwise edges, as at A-A. Place a pin on each ribbon 2 in. from one edge, as at B-B. Place a second pin 15 in. from first, as at C. Stiteh both ribbons in position, as shown. Fold ends of ribbon in toward center of square and pin them out of the way while you are stitching. Lay lining square right side down over right side of other square. Pin edges together. Stitch along four sides, leaving at D a 5-in. opening. Press seams open. Clip off corners. Turn right side out. Turn edges of 5-in. opening inside. Baste across this. Press case, then stitch around it, keeping ¼ in. from edge. Lay case flat with lining side up. Fold lengthwise edges over 4 in., as at E, and stitch across each end. Stitch also across each fold, about 12 in. down, as at F-F.

Shirts can easily be laid crosswise of case with underwear, ties, handkerchiefs, and other items tucked under sides. Bring top section down over center section, fold bottom over this, and tie ribbons, as shown in G.

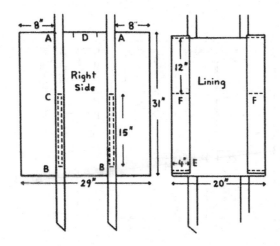

Stationery Holders

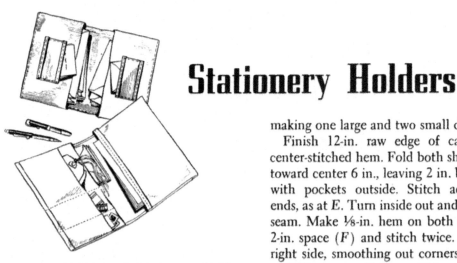

▶▶▶ THESE TWO fabric paper holders for men and women are not bulky and will keep correspondence supplies uncreased and readily available.

A man's writing case takes ⅓ yd. of 31-in. sailcloth. For the woman's, buy 1½ yds. of 4¼-in. grosgrain ribbon.

Center-stitched hem: Both cases make use of the center-stitched hem. Fold over one raw edge ¼ in. to right side; fold again ¼ in. and stitch through center, as in A, making hem on outside of case so that paper cannot catch on it.

Sailcloth case: Tear off 4½-in. strip from one selvage edge for pocket. Lay strip on larger piece, long raw edge of strip 4½ in. from selvage (B). Stitch as shown. Turn pocket piece toward selvage. For pocket sections, stitch through center (C) and again through one section (D), making one large and two small divisions.

Finish 12-in. raw edge of case with center-stitched hem. Fold both short ends toward center 6 in., leaving 2 in. between, with pockets outside. Stitch across all ends, as at E. Turn inside out and French-seam. Make ⅛-in. hem on both edges of 2-in. space (F) and stitch twice. Turn to right side, smoothing out corners.

Ribbon case: Cut one 10-in. and four 9½-in. lengths. For small pockets, divide remaining 6-in. piece in half. Finish long edges of small pockets with center-stitched hems, stitching one edge and basting other. Center pocket pieces on two 9½-in. pieces, as in G; stitch close to two sides and through center of one basted edge.

Finish raw edges of 10-in. piece with center-stitched hems (H). Lay one 9½-in. piece without pockets on each side of this piece, overlapping edges ⅛ in. Baste and stitch, as at I. (Ribbon may pucker if not basted first.) Join other 9½-in. pieces to side pieces along raw edges J and K, using French seams so that case, when finished, will appear as shown. Pocket openings should be toward center. Turn to right side. Stitch side edges together, as at L.

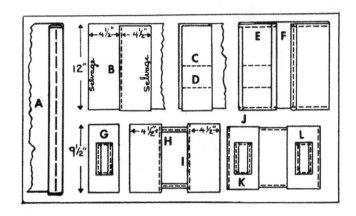

Map Case of Leatherette

▶▶▶ ONE-FOURTH yd. of 50-in. leatherette with ½ yd. of ½-in. elastic will make two cases. Buy leatherette in a desired color, possibly to match car color, or in bright color so that it is easily seen in glove compartment. Every person who drives a car is interested in a map case, one to hold three or four often-referred-to maps, possibly a half dozen for a long trip.

Pink or cut edges. Divide the ¼-yd. piece into four 12-in. sections. Fold one 9-in. piece in half lengthwise, right side out. Crease on fold to make a straight line. Lay second piece wrong side up and place creased fold ½ in. from edge, as at A in diagram. Use paper clips at points A and B to hold pieces together to prevent slipping while stitching. With top piece opened out flat, stitch from A to B, using a long stitch. Fold C over D, and stitch twice across each end through three thicknesses, as at E and F, thus making two compartments for maps. Bring flap G over to make cover.

Cut ½ yd. of elastic into two 9-in. lengths. Lap cut edges ½ in. and stitch three or four times to make a circular band to hold cover in position. Name or initials may be painted on freehand or with aid of small stencil, or metal initials may be secured to flap. This makes ideal gift or a good item for bazaar selling.

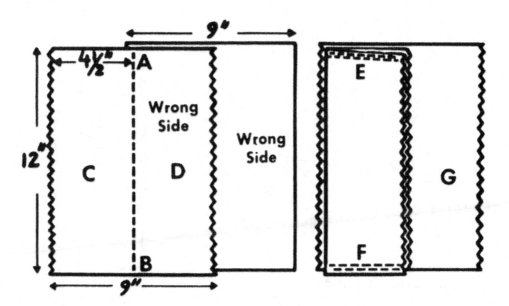

Bathing-suit Bag

▶▶▶ SOLVE THE PROBLEM of carrying home a wet bathing suit with this handy roll-up carrier. Convenient pockets for sun-tan lotion and other beach needs. Buy 1 yd. of 31-in. sailcloth and 6 yds. of No. 5 cotton bias binding to match or for contrast.

You can also make this bag of leatherette and use for traveling. Make it of moiré or brocade, line it throughout, and use as a container for knitting or sewing. Make a small version in tweed or flannel to match a suit and use it as a handbag.

Straighten fabric ends. Fold fabric in half crosswise. Pin selvages together at each side. Measure, as shown in diagram, and mark with pins or chalk. Round all corners, as indicated, for ease in binding edges. Cut on lines. Bind all around.

For pocket, cut one piece (A), rounding lower edge and corners and using selvage for top edge. Bind bottom and sides. Stitch to right side of one flap of carrier, as at B.

For strap handles, mark 2-in. strips, as at C. Cut through both fabric thicknesses. Seam together the four 12-in. and the two 10 in. strips into a continuous band. Turn raw edges in ¼ in. toward each other and stitch. Lay on right side of carrier. Pin, as indicated. Stitch from D to E, forming a box at each end.

Stitch pocket through center to form two divisions, or make three divisions to fit your own needs. Lay carrier right side down; place suit in center and fold in side flaps, B and F. Then bring G up and fold carrier in half at middle. Bring top flap H over and draw long front loop through short back loop, so that carrier appears as illustrated above.

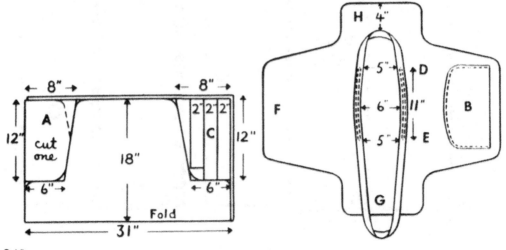

Beach or Camp Roll

▶▶▶ IN SUMMER, nothing is handier than a roll to stretch out on in the sun on roof, at beach, in shade, on picnic grounds.

Buy 4 yds. of waterproof sail cloth or awning fabric in a color pleasing to you. Buy one bat of comfort-type cotton. Roll should be made 2 yds. long and width desired—not less than 24 in. Cut a strip 3 in. wide from one selvage edge to make tie strings and handles. Turn raw edge of this strip over a scant one-third of its width lengthwise, turn selvage edge over a scant one-third, and stitch through center, as in A in diagram. Cut two tie strings and two handles, each 18 in. long.

Fold fabric in half crosswise, wrong sides together. Pin selvage edges together. Turn edges in on other side ½ in. and pin. Insert ends of ties and handles between edges on either side of pad at pillow end, as at B and C. Pin, then stitch each twice so that they will hold securely. Stitch with longest machine stitch from fold down one side, as at D, then across bottom, stitching ¼ in. from edge. Open out cotton bat. Cut a 2-yd. length. Fold one end over 12 in. Lay cotton inside folded fabric with double thickness of cotton at top fold for pillow section. Bat should be straight and smooth before stitching. Cotton will not reach bottom of pad. Let it come as far as it will.

Begin at fold again and stitch down selvage side, again ¼ in. from edge. Loosen top tension and stitch even rows across, spacing these 12 in. from fold, then 6 in. apart until all rows are stitched. This is to hold cotton in place. Since thickness of pad tends to crowd material forward on top, stretch underside and ease in top as you stitch crosswise. Fold roll up from bottom in five folds, like an accordion, so that all rest on pillow part. Square side edges together and tie strings at top. Carry by loop handles.

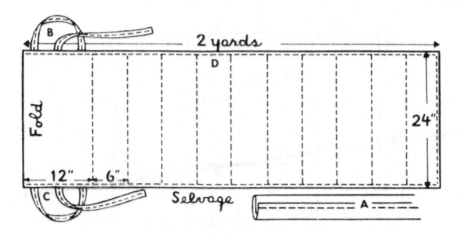

Rainy-day Accessories Holder

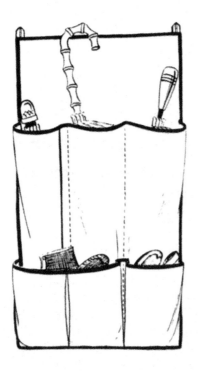

▶▶▶ YOUR FAMILY, as well as you yourself, will enjoy having one of these holders for umbrellas, boots, and rubbers. It can be hung on any door and helps keep these necessary nuisances out of the way.

You need ¾ yd. of 36-in. oilcloth, leatherette, or heavyweight plastic, plus 3 yds. of bias binding.

Lay cloth face down. With yardstick and pencil straighten edges; then mark and cut as diagram shows. Cut on line A, then on line B. Divide the 22-in. strip into three equal parts, as indicated. Divide bottom of 14-in. strip into thirds, marking each division 19 in. up from bottom edge.

Bind edges C, D, and B. Lay wrong side of D over right side of back piece, matching and pinning pencil divisions. Stitch two center lines, as at E and F; then stitch outside edges together (G), thus making three pockets.

Lay wrong side of B over D, bottom edges together and divisions again matching. Stitch on right-hand line H only, then on both edges, to make two pockets.

Lay pleats along bottom edge close to stitching lines, as indicated. Stitch across pleats to hold, as at I. Lay pleat in top of wide pocket and whip edges together, as at J.

Bind outside edges all around. Make two loops, for hanging, at top corners.

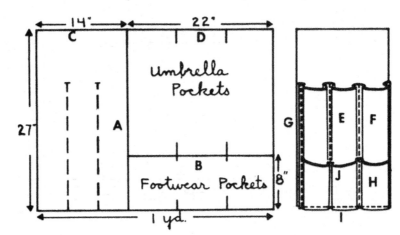

Card-table Cover

▶▶▶ DID YOU EVER have enough card-table covers? Have you often wished for a nice, fresh one when friends drop in for bridge or canasta? This type is the simplest ever to make. Thirty minutes will do it, and one square yard of felt in a color right for your room is all that it takes.

Take yardstick and a big book or newspaper, and make sure that your yard of felt is completely square. If it isn't, chalk true lines; then trim on them very carefully. If you have a pinking shears, pink edges, by all means.

Place felt over your table and pin corners. Most tables are 30 in., so that this size allows for a 3-in. drop on each side, as indicated in diagram. Pin each corner in a true miter. Stitch corners, stitching up and back, as at A. Cut away surplus fabric at each corner, allowing ¼ in. for seams. If you make cover a snug fit, you may not need tapes at the corner to tie around legs. If you prefer to have them, cut four pieces of twill tape each 12 in. long. Hunt through your button box for eight really pretty buttons that you cut from a dress —heaven knows when! Place each button about 2 in. from the corner. Catch tape on underside, as at B. The stitches that hold the buttons in place will serve to hold the tape at each corner.

If you have a very large card table, buy 4¼ yds. of 1¼-in.-wide matching or contrasting grosgrain ribbon, and stitch it all around outside edge to extend size of cover and make the overhang wide enough.

If you make the cover as a gift and feel ambitious, cut from bits of ribbon small card motifs—diamonds, hearts, clubs, and spades—and appliqué these to the corners instead of using the buttons.

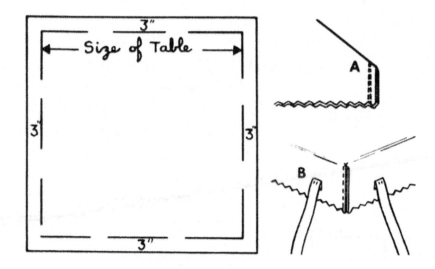

Man's Ascot Scarf

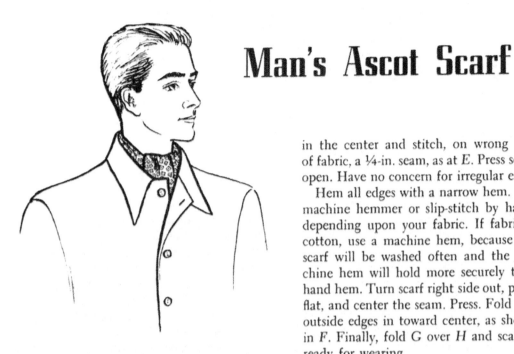

▶▶▶ MAKE THIS of washable cotton, Shantung or surah silk, with small, geometric design. It takes only ¾ yd. of 35-in. material.

Measure down 11 in. each way on selvage of two opposite corners, as at A and B in diagram, and cut a true triangle off each. Bring bias edges C and D together in the center and stitch, on wrong side of fabric, a ¼-in. seam, as at E. Press seam open. Have no concern for irregular ends.

Hem all edges with a narrow hem. Use machine hemmer or slip-stitch by hand, depending upon your fabric. If fabric is cotton, use a machine hem, because the scarf will be washed often and the machine hem will hold more securely than hand hem. Turn scarf right side out, place flat, and center the seam. Press. Fold two outside edges in toward center, as shown in F. Finally, fold G over H and scarf is ready for wearing.

This ascot makes a practical scarf for men to wear with cowboy shirts or flannel or other sport shirts when no necktie is worn. Men like these washable ascots, and if you choose a pattern as carefully as you would choose a necktie, you will undoubtedly make a gift that will give much pleasure.

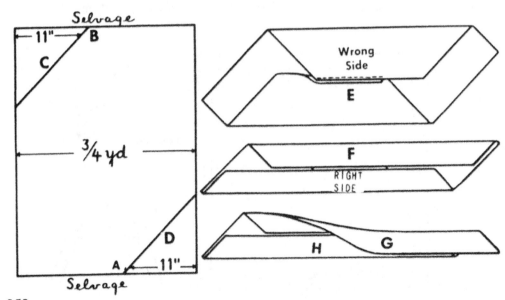

Washcloth Scuffs— Mother-and-daughter Dry-off Suits

▶▶▶ COST OF these scuffs? The price of two washcloths! Imagine using washcloths to make scuffs! And think how practical they are when you go from dressing room to pool or lie in the sun.

To make a scuff for a foot that needs a size 7 shoe: Fold a 12-in. wash cloth in half. Measure up from fold 4 in. as at A in diagram. Measure in 4 in. from A and place pins toward B. Slip the scuff on and place pins at the heel, C to D, at correct length for your foot.

Turn top edges down. Press foot down and see whether line C to D should move in or out from edge. This line should hug ankle. Place a pin crosswise of line A to B to indicate length of foot. Make any readjustment of pins so that scuff is comfortable.

Remove scuff and stitch line A to B as deep as desired, or about 4 in. Stitch line C to D. Flatten scuff so that seams are centered, as at E. Stitch across front (you placed pin to denote length) in a curved line F to G. Open heel seam and stitch across, as at H. Fold heel into point, as at I, and stitch across, as shown. Make two scuffs, and enjoy them the summer through!

Dry-offs: Have something different, comfortable, useful, and economical to wear when you come out of a swim. Towels can be in any favorite color or white.

To make dry-offs: Buy four towels; two in size 18 by 36 in. for mother, two in size 16 by 27 in. for daughter. Simply tack or stitch each pair of towels together at each shoulder for a distance of 2 in., sewing securely. Slip over the head and tie around waist with a ¼-in. cord that equals twice waist measurement. Easy, isn't it? When summer is over, out with the shoulder stitches and return the towels to the linen closet. These dry-offs are wonderful to take on a vacation, ideal to make as a gift for swimmers who want to look smart.

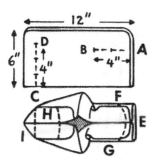

Man's Summer Nightshirt

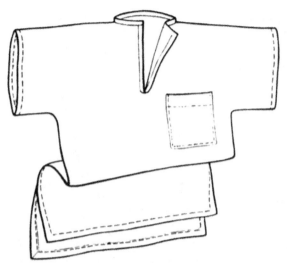

▶▶▶ A NIGHTSHIRT is cool, easy to wear, makes an ideal gift, costs little, depending upon quality of fabric you use. Buy 2 yds. of plain 36-in. percale or broadcloth and matching thread.

Straighten both ends by tearing across. Fold material lengthwise. Mark A at center of fabric on fold, as in diagram, and B on selvage straight up from A. At A, slash in from fold one-fourth neck measurement. For front opening slash down on fold one-half the neck measurement.

Measure each way from B one-fourth chest measurement for C and D. Measure in from fold, at each end, one-fourth chest measurement plus 2 in. for E and F. For example, for a 40-in. chest you measure 10 in. plus 2 in., or 12 in. Place a pin for E and F. Draw lines C, D, E, and F. Cut on these lines.

From surplus pieces G and H cut two bands, each 2 in. wide and as long as underarm. Use these to band center-front and neck opening. Stitch band on center-front opening with ¼-in. seam; then apply neckband. Finish corners by turning ends in and stitching across. Put a ⅝-in. hem in each sleeve.

Piece a pocket 6 by 8 in. Make a 1¼-in. hem. Turn raw edges under and pin on left side front, as shown. Open out shirt and stitch pocket in position. Bring side seams together. French-seam sleeves and underarm. Stitch to within 10 in. of bottom on each side seam. Hem side openings and bottom, mitering corners as illustrated, and press shirt to finish. Some like to fold a 2-in. square and place it diagonally at end of side seams as a gusset to prevent seams from tearing out. If these are used, pin them in position and catch them in the hems you put at each side of openings.

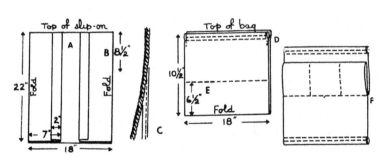

Bimini Beach Bag and Slip-on

▶▶▶ MAKE THESE attractive accessories for yourself and for gifts from 1⅛ yds. of 36-in. terry cloth and 6 yds. of ¼-in. cotton upholstery cord.

Terry slip-on: Straighten ends of fabric. Cut one crosswise piece 22 in. long. Fold selvages to center and turn back 2 in., as shown at A in diagram. For armhole, slash on outer folds 8½ in. from one raw edge, as at B. Make French seam from slash to front fold for shoulder seam. Turn neck and armhole edges ¼ in. to right side; stitch. Cut two lengths of cord each 30 in. for armhole; cut one length 40 in. for neck. Center cord; whip over stitching around armhole and across back of neck, as at C. Tie knots in ends of cord. Put a ⅜-in. hem in bottom.

Terry bag: Turn in raw edge at each end of selvage ⅛ in. for a distance of 3 in. Stitch. Turn selvages over 1½ in. Stitch on selvage and again 1 in. above to form casing, as at D.

Fold fabric in half crosswise, right sides out; stitch through two thicknesses 6½ in. from fold, to make pocket piece, as at E. Fold this up toward casing. Pin in place. Divide this into three even pockets; then stitch pockets against one piece of the bag and through three thicknesses of terry, as at F.

Bring casing edges together, right sides in. Starting at bottom of casing, stitch side seams three times, to prevent raveling. Turn to right side.

Cut remaining cord in half. To make drawstrings, run one end of cord through casing on one side and back through other side. Knot the two ends. Beginning at opposite end, run other cord through casing and back, and knot ends.

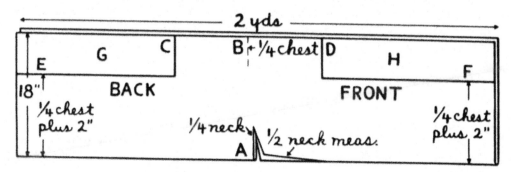

Ponchos Made of Towels

▶▶▶ *One-towel poncho:* Make a towel-poncho for the man in your life to wear after swimming or for sunning or relaxing, in perennially approved white. Buy, for an average size, the large-size towel, about 72 by 36 in. For a smaller man, or for a woman, you can use a towel approximately 50 by 30 in. Buy 2¼ yds. of ⅜-in. heavy cotton upholstery cord and two matching tassels.

Fold the towel in half lengthwise. Find center of fold and on lengthwise thread, cut a slash each way one-half the head measurement plus 2 in. Turn a ¼-in. hem on each cut edge and stitch, stitching across each end of slash so that it cannot tear out or ravel. Use your longest machine stitch, and do not stitch too fast so that thicknesses will feed easily under your presser foot.

Mark the waistline. (Either try poncho on the proud owner or measure one of his suits.) One inch below waistline on each selvage edge of back, apply a 2-in. strip of tape or cording for belt straps by stitching strip on across each end. Run cord ends through these loops and sew on tassels, ready to bring to front and tie.

This same method can be used to make a poncho for a woman. If a novel note is desired, buy 2¼ yds. of 36-in. terry in a becoming color and 4½ yds. of matching cotton fringe about 1½ in. wide, from the drapery department. Turn under all raw edges and stitch fringe over them for a decorative finish. Finish the neck and make belt straps and use a cord tie in the same way as for the man's poncho.

Terry cloth may be made into stoles, into blouses and robes—so many lovely, useful things. The washing machine fluffs terry clean, and the breezes make ironing unnecessary.

Two-towel poncho: This is a practical poncho to wear over a bathing suit, since it gives protection from sun and can be used as a towel afterward.

Take two medium-weight terry cloth towels, 20 by 40 in. Cut one towel in half crosswise to use for front and back sections. At the center of one side of second towel make a slash in half the width, as at A in diagram, and then cut each side of this slash in 2 in., as at B and C. This is for the neck opening. Turn slashed part back 2 in. Turn raw edges in and stitch along edges as shown. Make narrow hem across the line D to finish back neckline.

Take the towel that you cut in half and center one cut edge 2 in. from back edge of shoulder piece, as at E and F. Stitch. Put poncho on; bring front neckline edges together to make a V, as at A. Pin the second half towel to front of shoulder piece; stitch line G to H, as shown. The size of the bust will influence slant of front stitching line G-H.

Buy one yard of heavy cord to use around waist. Cut in half. Tie knot in one end of each piece. Sew other ends of cord pieces to each side of back section, at waistline. Stitch across cord ends a couple of times by machine, or whip them in place by hand. Put poncho on, bring cord ends to front, and tie as shown.

Many will find this ideal to wear for shampooing their hair; it also makes a thoughtful gift for someone going on vacation.

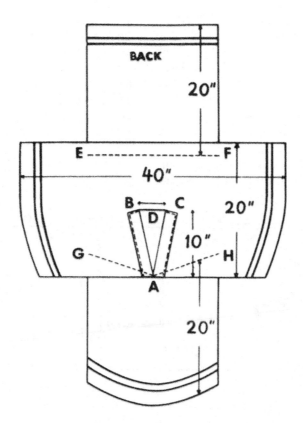

Terry Shaverong

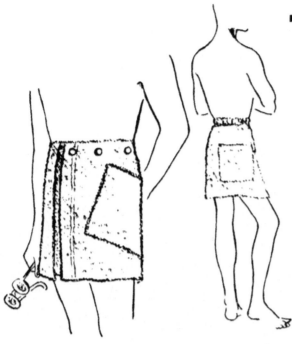

▶▶▶ MOST STORES have a medium lightweight 19-by-40-in. bath towel. Two such towels usually cost very little, and, in addition, you need only ⅜ yd. of ½-in. elastic, three buttons, and one spool of thread to make this shaverong. Once you've made one of them, you will want to make one each for father, son, brother, uncle.

Lap the towels as shown in the diagram, in this case the width of the border, and stitch the two thicknesses crosswise of the towels, as shown. Measure the waist. For a 36-in. waist you would need approximately 60 in. for fullness across the back and for overlap in the front. Thus you would cut the under towel in half, using the second half for small shaving towel and pockets.

Hem the two pocket pieces. Turn the three raw edges in ½ in., and place pockets as shown. Make a ⅝-in. hem across the top edges of the towel. Measure across center-back for a distance of 21 in., as indicated. Insert elastic and draw up to 13½ in. Stitch ends of elastic securely. Lap the front edge over underlap so that all measurements are according to the required waist measurement. Mark for buttonholes. Stitch these in the hem, stitching and pivoting to get a secure edge. Cut between the stitching of each buttonhole; then overcast the raw edge. Place the buttons so that they will be right for the buttonholes and also for the correct waist measurement.

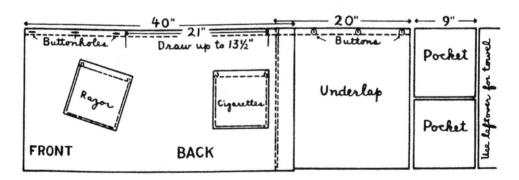

Jersey Cardigan

▶▶▶ CARDIGANS MADE of 54-in. tubular jersey are soft, suitable for either men or women, and can be had in so many lovely, soft sweater colors that you will want to make several.

You need one length measured from shoulder to wrist, plus 2 in., plus one sleeve length. Average requirement is only 1½ yds. Buy jersey of a quality good enough not to sag. Since sleeves are straight at the top, they go into the armhole as readily as the straight crosswise banding goes on the edges.

Straighten fabric. Lay one fold toward you. Following the diagram, A is lower left-hand corner; B is the measurement from shoulder to wrist to right of A on fold. Chalk line straight to opposite fold for C. D is one-half the chest measurement plus 1 in. from A. E is halfway between A and D. F and G are one-fourth neck measurement from D and A, on edge. H is 1 in. to right of E; I, one-half the armhole measurement plus 2 in. from H; J, 11 in. to right of D.

Chalk lines G-H, H-F, F-J, H-I. Shape neckline F-J as shown. Back neck G-A can be shaped slightly if desired. Cut from B to C; G to H; H to F; F through J to line C-B. Cut H to I.

K is lower right-hand corner; L, upper right-hand corner; M, one-half the armhole measurement plus 2 in. above B; N, one-half the armhole measurement less 2 in. above K. O is 1 in. to right of M. Connect N and O. Connect O and B. Cut B to O to N. Turn sleeve around and lay fold B-K along C-L. Cut second sleeve.

French-seam shoulders and sleeves, making ¼-in. seams. Make 1¼-in. hems in bottom of sleeves. Pin sleeves in armhole, matching fold in sleeve to shoulder seam. Stitch sleeves. Make 1¼-in. hem in bottom of jacket.

Cut 3-in. band strips (lengthwise) from remaining fabric, and seam together for necessary length, piecing so that seam comes at back of neck.

Pin right side of band to wrong side of front edges. Stitch, making ¼-in. seam. Bring other edge of band to right side, turn under, and pin along stitching line. Baste carefully so that band is smooth. Turn in ends at bottom to make neat finish, and stitch close to edge.

Cut pockets to size desired. Hem top edges. Turn sides and bottom under. Topstitch. If owner wears reading glasses, a 5-in.-deep welt pocket on the left chest will be appreciated. Press jacket carefully.

Use a buttonhole maker or have the buttonholes done at your local sewing center. After buttonholes are made, mark position of buttons and sew on.

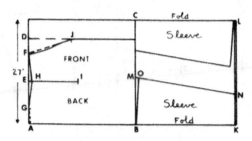

Man's Slip-on of Fake Pony

▶▶▶ MEN SEEM TO like fake fur as well as their womenfolk do. Many jackets, waistcoats, and scarves for men are made of this fabric.

The waistcoat shown (pronounced *weskit*) is easy to make and costs very little in comparison with ready-mades.

The original was made of fake pony fur, which is available in black, brown, and palomino, all with white.

You need one length measured from shoulder to waist, plus 4 in., or from ⅝ yd. to ¾ yd. of 54-in. fabric, plus ⅛ yd. of wool jersey in matching color for facing.

Straighten fabric. Fold lengthwise, wrong side out, bringing edges to center, as at A in diagram. Pin. B is lower left-hand corner. C is desired depth of V from B. D is one-half the armhole measurement plus 2 in. from B. Chalk a line straight across from D to opposite fold for E. F is lower right-hand corner. G is one-fourth neck measurement from B. H is length of shoulder from G. I is 1 in. to right of H. J is one-fourth chest measurement plus 2 in. in from D. K is one-fourth chest measurement plus 1 in. from F.

Chalk lines C-G and G-I; make armhole curve from I to J; connect J-K. Cut out front, cutting from C to G; G to I; I around to J; J to K.

Lay front over back section, folds together and edges meeting. Cut back to match front, except neckline. L is upper left-hand corner. Cut back neck curve 1 in. to right of L, tapering to shoulder line as shown.

Cut paper patterns for fitted facings for armhole and neckline, as indicated by broken lines. Make facing 1 in. to 1¼ in. wide. Lay pattern pieces on double jersey, as shown in diagram M. Cut out facings.

French-seam shoulders and underarms. Lay facing pieces for V neck and armholes right side down on right side of pull-on. Pin, mitering V as at N and making shoulder seams as at O. Stitch miter and shoulder seams. Stitch all around neckline ¼ in. from edge, as shown. Turn free edge over ¼ in. and stitch. Finish armholes in same way. Press facings to wrong side and slip-stitch them in position.

Around bottom edge, turn hem of same width as facings. Turn edge under and stitch free of garment. Slip-stitch in position. Press.

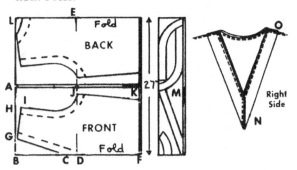

Night Reader

▶▶▶ MANY MEN like to read in bed. When the heat is turned down for the night sometimes extra warmth over shoulders is highly desirable. This little wool-jersey jacket solves the problem admirably. Jersey is soft, easy to handle, and ideal for this type of jacket. The design shown requires only 1 yd. Such a jacket can last for years and provide much comfort.

Choose a color that is becoming and that is a favorite—pajama blue, wine red, gold, grey, or a pleasing pastel. Jersey comes in many lovely colors.

The diagram and measurements here are for an average figure, size 14½ and 16½ neck. Lay tube out folded into four thicknesses, the two creased folds away from you, the fold you have made toward you. Point B is one-sixth of the neck measurement above corner A. C is one-fourth neck measurement plus 3 in. right of A.

To left of corner D, mark for two 2-in.-wide binding strips. Cut these off straight across. Measure to left of E 10½ in. Cut from this point (F) straight across to make bottom of jacket. Take the sleeve pieces cut from between E and F, and place them alongside edges, as at G and H. Locate I 1 in. to right of sleeve edge. Draw a chalk line from I through G to B; cut on this line to make a slanting shoulder line.

Cut tube of jersey G to H, and cut center-front line, single thickness C to F. Open jersey out and cut a straight neckline, as dotted line shows, from C to B. Binding is easier to apply if you round this edge slightly at C.

Stitch underarm sleeve seams H to J, using a ⅜-in. seam. To join sleeves to the jacket, begin at H and baste up on each side; then stitch. Press seams open. Stitch shoulder seams B through G to I. Press these open.

Apply the binding to the center-front. Begin at F, place right side of binding to wrong side of jacket, stitch binding all the way up front and around neck and down the opposite front edge, as in K, making a ¼-in.-wide seam. Turn the free edge of binding down on right side and baste it evenly all around, as in L; then stitch it in place. Finish bottom of sleeves with binding in the same way as neck is finished, making a ⅛-in. hem turn; make a ¼-in. hem in bottom of jacket. Press, and jacket is ready to wear.

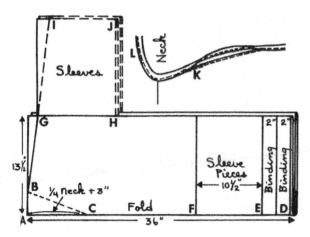

Hideaway Lap Robe

▶▶▶ HOW OFTEN, when you are in the car, do you wish for a lightweight robe for warmth, or one to wrap a sleepy child in, or a tired older person. The hideaway lap robe solves the problem.

Buy a remnant of 1½ yds. of 50-in. wool —something that is bargain-priced, that is warm and without bulk. Fold this in half lengthwise, then in flat folds, as shown, and you can wrap it in plastic and place it under the front seats where it will be handy when needed.

There are two ways to finish crosswise edges of such a robe, in addition to making plain hems.

Fringe finish: Straighten your fabric Fringe ends for ½ to ¾ in. simply by pulling the crosswise threads away. With double thread of raveled yarn in your needle, blanket-stitch the edge at top of fringe. This prevents fringe from raveling farther and gives a practical finish.

To make blanket-stitch: Secure thread with small back-stitch. Insert needle about ¼ in. above top of fringe; bring it out over thread at bottom, as in A. Draw needle through. Repeat until entire crosswise edge is finished. Finish off, when selvage is reached, with a back-stitch. Finish both ends in the same way.

Binding with ribbon or braid: If you wish to make such a robe as a gift, it can be dressed up with a ribbon or braid finish. Choose trimming that is at least 1 in. wide, and buy 1 yd. more than robe measures all around—this because it must be eased on. Fold and press ribbon or braid through center lengthwise, with top edge slightly narrower than lower. When placed along edge of fabric, with lower edge underneath (B), this ensures catching both edges in basting and stitching. Begin at center of one side of fabric, and baste as you proceed. When binding all four sides, use mitered corners. To miter corners, fold binding, as at C. When corner is folded true and square, bring edge up, as at D. Stitch binding in position close to edge. Whip mitered fold as shown. To finish, lap ends of binding, turn under free end, and whip in place.

Plain hemmed edge: If time for finishing is short, or you prefer a simpler finish than those given above, make a ⅜-in. machine or hand hem along both crosswise edges.

A plastic or washable envelope-type case can be made to slip robe in to keep it clean and neat.

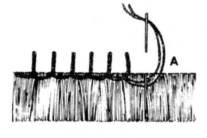
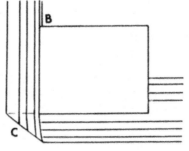
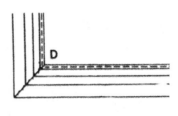